FinTech

for dummies®

A Wiley Brand

FinTech

by Susanne Chishti, CEO, FINTECH Circle and FINTECH Circle Institute, Ltd.; Steven O'Hanlon, CEO, Numerix, LLC; Brendan Bradley, Advisory Board Member, FINTECH Circle; James Jockle, CMO, Numerix, LLC; and Dawn Patrick, COO, Numerix, LLC

A Wiley Brand

FinTech For Dummies®

Published by: **John Wiley & Sons, Inc.**, 111 River Street, Hoboken, NJ 07030-5774, www.wiley.com

Copyright © 2020 by John Wiley & Sons, Inc., Hoboken, New Jersey

Published simultaneously in Canada

For general information on our other products and services, please contact our Customer Care Department within the U.S. at 877-762-2974, outside the U.S. at 317-572-3993, or fax 317-572-4002. For technical support, please visit https://hub.wiley.com/community/support/dummies.

Wiley publishes in a variety of print and electronic formats and by print-on-demand. Some material included with standard print versions of this book may not be included in e-books or in print-on-demand. If this book refers to media such as a CD or DVD that is not included in the version you purchased, you may download this material at http://booksupport.wiley.com. For more information about Wiley products, visit www.wiley.com.

Library of Congress Control Number: 2020936884

ISBN 978-1-119-42726-1 (pbk); ISBN 978-1-119-42724-7 (ebk); ISBN 978-1-119-42725-4 (ebk)

Manufactured in the United States of America

SKY10020252_080320

Contents at a Glance

Table of Contents

Introduction

Welcome, FinTech friends! Thanks for picking up this book, in which we explain the ins and outs of Financial Technology, or FinTech for short. *FinTech* is all about bringing transformative and disruptive innovation to financial services by applying new and emerging technologies and satisfying consumer and business needs through automation. We're passionate about FinTech, and we hope we can pass on some of our enthusiasm and knowledge to you.

For better or for worse, the financial industry has been going through some highly disruptive and substantial transformations in the last few years, and most of these are related to technology. Many traditional financial institutions aren't equipped for the digital future, for a variety of reasons, and are at risk of being displaced by newer and more agile competitors. We hope in this book to guide leaders in such institutions to help them implement cutting-edge financial technologies. But that's just half of our target audience here. We also hope to guide people on the other side of that competitive equation, who are part of the FinTech disruption — or who aspire to be.

About This Book

As we were preparing to write this book, we started out by looking at the competition. What books on FinTech already exist, and how can we improve on them? We found that there really wasn't any direct competition to what we wanted to do. Many of the existing FinTech books were very broad in covering this topic, particularly from a retail consumer perspective. Some others were too specific, focusing on single issues such as blockchain or digital currencies.

Our vision for this book is to provide a pragmatic look at the most important aspects of FinTech, particularly in the business-to-business (B2B) area. B2B is especially interesting because it's less about FinTech disruption and more about collaboration with established institutions to jointly achieve the needed transformations.

Sidebars (boxes of text) in this book give you a more in-depth look at a certain topic. Although they dig deeper into a particular point, these sidebars aren't crucial to your understanding of the rest of the book. Feel free to read them or skip them. You can also pass over the text that accompanies the Technical Stuff icon. The text marked with this icon gives some technical details about FinTech that are interesting and informative, but you can still come away with the information you need without reading it.

One last note: Within this book, you may note that some web addresses break across two lines of text. If you're reading this book in print and want to visit one of these web pages, simply key in the web address exactly as it's noted in the text, pretending as though the line break doesn't exist. If you're reading this as an e-book, you've got it easy — just click the web address to be taken directly to the web page.

Foolish Assumptions

This book is basic enough that almost anyone can understand it, but it was written largely for a few specific types of people. As we wrote this book, we had the following audiences in mind:

» Financial services professionals who want to educate themselves in FinTech instead of bluffing their way through

» FinTech firms that are looking to engage with financial institutions

» Venture capitalists and other investors looking for a broader view of the market than the next challenger bank or payments provider

» Corporate clients that receive B2B FinTech services

» Professional services providers such as accountants, consultants, and lawyers who are trying to define their places in the FinTech ecosystem

Our general assumption is that you'll have some experience with and understanding of FinTech, but you can build your understanding as you progress or dip into certain chapters that are more specific to your role or interest.

Icons Used in This Book

As you read through this book, you'll come across icons in the margins that call out blocks of information you may find important.

TIP

The Tip icon marks helpful advice for saving time and money or enhancing the experience as you begin to explore FinTech.

REMEMBER

The Remember icon calls out a key piece of information to retain. If you don't remember anything else from the section or chapter you just read, remember the material marked here.

WARNING

Warning icons point out hazards, drawbacks, or gotchas.

TECHNICAL STUFF

Although this book doesn't require any advanced technical knowledge, items called out by this icon will take a deeper look at a particular technical detail. Feel free to skip the information marked with this icon if it doesn't appeal to you.

Beyond the Book

In addition to the material in the print or digital book you're reading right now, *FinTech For Dummies* comes with other great content available online. To get the Cheat Sheet, simply go to www.dummies.com and search for "FinTech For Dummies Cheat Sheet" in the Search box.

Where to Go from Here

You don't have to read this book in order. Each chapter is self-contained, so you can jump around as much as you like. Flip to the table of contents and the index if you're looking for a specific topic.

If you want to find out more about FinTech, you can join FINTECH Circle, one of the leading FinTech ecosystems in the world. You can become a member online for free (https://fintechcircle.com/become-a-member) and then automatically receive daily updates on global FinTech trends.

If you want to keep up on general FinTech news on a daily, weekly, or monthly basis, check out these websites:

>> www.finextra.com

>> www.fintechfutures.com

>> www.fintechweekly.com

>> https://thefintechtimes.com

>> https://fintechcircle.com/fintech-insights/

Wiley has also published The FinTech Book series, through which you can delve deeper into various FinTech verticals. The available books are

>> *The FinTech Book* by Susanne Chishti and Janos Barberis

>> *The InsurTech Book* by Sabine L. B. VanderLinden, Shân M. Millie, Nicole Anderson, and Susanne Chishti

>> *The WealthTech Book* by Susanne Chishti and Thomas Puschmann

>> *The RegTech Book* by Janos Barberis, Douglas W. Arner, and Ross P. Buckley

>> *The PayTech Book* by Susanne Chishti, Tony Craddock, Robert Courtneidge, and Markos Zachariadis

>> *The AI Book* by Ivana Bartoletti, Susanne Chishti, Anne Leslie, and Shân M. Millie

>> *The LegalTech Book* by Sophia Adams Bhatti, Susanne Chishti, Akber Datoo, and Drago Indjic

WARNING

We were just in the process of finalizing this book when the Corona Virus pandemic took hold! Therefore, these comments are made in late July 2020, before publication in September, as we wait for clarity on the repercussions of the first wave of the virus and whether there may be a second wave lock down as new virus cases begin to spike in certain locations. As you read this, are you a 'glass half full or half empty' type of person?

Those in the 'half empty camp' will point toward the fallout from the pandemic and the resultant challenges that will imply for FinTech firms. We are likely to see some FinTech casualties due to the range of pressures they will face from a cash flow perspective as larger financial institutions will still be slow to take decisions on new technology. This may also lead to consolidation.

However, in the 'half full camp' the mantra is that COVID-19 will fast-track the digital transformation of financial services and spur firms to innovate their way out of the malaise. Therefore, greater acceptance of digitalization will present huge opportunities in the FinTech space as we build into the 'new normal.' These opposing thoughts are further elaborated on at the back of this book (pages XYZ-ABC), under the strapline, 'The future of Fintech post the Corona crisis?'

1

Getting to Know FinTech

Chapter 1

Navigating the FinTech Landscape

FinTech has undoubtedly become one of the hottest topics in business. Web searches for the term *fintech* in Google have grown exponentially in the last several years, so it's obvious that people are curious about it. But what is it, and why is it relevant to today's financial industry? This chapter looks at those very basic questions, helping prepare you for the more detailed information you discover later in this book.

REMEMBER

Having FinTech knowledge gives you a competitive advantage in your personal career, because FinTech experts are in high demand globally. Reading this book will also empower you to help your institution innovate and develop its services faster than your competitors. Globally, the FinTech market is booming, and we see investors investing across all stages of FinTech companies' life cycles.

THE BIRTH OF NUMERIX

In 1996, Michael Goodkin, Mitchell Feigenbaum, Nigel Goldenfeld, and Alexander Sokol teamed up to form Numerix, a software company created to supply the finance industry with quantitative research and tools.

Each founder had already had great success in his own right. Michael Goodkin was a quantitative analyst and author of the book *The Wrong Answer Faster*. Mitchell Feigenbaum was a MacArthur Grant recipient and one of the pioneers of chaos theory. Nigel Goldenfeld was a statistical physicist and director of NASA Astrobiology Institute for Universal Biology. Alexander Sokol was a writer and professor at the University of Illinois.

Numerix was initially a think tank for mathematicians, computer scientists, and theoretical physicists in search of uses for a series of financial industry–specific projects. The first Numerix product was a software tool kit leveraged to speed up Monte Carlo simulations, tree and difference finite methods, and value-at-risk calculations. It sped up the computation time by factors of four, while not negatively impacting the accuracy of the results. Merrill Lynch and Price Waterhouse were the first companies to deploy this product in 1998.

The use of the Numerix Monte Carlo method provided more accurate pricing faster. This enabled banks to mitigate their intra-day risk more effectively.

Between 1998 and 2003, Numerix focused on creating many projects, some paid for by clients but most based on a desire to solve perceived financial industry–related problems. By 2003, the company had amassed 20 different kinds of potential products in search of clients. However, the company was distracted and unfocused and had spent more than $25 million to create a business that was barely generating $4 million in annual billings. During the summer of 2003, a multibillion-dollar financial service company attempted to buy Numerix for $5 million, only to have its offer rejected by the primary shareholder. The company at that time was a broken start-up building "cool" technology for the sake of it rather than solving real market problems. At this stage, it was going out of business unless it could get backing from committed investors to pivot into a new product or approach. Sometimes parallel changes in the market environment enable your pivot timing.

What Is FinTech, Anyway?

There are many definitions of FinTech, but for the purposes of this book, this one is the most relevant: FinTech companies are businesses that leverage new technology to create better financial services for both consumers and businesses. Of course, that begs another question: What is *financial technology*? We define it as all parts of technology that help provide financial services and products to customers. Those customers can be individuals, companies, or governments.

FinTech is also frequently used as an umbrella term for various subcategories, such as WealthTech and RegTech. You find out more about these subcategories in Chapter 2.

NUMERIX: THE PIVOT

The desire for greater profits drove the financial industry to create new instruments that were of significantly higher risk. Credit default swaps (CDS) and mortgage backed securities (MBS) became the instruments of choice for many hedge and investment funds that were promising high rates of return to their investors. However, these instruments were complex and not easy to price. MBS and CDS often had many different components bundled within them, making it hard to determine the true value of what was being sold or bought. This was a real market problem that Numerix could solve.

Coauthor and Numerix CEO, Steve O'Hanlon joined Numerix in January 2002 to lead global sales, marketing, and support. In 2004, Greg Whitten, chairman of the board and CEO, appointed Steve to run the day-to-day operations as president and COO. Steve's primary goals were to refocus the company and eliminate all the distractions. Steve set forth five tenets of operations to bring clarity of purpose and focus to the 50 employees:

- Evolve as a financial-focused software analytic company for derivatives.

- Replace the "term software pricing model" with "recurring software subscription model."

- Complement direct sales initiatives with a partner strategy that licenses some or all financial asset class pricing capabilities to financial software companies that require Numerix's caliber of analytics.

- Eliminate 17 of their then-20 products. Take the three remaining products and merge them to create a groundbreaking multi-asset class pricing tool.

- Shut down CrossAsset software, a majority owned Numerix company, to eliminate a $5 million annual spend.

Analyzing FinTech's Dimensions

REMEMBER

FinTech may sound simple from the definition you read in the preceding section, but there are multiple dimensions. You need to think about each of these factors:

>> Which part of finance is being impacted (financial sector)?

>> Which business model is being used?

>> Which technology is being used?

FINTECH Circle has coined the term *Fintech Cube* to describe the intersections of these factors. Figure 1-1 illustrates this cube, in which there are three axes: the financial sector on the x-axis, the business model on the y-axis, and technology on the z-axis.

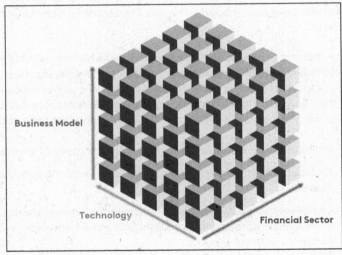

FIGURE 1-1:
The Fintech Cube combines financial sector, business model, and technology factors.

Source: FINTECH Circle, 2020

Each of these dimensions can be further categorized. For example, Figure 1-2 expands on the concept by adding key areas of financial services that can benefit from FinTech. All financial sectors are shown on one side of the cube, including retail banking, trading, and insurance (among others).

Figure 1-3 summarizes the most important business models from business-to-consumer (B2C), business-to-business (B2B), business-to-business-to-consumer (B2B2C), to business-to-government/regulator (B2G), to platform-based business models, crowdfunding, and peer-to-peer (P2P) lending.

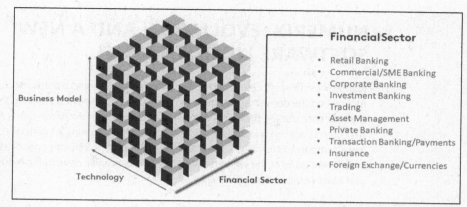

Source: The Fintech Cube, FINTECH Circle, 2020

Financial Sector

- Retail Banking
- Commercial/SME Banking
- Corporate Banking
- Investment Banking
- Trading
- Asset Management
- Private Banking
- Transaction Banking/Payments
- Insurance
- Foreign Exchange/Currencies

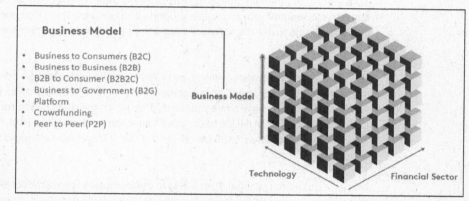

Business Model

- Business to Consumers (B2C)
- Business to Business (B2B)
- B2B to Consumer (B2B2C)
- Business to Government (B2G)
- Platform
- Crowdfunding
- Peer to Peer (P2P)

Source: The Fintech Cube, FINTECH Circle, 2020

Figure 1-4 shows the third dimension — the technology being used, which can range from cloud computing, big data, artificial intelligence (AI)/machine learning (ML), blockchain (distributed ledger technologies), the Internet of Things (IoT), and quantum computing, to augmented and virtual reality. Part 2 covers these technologies in more detail.

FinTech start-ups, for example, can now be more easily categorized and compared. For example, you may have a retail banking (financial sector x-axis) solution focused on the business model of B2C and using various technologies, such as cloud, big data analytics, and AI. Such a company would be called a challenger bank, sometimes also referred to as digital bank or neo-bank.

NUMERIX: EVOLUTION AND A NEW SOFTWARE LICENSE MODEL

Numerix established clear internal and external branding as a software company focused on the derivative and over-the-counter (OTC) markets, servicing the needs of the four core trading desks: fixed income, equity, foreign exchange, and credit. Its internal communication was constant and consistent about being a financial analytic software company. Externally, it participated in 15 different industry-specific trade shows in different parts of the world to make itself known, while developing industry contacts and leads resulted in product sales.

The financial software industry was fraught with legacy sales models. One of the most common was the perpetual license model (PLM), which involves an initial license fee (ILF) upfront and then an annual maintenance fee (AMF) of about 20 percent of the ILF for each subsequent year to receive supports and updates. The ILF payment ensures perpetual rights to use the software even if the client stops paying annual maintenance.

The other popular software license type in 2004 was the term license model (TLM). It required an ILF similar to a PLM, but generally the ILF for a TLM was lower, because a TLM would generally have a five-year term, after which the client had to renew by paying the original TLM ILF fee to continue to use the product. Like a PLM, the TLM would have an AMF equal to 20 percent of the TLM ILF, and this too would be paid annually.

Numerix successfully shifted from a TLM to a subscription license model (SLM), which at that time was common for enterprise software but not for financial software. Since Steve O'Hanlon came from the Enterprise software world, he moved Numerix into the new world of a SLM. This change shifted the way clients paid for Numerix products. For existing TLM Numerix clients, Numerix took the sum of ILF and five AMF periods, added them together, and then divided by 5 to determine what the SLM would be for renewing clients. For example, if a client originally paid an ILF of $100,000 and an AMF of $20,000 each year for five years, where the client's first-year payment would be $120,000 and each subsequent year would be $20,000, the client would have spent over five years the sum of $200,000, Numerix divided the $200,000 by five years, making the SLM price $40,000 per year. Numerix then used the same logic when re-creating the TLM as an SLM price book. This SLM enabled Numerix to have recurring billings of 83 percent of the gross in 2019.

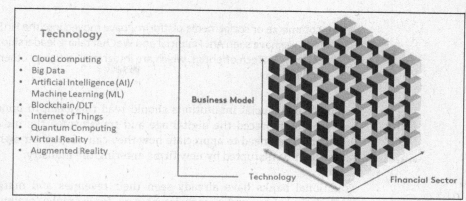

Source: The Fintech Cube, FINTECH Circle, 2020

FIGURE 1-4:
The key technologies used to achieve change.

As another example, you may have a WealthTech company that sells its software to hedge funds. You could describe it as being focused on asset management (x-axis), B2B business model (y-axis), and using several types of technology from the z-axis in combination.

Understanding What Has Changed in FinTech

There have been tremendous changes in the financial technology landscape in the last decade. We look at these changes and their effects in detail in Chapter 2, but it may help to survey the basics here as well. Consider the following:

>> Just 20 years ago, it would have been very expensive to launch a FinTech company, whereas today the required expenditure is much more affordable. The decreasing technology costs have reduced the barriers to entry.

>> The funding landscape is also different now. Twenty years ago, there was little funding available for early-stage FinTech firms, but today venture capitalist and corporate venture arms of both financial institutions and tech companies invest large sums in scalable FinTech companies. (See Chapter 16 for more information.)

>> The industry dynamics have also changed. Previously, technology suppliers to financial services firms were seen as pure vendors. Lately, there has been a powershift in which FinTech companies, larger scale-ups, and unicorns are clearly seen as partners or competitors to established financial players. Even tech giants such as Facebook and Google, which have historically focused on

e-commerce or social media platforms, have moved into the FinTech arena. In China, we have seen Ant Financial and WeChat taking leadership positions with their FinTech offerings, which are integrated into their other services in a seamless way.

REMEMBER

Established financial institutions should read this book to understand how the tech giants embraced the digital age and transformed the industries they now dominate. They need to appreciate how they can adopt their own transformation rather than be disrupted by new firms entering the industry.

Traditional banks have already seen their revenues and margins decrease as FinTech firms have undercut their prices on, for example, foreign exchange, lending, payments, and traditional banking services, particularly as open banking is promoted by regulators.

NUMERIX: THE "INTEL INSIDE" STRATEGY

Coauthor Steve O'Hanlon worked in the enterprise software arena before he came to Numerix. He leveraged the skills from those experiences to make Numerix an early adopter in the financial software markets by implementing an SLM. The concept of Software-as-a-Service (SaaS) was still in its infancy, and the cloud offerings that are available today weren't offered (see Chapter 6 for more about the cloud). Introducing an SLM (which was more common in enterprise software sales) to the financial software market enabled Numerix to become an early adopter of a license approach that the industry embraced. It's still the approach Numerix uses with its products today. This very early approach brought greater market value for Numerix investors.

Having witnessed the growth of Intel with its *Intel Inside* strategy, Steve reasoned that Numerix pricing analytics could be licensed in part or whole to financial software companies that lacked the ability to price complex derivatives. His mandate in January 2004 was to complete the software development kit (SDK) for the pricing analytics so that any financial software vendor could easily consume Numerix pricing analytics. This strategy has endured since 2004 and has resulted in 90 global partners that represented nearly half of Numerix revenue in 2019.

Many FinTech firms today should investigate the potential to partner with complementary software providers, especially larger firms that have established sales with large financial institutions, to piggyback on their success, while also reducing their own dedicated sales force requirements.

Asset managers have already seen their margins reduced by a move to passive rather than active asset management, but this has further developed into robo-advisors that use algorithms to disintermediate financial advisors and portfolio managers. Equally, the insurance industry has found that companies using predictive analytics, based on big data access, are better able to price and manage risks than they have.

In all of these organizations, boards need to develop new strategies based around digital transformation and innovation teams that will work in conjunction with existing product and business development. They must also work with technology teams to help them determine how they compete in this new environment. Of course, one of their biggest hurdles will be themselves as they need to instill a new culture that embraces change from the top down. Flip to Chapter 17 for more discussion on this topic.

Highlighting the Size of Global FinTech

Figure 1-5 shows some data from the "Innovate Finance 2019 FinTech Investment Landscape Report," published in partnership with PitchBook. It shows that FinTech hubs are globally diversified, but some are more dominant than others, particularly China, the United Kingdom, and the United States.

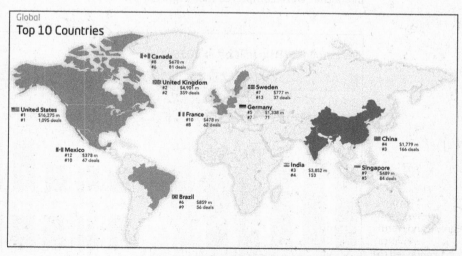

FIGURE 1-5: FinTech hubs are globally diversified.

Source: Innovate Finance, 2019 FinTech Investment Landscape Report, PitchBook. Data has not been reviewed or approved by PitchBook analysts.

Although FinTech investment fell to $35.7 billion in 2019, as shown in Figure 1-6, this was largely driven by a sharp fall of funding to Chinese FinTech firms.

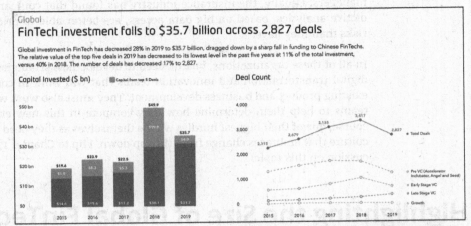

FIGURE 1-6: A 2019 drop in global FinTech investment.

While FinTech investment decreased in Asia in 2019, long term we believe that Asia will be a growth engine for the global FinTech sector. Meanwhile, all other regions' total investment increased, primarily due to the number of large size deals that were completed (see Figure 1-7).

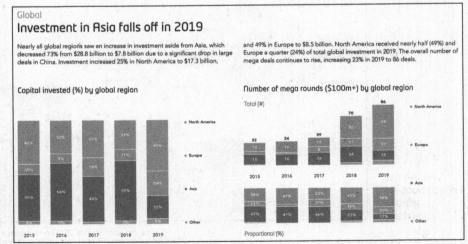

FIGURE 1-7: FinTech investment in Europe and North America continued to increase in 2019.

NUMERIX: A FOCUS ON FEWER PRODUCTS

When Steve O'Hanlon took the helm in January 2004, Numerix was distracted and unfocused and was building more products than it could possibly ever sell through its four direct salespeople. Steve, a veteran of seven software start-up companies over 37 years, believed that focus was the only way a start-up would have a chance to grow into a larger company. He determined that at least 17 of Numerix's 20 products had a completely different market focus or would need a different sales approach. Four salespeople could never focus on more than one of these products. In addition, none of the products were complete and were in various stages of product maturity. This lack of focus was the main reason Numerix sales weren't growing significantly enough for the size of company it was. Steve made the choice to eliminate 17 products and focus on the three core pricing analytic products: Numerix Toolkit, Numerix Engine, and Numerix Library.

The Numerix Toolkit was sold to financial quants as a stand-alone tool where they would use an SDK to create their own applications on top of the Toolkit. Its sluggish sales led Numerix to create the Numerix Engine product, a full application for pricing fixed income, credit, equity, and foreign exchange derivatives. The Engine was built on top of the Toolkit, so it effectively rendered the Toolkit product obsolete.

In 2002, Numerix's then-CEO hired a financial software quant to build the next generation of the Engine, which was dubbed the Numerix Library. This dual focus of building the same product twice became known in Numerix as the "Pepsi Challenge." The then-CEO created competition between the Engine and Library development teams. This meant that the four sales reps were attempting to sell both the Engine and the Library. When clients asked about the difference between the two products, the sales rep would state that the Engine was legacy with more features, but the Library was next-generation and would eventually catch up to the Engine features. Potential clients were understandably not thrilled with that answer, and it was yet another reason for insignificant billing growth at Numerix.

Steve identified the problem in the sales approach and sought to rebrand the products to stop the confusion. He immediately took the Toolkit out of the price book so that salespeople could no longer sell it as a separate product. He eliminated Toolkit, Engine, and Library product names and instead began using the company name, Numerix, as the product name.

Steve then renamed the Engine Numerix 3.0 and renamed the Library Numerix 4.0. He refocused the Numerix 3.0 product (the Engine) developers on Numerix 4.0 (the Library). Just a couple of developers were left to maintain Numerix 3.0. His goal was to speed up the process of enhancing Numerix 4.0 with new features and features that were only in Numerix 3.0.

(continued)

(continued)

All this new work became known as Numerix 5.0, which was delivered at the end of 2004. The sales team could show the road map that took all the features of Numerix 3.0 and moved them to Numerix 4.0, resulting in Numerix 5.0. This sales story was very focused, and prospective customers could clearly understand the benefits of licensing 4.0 knowing when they would get the gap fillers from 3.0. It was this single focus that caused Numerix billings in 2004 to nearly double over the prior year!

The process Numerix went through in its analysis of the effect of conflicting software and market perceptions is not unlike the analysis FinTech companies provide to their banking customers. The need to identify redundancy, consolidate functions, and provide clear messaging both internally and externally is key to the modernization of financial institutions and a service that FinTech is integrally involved in.

Discovering a Few Important FinTech Terms

REMEMBER

Throughout this book, you find many terms to describe the various parts of the FinTech industry and its inner (and outer!) workings, and we try to make this as digestible as possible. To get started, though, here's a core set of definitions that it may help to have in your back pocket at the outset:

>> An *application programming interface (API)* is a software intermediary that enables two applications to talk to each other. It delivers your message request to a provider and then delivers the response back to you. (See Chapter 4.)

>> *Data management* means to collect, cleanse, manage, and analyze data to generate additional business intelligence. (See Chapter 4.)

>> A *decentralized application (DApp)* stores data in a decentralized database and uses decentralized computing resources in a peer-to-peer network. This open source code can be accessed by all network members. (See Chapter 5.)

>> *Digital transformation* is the change that happens to a business when you apply and integrate digital technology. It includes changes to business processes, business models, domain expertise, technology, and culture.

>> *Disruption* refers to the way emerging FinTech firms and technologies are interfering or competing with the traditional way business has been done in the past.

>> *Microservices* is an approach to application development in which a large application is built as a set of modular components. (See Chapter 4.)

>> *Open source* is software for which the source code is freely available to anyone. Any capable programmers can then use, modify, and distribute their own versions of the program. (See Chapter 10.)

NUMERIX: CLOSING CrossAsset LLC

In addition to building 20 software products pre-2004, Numerix had also created a company called CrossAsset Software LLC. Numerix owned 70 percent of it, and Toronto Dominion and ICAP each owned 15 percent. CrossAsset Software focused on building a front-to-back office trading system for Toronto Dominion. There were only 15 developers, and they were tasked with not only building the system but also building a Bloomberg-like terminal.

CrossAsset software was losing $5 million per year, and there was no deliverable product anywhere on the horizon. Therefore, when coauthor Steve O'Hanlon took over Numerix in January 2004, one of the missions was to shut down CrossAsset Software without incurring legal damage from ICAP or Toronto Dominion. By the end of March 2004, the partnership was successfully terminated and Numerix retained the rights to the name CrossAsset Software, which was trademarked. The name CrossAsset eventually became the product name that replaced Numerix 5.0.

The company's new approach focused developer efforts on creating a single pricing platform that hedge funds, second tier banks, and partners could all use. During this pivot, Numerix developed and used a tool kit of creative analysis that provided a way forward to new and definitive software and services that would be utilized in the future to support its FinTech customers in their transitions.

The problem the Numerix software was set to solve was to provide consistent and fast pricing information across an entire institution's workflow process. It was driven by these considerations:

- Mass process analysis was nonexistent.

- Customers needed information on-demand.

- Financial deal structures were extremely fluid and ill defined.

- It was difficult to assess the impact of different models when pricing.

(continued)

(continued)

- Customers needed to create dealer quality models that were flexible and provided for customization.

- Traders required nearly instantaneous response time.

- End users wanted customizable views.

- Data needed to be mutable, delivered in the forms the user wanted.

Numerix software had the flexibility required to price the most exotic instruments and was built on a world-class analytics library that had models in every asset class.

The Numerix differentiators were

- Depth of instrument coverage

- A wide range of models for each asset class

- Depth of domain knowledge within Numerix

- Ability to price exotics for the business lines they cover (Equity, FI, Credit, and FX)

- Instrument building capabilities

- A consultative approach to selling and deployment

- Ongoing support for the product after deployment

- A historical precedent of excellence

- A flexible technological infrastructure that addresses the needs of partners as well as financial institutions

The way forward would incorporate

- Attacking the hedge fund market with analytics

- Capitalizing on the emerging market: credit

- Partnering with companies that could embed their analytics

- Moving upstream to second-tier banks with analytics

- Becoming the most pervasive analytics company in the world

In Chapter 2, we continue the story of Numerix, and you discover how this path forward took shape.

Chapter **2**

Understanding What's Disrupting the Financial Industry (and Why)

uring this era of post-financial- crisis, the financial services industry has been thrown into a state of massive disruption. Venerable, traditional financial institutions are on the defensive as new upstarts change the playing field in fundamental ways. This disruption is a growing concern for financial services firms at risk from potential displacement by nimbler, data-driven competitors, including those in banking, capital markets, insurance, and wealth management, and is forcing them to evolve to remain competitive.

Some of this disruption is coming from the perception that BigTech giants, such as Amazon, Ant Financial, Apple, Facebook, and Google, are likely to roll out industry-changing platforms and technologies that compete with more traditional offerings. However, emerging FinTech start-ups are also challenging the status quo by providing innovative services and increased personalization, particularly in the consumer space rather than the wholesale arena.

REMEMBER

FinTech, which is shorthand for "financial technology," is the drive to bring transformative and disruptive innovation to financial services by applying new and emerging technologies and satisfying consumer needs through automation. Flip to Chapter 1 for an introduction to FinTech.

Traditional financial services institutions are right to be nervous about the growing successes of FinTech firms. By their very nature, FinTech start-ups have a number of advantages. Here's a brief comparison:

» For starters, FinTech start-ups are nimble. Because they aren't disadvantaged by inherited older systems and methodologies, they can move faster to create new solutions. Their top leadership is also focused on creating the future, rather than maintaining the status quo, so they aren't resistant to investing heavily in technological development and innovation.

» In contrast, traditional banks, brokers, and asset managers have weighty existing systems to support, limiting what they can spend on innovation. They are also subject to greater regulatory and institutional constraints that limit their ability to fully focus resources on new technology.

In this chapter, you find out about the key competitors in the financial services market today, the challenges they face, and what they bring to the table.

Providing Trust and Value

Both consumers and businesses select financial services using two basic criteria:

» Is it a trustworthy institution?
» Do the services offered meet my needs at a competitive price while providing value-added services that make my life easier?

Because of this, every financial sector firm faces the same basic challenges today. They are all trying to restore public trust in a post-financial-crisis environment, deliver the services that customers want, and offer the customer an attractive value — all while still making a profit.

Trust

In today's environment, a "trustworthy" financial institution is one that can be relied on to hold up its end of the relationship by being a responsible steward of the customer's assets and information. This means safeguarding every aspect of the relationship, preventing harm from both internal and external sources. This can include

>> Maintaining the financial services company's ongoing solvency and success. Nobody wants to use a financial services company that might go out of business at any moment or that doesn't have the resources to invest in the latest and best capabilities.

>> Safeguarding the customer's investment, both physically and digitally, maintaining effective vigilance against data thieves and saboteurs. Cybersecurity is critical for this point; a cybersecurity breach that exposes customer or supplier data can damage an institution's reputation irreparably.

>> Safeguarding the customer's privacy. Customers want to know that their sensitive financial data is going to stay private and not be compromised by hackers or careless internal handling.

So who has the edge in this area: traditional institutions or FinTech start-ups? It's a mixed bag, because they both bring advantages to the table. Customers may perceive large, traditional institutions as being more trustworthy because of their history and gravitas, and a large, well-established business may be more solvent and less likely to crash and burn (although it's no guarantee, as we've seen in recent years). However, FinTech start-ups may actually have an edge on the data-safeguarding front because of their focus on the latest technologies.

Value

The second part of the equation is the services and their value. What does the financial service provider bring to the table that the customer wants? In an ideal world, the customer wants all the services, and all the options for receiving them, for the lowest possible price. The challenge, then, is to be the provider that best meets that demand.

REMEMBER

One way that providers are able to offer greater value to customers is through disintermediation. To *disintermediate* means to cut out some or all the steps between two points — in other words, to "cut out the middleman." Financial services has traditionally had lots of intermediate steps between a consumer's need and its fulfillment, creating lucrative careers for stockbrokers, tellers, credit card processors, personal bankers, and even check-printing companies. However, in today's market, disintermediation is becoming not only the norm but a near imperative to keep up with demand for lower costs and better value.

Fortunately, advancing technology has made it possible to automate many areas of the financial services value chain that were strictly manual operations in the past. This has enabled companies to economically provide services to customers that were expensive in the past due to the labor involved. In this endeavor, FinTech companies are better positioned than their traditional counterparts. They can be more responsive, more focused, and less distracted by legacy issues such as fixed cost, old infrastructure, and dated technology.

The established players have been slow to respond to FinTech's disintermediation and disruption because they haven't wanted to cannibalize their legacy franchises. Many have attempted to offer digitalization only in noncore businesses or geographical areas. For example, some large banking institutions have experimented with offering new experiences such as payment services that compete with FinTech payment providers. However, these new offerings often require significant investment in new technologies to "get in the game," such as mobile-friendly site design, cryptocurrency, and digital wallets. They must respond to continually advancing technology, changing consumer habits, and in some cases underserved and underbanked markets.

TECHNICAL STUFF

In China, the most successful FinTech firms have been BigTech companies that developed financial ecosystems in conjunction with their highly engaged consumers. One example, Ant Financial, was created on the back of Alibaba's e-commerce platform, offering online payments, investments, digital banking, lending, and wallets. This was possible because China's FinTech ecosystem is fundamentally different from those of the United States and Europe. In Western economies, successful FinTech firms have been disruptors, particularly in the payments, lending, and wealth management sectors. They have benefited from extensive consumer adoption of mobile technologies and Internet access. Ant Financial is closer to the notion of TechFin rather than FinTech, where a large technology firm leverages its technology prowess to deliver financial products within its more efficient, broader service offering. It can also do this because it has generated a level of trust with clients that was previously reserved for traditional financial institutions.

2008: THE MARKET COLLAPSES

On July 30, 2007, Jeff Larson, the fair-haired child of the hedge fund world, closed his famous fund, Sowood, after it lost half its value in just one month. Sowood had gained fame and investors because of its tie to Harvard University's endowment fund. In the month of July, Sowood's two funds declined by 57 percent and 53 percent, and Citadel, LLC, bought Sowood's position, taking over its credit portfolio at a huge discount. This sale allowed Sowood to return the remaining $1.5 billion to its investors. The closing of these funds followed the Bear Stearns bailout, a failure tied to the subprime mortgage failures.

The fears over the subprime fiasco widened credit spreads (the difference between corporate and government debt) and tightened cash. The gamble that Sowood made through the use of derivatives resulted in its unrecoverable loss. Debt securities went into free fall, and Larson couldn't fully repay his lenders. The bailout of Bear Stearns and failure of Sowood caused the cost of private debt to skyrocket. From 2005 through 2006, Larson's strategy had yielded more than 16 percent returns per annum — twice the historic rate. His strategy was predicated on the difference between a company's debt and its stock value. The hedge was in the short selling of a company's stock against its debt. This strategy wasn't considered risky at the time and would probably not have brought the company down had he not borrowed excessively to offset his risks and increase his positions. Larson had insufficient cash to repay all debts when the sub-prime crisis was exposed. This crisis caused investors to retract support for all corporate debt indiscriminately. Sowood's hedge failed as a result.

At the time in which this was transpiring, Sowood was a customer of Numerix, with a five-year contract. It was this defining moment when Steve O'Hanlon heeded this early warning yet at the same time did something about it. He attempted to fully understand the extent of what was taking place in the industry, and he embraced the bad news. Seeing that Sowood's pedigree founder had been caught in this market collapse along with the prestigious Bear Stearns, he began quickly reflecting on what just happened and became more concerned about the derivative marketplace, a market to which Numerix was completely dedicated. In fact, Numerix was on the verge of being recognized by Celent as the industry leader of multi-asset class derivative pricing, and Steve wanted to be certain that the business would still have legs.

He recognized that Numerix was providing Risk Greeks, an important component used by traders and portfolio managers to hedge and to create scenarios that predict the potential changes on the profit and loss based on different pricing stresses, as part of the Numerix pricing system for free. Steve and his senior management team quickly started to analyze the risk market and realized that a pivot into that market was possible. Numerix separated out the risk technology from the pricing and offered two different kinds of licenses. This reorganization and product positioning set Numerix on the road to becoming a leader in Risk years later. It was because he got Numerix intimately involved and engaged in Risk deals that he learned a lot about what banks would need, and this knowledge set the basis for what later on became known to the market as a front-to-risk product called Oneview.

Weighing Wall Street against Silicon Valley: Where Disruptors Live

As you discover earlier in this chapter, recent disruptions in the financial industry have led both businesses and consumers to consider alternatives. This section reviews some of those alternatives and where they reside.

When people think about the financial services industry, many think about Wall Street, New York City. However, an important secondary concentration of budding financial services companies can be found in Silicon Valley, a region of the San Francisco Bay area that serves as a global center for high technology, innovation, and social media. In fact, some of those Silicon Valley companies have far larger balance sheets and market capitalization than traditional financial services firms.

Moreover, the success of Silicon Valley as a focal point for new technology innovation has resulted in imitators in the financial services industry somewhat closer to their traditional financial roots, in areas such as Silicon Alley, a growing community of FinTech businesses in downtown New York City, and Silicon Roundabout, a cluster of high-tech companies located around the Old Street Roundabout in London. And let's not ignore the rise of Asian FinTech firms, given some major household names already exist, such as Ant Financial and Tencent.

In addition, FinTech hubs are growing globally, as the map in Figure 2-1 illustrates based on a 2018 research study. While the "usual suspects" in China, the United Kingdom, and the United States are well publicized, some other hubs deserve a favorable reference. In Europe, centers such as Berlin and Tel Aviv have built up their presence in recent years, while in Asia and Australia, Singapore and Sydney have dedicated huge efforts to attract more global focus. Last but not least, in North America, Chicago has leveraged its traditional futures market ties, and Toronto has grown a dedicated expertise in artificial intelligence.

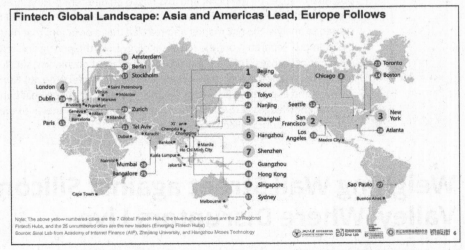

FIGURE 2-1: An overview of the global ranking of FinTech centers relative to funds invested in 2018.

Source: Sinai Lab from Academy of Internet Finance (AIF), Zhejiang University, and Hangzhou Moses Technology, 2018

2008: THE LEHMAN BANKRUPTCY

The subprime mortgage failure went on to take down other organizations, the largest of which was Lehman. On September 15, 2008, Lehman filed for bankruptcy. Lehman had $639 billion in assets and $619 billion in debt. A large amount of those holdings and debt were tied to mortgage-backed securities and illiquid trades. The valuation of its assets and liabilities was a difficult Gordian knot to untie.

When Lehman Brothers collapsed in 2008, Steve O'Hanlon saw how this event exposed serious gaps in the risk-management practices of financial institutions. He became determined to improve risk management and create the tools financial institutions needed to best structure their risk controls. He quickly spearheaded Numerix efforts to introduce new risk analytics offerings, which soon became game changers for the firm and the financial services industry.

The fall of Lehman Brothers was a watershed moment that continues to shape Numerix to this day. With trillions of dollars in outstanding derivatives needing to be reconciled with counterparties, Numerix was selected on behalf of the Lehman creditors to value millions of terminated trades. This was arguably the most complex and one of the largest derivatives portfolios in the world.

Not only did Numerix facilitate the unwinding of these positions, but because of its work, Lehman was able to return billions of dollars to creditors.

As Numerix worked side-by-side with the Lehman traders and IT staff, beginning January 2, 2009, it was clear that a more integrated and holistic approach for managing risk was a requirement, not just something that was nice to have. Through this experience, Steve recognized an opportunity to look at risk differently. He made the key decision to reevaluate Numerix's core analytics solution and creatively determine how it could be maximized to pivot the organization into what became a rapidly changing market of derivatives risk management.

The first deliverable was front-office credit value adjustment (CVA) calculations. When Numerix delivered this, it was quickly embraced by the marketplace as a game changer. This led Numerix to calculate all the value adjustments, now commonly referred to as XVA. At the same time Numerix created these calculations, it had immediately, under Steve's direction, begun building out an entirely new Java stack from the Numerix Analytics to the presentation layer. As XVA was being adopted, the new stack enabled financial institutions to leverage the "cloud" like Microsoft Azure, to enable economy of scale.

Today, the pivot to risk, and the creation of a next-generation technology stack leveraging Java so that Numerix could be cloud agnostic, was the most visionary accomplishment for Steve, propelling Numerix from a "multi-asset class pricing leader" to the leader in "front-to-risk enterprise systems."

Examining the Role of BigTech

In addition to companies that specialize in technologically advanced financial services (FinTech), several very large tech companies, such as Apple, Microsoft, Amazon, and Google, provide products and services across multiple industries. We'll call those *BigTech* as a shorthand. Whereas FinTech companies are focused on financial services activities, BigTech firms can offer financial services as part of their much wider offering.

REMEMBER

Financial services represent a relatively small percentage of a BigTech company's customer base, but the services that BigTech can provide match up well with what financial companies need more of to stay competitive. For example, Amazon Web Services (AWS) provides financial companies (and others) with a cloud presence without them having to reinvent the wheel by building their own cloud infrastructure. Other useful BigTech services of interest to financial companies include data analysis and customer relationship management. Therefore, BigTech's entry into financial services can be seen not only as a potential competitive threat but also as an opportunity for win-win partnerships that allow financial companies to focus on what they do best and outsource some of the technology aspects.

BigTech and payment platforms

To date, the main focus of most BigTech companies has been to provide basic financial services to their large, global ecosystems of clients. They have also acted as a delivery channel for established wealth management and insurance providers, largely driven by advertising revenue associated with search engine or targeted advertising.

However, some BigTech companies have moved into actively providing payment services to help increase the confidence level between buyer and seller on e-commerce online platforms. Payment services, such as Alipay (of which Alibaba is still a minority shareholder) or PayPal (owned by eBay), can provide secured settlement at delivery by buyers and are fully integrated into e-commerce platforms. In fact, the payment services market has developed to a point where buyers and sellers often use it as a replacement for other electronic payment channels such as credit and debit cards.

While BigTech payment platforms compete with those that banks provide, they still predominantly depend on banks. Services such as Apple Pay and PayPal, for example, need established suppliers of given infrastructure, such as debit/credit cards or trade payment systems, to manage and reconcile payments. Even where they allow payments that are processed and settled on their own proprietary system, such as Alipay, users still require a bank account or a credit/debit card to direct money into and out of the network and hold the funds in their bank accounts until they request repayment.

In addition, BigTech companies also need the banks' services to settle between banks, because the BigTech companies don't participate in interbank payment systems for settlement in central bank money. Therefore, for payment services, BigTech both competes and cooperates with established banks.

TECHNICAL STUFF

It will be interesting to see how Facebook's launch of its own digital currency, Libra, may change this dynamic. Interestingly, credit card behemoths Mastercard and Visa and payment specialists eBay and Stripe were among the initial collaborators announced among the Libra partners, but they have all subsequently stepped back, waiting for the "association to satisfy all the requisite regulatory requirements."

BigTech partnership opportunities

BigTech companies are approaching their financial services engagement from several different angles, and these are likely to develop further over time. BigTech typically enters areas of financial services where they have acquired an established customer base and brand recognition. This reflects crossovers between financial services and core nonfinancial activities, where they identify enough economies of scale. For example, companies such as Apple, Google, and Microsoft are application-centric and data-centric, providing financial cloud computing from data management and technology perspectives. E-commerce firms such as Alibaba and Amazon are more focused on delivering frictionless client experience, using customer data to better manage credit risk and working capital.

REMEMBER

As a result, rather than seeing BigTech as an imminent threat, many financial institutions are looking at potential partnerships and collaboration benefits. According to various reports, many financial institutions have started to partner with some of the BigTech giants, such as Apple with Goldman Sachs and Google with Citigroup, while others are planning to develop such partnerships in the near future. Some of the key features of their business models are those that financial institutions are hoping to replicate, largely because they haven't been so successful at implementing them internally.

How BigTech can help utilize data

Traditional financial institutions have always had huge amounts of data at their disposal, yet they have mostly failed to exploit it in the way that BigTech has. Banks, asset managers, and insurance companies have all developed their own internal platforms from which customer data can be leveraged. The more transactions facilitated on the platform, the more data available for analytics that can enhance existing services and attract further users. The potential for improvement industry-wide is huge in this area.

REMEMBER

BigTech companies have been masters at increasing the number of users on their platforms, which provides the critical mass of customers to further offer a broader range of services, which in turn develops even more data. Offering financial services in addition can supplement and strengthen BigTech's commercial activities. Payment transactions, consumer loans, and credit scoring are all examples of data generated from transactional activity. The synergies to be leveraged depend on the type of data collected, but BigTech companies, with their large user bases in social media or Internet search, can record user preferences and use them to promote, distribute, and price third-party financial services such as wealth management or insurance products.

TECHNICAL STUFF

Large financial institutions also have many customers, to whom they offer a broad range of services, but they have not been as effective as BigTech in exploiting the feedback benefits. One reason for this is the mandatory separation of banking and commerce data in many jurisdictions, which limits the data that banks can access to transaction data. In addition, legacy IT systems have not been traditionally linked to various other services through application programming interfaces (APIs).

By using more advanced technology, coupled with richer data and a clearer customer focus, BigTech companies have more proficiently developed and marketed new products and services. As a result, they have lowered the barriers to delivery by reducing information and transaction costs, and they have enhanced financial inclusion by making financial accounts more widely available (in other words, "banking the unbanked"). However, the gains available through these actions may vary by service and could generate new risks or market failures.

Barriers to greater BigTech participation

WARNING

BigTech companies will face a lot more regulation if they want to enter the financial services arena in a more meaningful way. Consider the following:

>> Policy regulators will have to create a level playing field between financial institutions and BigTech, particularly considering their established client base, the ability to access information, and wide-ranging commercial models. Many observers question why BigTech would want to threaten their dominant position across many industries if they must overcome many prospective obstacles to direct entry into the financial institution community.

>> There are also many examples where BigTech companies have shown themselves to be averse to regulation and wouldn't want to face a potentially strong anti-trust backlash.

>> Moreover, their entry will raise many new and multifaceted trade-offs between financial strength, rivalry, and data protection.

>> It's also uncertain whether BigTech companies will have the required domain expertise in the complexities of financial services. In other words, just because a company *can* do something technologically doesn't mean it will automatically be good at it.

2008: SUCCEEDING AGAINST ALL ODDS

Since 2004, when Steve O'Hanlon took leadership of Numerix, it has always taken bold moves and never worried about stagnating around one offering for too long. Inherently, Steve knew that Numerix possessed many of the key attributes (analytics) that both Bloomberg and Blackrock possessed. As a result, climbing hills to take ownership of a product category has always been Steve's style.

In 2008, before Lehman's collapse and two years after signing an incredibly exciting partnership with Bloomberg, Numerix became the recognized leader of multi-asset class pricing. Having achieved this stature and after the collapse of Lehman, Numerix reinvented itself as both a pricing and risk company. This was a bold move; to be able to build out a significant Enterprise Risk product from the Numerix Pricing analytics stack to the presentation layer was the boldest move ever. Maintaining a significant pricing business while investing in a completely new path was possible only because Numerix became Lehman's partner in bankruptcy and Numerix invested all of that money into the pivot to risk.

Steve always believed that making choices that are managed is just as critical as willing a new direction or initiative to happen. In other words, we must always attempt to do new things while succeeding against all odds, both morally and ethically. The journey that Steve has been on with Numerix since 2002 is living proof that if you want something badly enough, if you're willing to do what it takes, and if you take an unorthodox approach but get a team to follow you into the heat of battle, then you can succeed against all odds!

Understanding Where the Disruptions Are Happening

REMEMBER

As mentioned earlier, *FinTech* is an overarching term for the combination of finance and technology. However, within FinTech, many subcategories apply to specific sectors of the financial world. Here's a quick summary of them:

>> **Capital Markets Tech,** in which companies leverage newer technology such as artificial intelligence, machine learning, and blockchain, is led by seasoned capital markets veterans and is both collaborating with and disrupting the financial services incumbents.

>> **WealthTech** unites wealth and technology to provide digital tools for personal and professional wealth management and investing. This sector includes brokerage platforms, automated/semiautomated robo-advisors, and self-directed investment tools for individual investors and advisors to navigate the changing landscape in wealth management. For more information, check out *The WealthTech Book,* edited by Susanne Chishti and Thomas Puschmann (published by Wiley).

>> **InsurTech** is a combination of insurance and technology. It refers to innovations that generate efficiency and cost savings from the existing insurance industry model. For more information, see *The InsurTech Book,* edited by Sabine L. B. VanderLinden, Shân M. Millie, Nicole Anderson, and Susanne Chishti (published by Wiley).

>> **RegTech** is a community of technology companies that solve regulatory challenges through automation. The increase in major regulatory policy and the rise in digital products have made it imperative for companies to check for and implement compliance issues, and this can be difficult with old, manual processes. For more information, refer to *The RegTech Book,* edited by Janos Barberis, Douglas W. Arner, and Ross P. Buckley (published by Wiley).

>> **PayTech** refers to the combination of payments and technology. Innovative payment services now form part of the PayTech ecosystem and have dominated the early days of the FinTech revolution through mobile, cross-border, peer-to-peer, and cryptocurrency payments. Financial institutions have had to digitize their current offerings to create new channels linked to a digital platform. For more information, see *The PayTech Book,* edited by Susanne Chishti, Tony Craddock, Robert Courtneidge, and Markos Zachariadis (published by Wiley).

>> **AI in Finance** refers to how artificial intelligence, machine learning, and deep learning are applied across financial services companies today and how they could be used in the future. For more information, see *The AI Book*, edited by Ivana Bartoletti, Susanne Chishti, Anne Leslie, and Shân M. Millie (published by Wiley).

>> **LegalTech** combines the nature of legal technologies and their relationship with data, the Internet of Things (IOT), cybersecurity, and distributed ledger technologies as well as ethical considerations of the technological advancement. For more information, refer to *The LegalTech Book*, edited by Sophia Adams Bhatti, Susanne Chishti, Akber Datoo, and Drago Indjic (published by Wiley).

In the following sections, we look at some business types in more detail to see how traditional financial firms are being shaken up — and improved — by FinTech disruptions.

Banks

Some larger financial institutions have adopted the phrase "We're just a technology company that happens to have a banking license." This is mostly a marketing gimmick, although it's perhaps partially true for some of the new challenger banks that are attempting to disrupt the incumbent banks. However, with customer acquisition costs high and increasing regulatory hurdles to surmount, new challenger banks need to decide whether they will build their technology stack themselves or work with FinTech partners to develop the innovation required to topple the incumbents.

REMEMBER

The financial institutions that are effectively managing this move to become FinTech companies are those that understand how to move quickly to deliver what the consumer needs in an industry on the verge of further change. Most of those who succeed have taken a hybrid approach, focusing on partnerships, acquisitions, and internal initiatives.

Several incumbent banks are known to be developing new digital-first products in a bid to keep the new wave of challenger banks and providers in the background; an example is Bo from the Royal Bank of Scotland. They are also gradually adopting much more ambitious cloud-based platforms (despite their paranoia about their data being hacked) on which they can offer or launch numerous products. These initiatives are being supported by the likes of Amazon, Google, and Microsoft, which provide cloud hosting services and enable banks to develop core banking Software-as-a-Service (SaaS) platforms with the required encryption security.

Asset managers

Traditionally, serious investors have valued personal investment advice from human experts, and they haven't minded paying for it. However, the asset management industry has been attacked from two different angles:

» One of these is the march toward passive investments (such as exchange traded funds, or ETFs) over active asset management. ETFs are traded like stocks where the holdings track to some well-known index, such as the Standard & Poor's (S&P) 500.

» The other is the rise in popularity of robo-advisors, which use ETFs as a strong part of their strategy. A robo-advisor is an investment selection tool that uses algorithms and machine learning to offer investment advice and management to users.

The trend toward passive asset management has been apparent for some time in the retail/business-to-consumer (B2C) space, but we're lately also seeing it with the larger business-to-business (B2B) investors as the stock market index returns continue to rise and they are looking to cut costs to further enhance returns for their clients.

REMEMBER

WealthTech firms are enabling investors to self-manage their portfolios by offering users technology-enabled tools to help make investing decisions. These tools can include full-service brokerage alternatives, automated and semiautomated robo-advisors, self-service investment platforms, asset class specific marketplaces, and portfolio management tools for both individual investors and advisors. They consider not only investment opportunities but also factors such as a user's goals, income, marital status, and risk aversion to differentiate on their offering. They enable those who can't afford a traditional financial advisor to have similar — if not more informed — advice at a lower cost.

Insurance

If the banking and asset management firms think they have it tough with the rise of FinTech firms, there are many that believe that the insurance industry is even more prone to disruption — and innovation.

InsurTech firms initially started to explore offerings that large insurance firms had little incentive to pursue. For example, they offered customers the ability to customize their policies, and they used Internet-enabled devices to collect information about behavior (such as driving habits) that could be used to dynamically price insurance premiums. Traditionally, the insurance market has worked with relatively basic levels of data to group respective policyholders together to generate a diversified portfolio of people. However, InsurTech firms are tackling their data and analysis issues by taking inputs from various devices, including GPS tracking of cars and activity trackers on wearables so that they can monitor more defined risk grouping and therefore allow certain products to be more competitively priced.

In addition to better pricing models, InsurTech firms are using highly trained artificial intelligence (AI) to help brokers find the right mix of policies to complete an individual's insurance coverage and credit score. In some cases, they can replace brokers entirely, further disintermediating the process (and saving costs). Apps are also being developed that can combine contrasting policies into one platform for management and monitoring. Some of the benefits of that might include enabling customers to purchase on-demand policies for micro-events and enabling groups of individual policyholders to become part of a customized group that is eligible for rebates or discounts.

REMEMBER

Insurance is also a highly regulated industry. Major brokers and underwriters have survived by being both prudent and risk averse. They are therefore suspicious of working with InsurTech start-ups, particularly those that want to disrupt their stable industry. Many InsurTech start-ups require the help of traditional insurers to handle underwriting issues, so the incumbent players here are likely to collaborate with and invest in their junior partners.

Regulation and legal work

RegTech is the management of and compliance with regulatory processes within the financial industry, using technology to address regulatory monitoring, reporting, and ongoing compliance. The predominantly cloud-based, SaaS offerings to help businesses comply with regulations efficiently and more cheaply act as the glue between the various sectors of the financial services industry described earlier.

LegalTech describes technological innovation to enhance or replace traditional methods for delivering legal services across financial services and beyond. This innovation includes document automation, predictive artificial intelligence, advanced chat bots, knowledge management, research systems, and smart legal contracts to increase efficiency and productivity and reduce costs.

With the use of big data and machine-learning technology, RegTech and LegalTech firms reduce the risk to a financial institution's compliance and legal departments by identifying potential threats earlier to minimize the risks and costs associated with regulatory breaches and any legal work. RegTech firms can combine information from a financial institution with precedent data extracted from prior regulatory events to forecast probable risk areas that the institution should focus on.

LegalTech firms can help financial institutions draft documents, undertake legal research, disclose documents in litigation, perform due diligence, and provide legal guidance.

These analytical tools can save institutions significant time and money, including saving them from having to pay fines levied for misconduct. The institutions also have an effective tool to comply with ongoing rules and regulations specified by financial authorities, which are constantly prone to amendments.

Payments

From banknotes to coins to plastic cards and mobile devices, payments have evolved over the centuries to include a number of ways to help financial transactions take place between individuals, institutions, and governments. Payment technologies and global infrastructures that facilitate payments around the world also are changing.

Over the last few years, mobile money has helped millions of people in developing countries get access to the financial system and tackle the goal of financial inclusion. Digital and cryptocurrencies such as Bitcoin, Ripple, and Ether have also entered the payments sector, which is innovating more rapidly than ever with the goal to move value cost-efficiently in real time and at near zero cost. As a result, the PayTech sector is booming; established players closely work with newcomers as there is no end to the creativity of the PayTech and payment industry.

Looking for the Opportunities

REMEMBER

Disruption isn't a bad thing necessarily, as we hope you've picked up in this chapter. In fact, another word for it is innovation. Disruption interrupts the status quo, inviting traditional businesses to adopt new approaches as well as opening the door for new businesses to try their hand at it. Here are some ways that FinTech is opening the door to innovation for all financial services companies.

Partnership opportunities

Traditional financial institutions and FinTech firms are increasingly combining their strengths in partnership models. Even some of the business-to-consumer (B2C) retail-driven FinTech firms realize that they may reach a saturation point with their digital marketing coverage before they meet their revenue targets, so they need distribution partners to grow their business. FinTech companies offer greater speed, risk tolerance, and agile processes to react to change, while larger institutions bring the depth and breadth from their core businesses to the table.

Exploiting digitalization with AI

Digitalization has generated huge amounts of data, which FinTech firms have been quicker to exploit. New data feeds and evolving AI know-how have made labor-intensive workflow processes more efficient and have produced new insight into financial services applications and products. AI and machine learning technologies are critical for both small and large players within the expanding FinTech ecosystem. These technologies make it possible to extract unique and relative insights from data, and companies that invest in it will be able to exploit its capabilities in years to come.

WARNING

AI isn't without its drawbacks, however. For example, many industry experts have said that managing the security risk of AI systems will be a challenge. In addition, developing AI tools that can improve decision-making, but are also transparent to the user in how they operate, could be potential barriers to the technology's development if users don't feel the results have been clearly explained.

Introducing some additional rules regarding privacy of data, while simultaneously allowing users to selectively determine the types of data to be shared, could enlarge the efficient analysis of AI and the new products it creates. This would ensure that customers determine which of their data sets are used and providers have sufficient data to improve their products.

Enhancing data portability

Data portability, whereby clients are allowed to transfer personal data seamlessly across multiple services, will also be key in defining the terms of competition in the financial sector. For example, open banking regulations subjectively limit what data can be communicated (for example, only financial transaction data), as well as the sort of organizations among which this data can be shared (for example, only certified deposit-taking organizations). Likewise, the European Union's General Data Protection Regulation (GDPR) requires clients' active consent prior to a financial institution using their personal data.

Chapter **3**

The Role of Regulation in FinTech

The financial crisis of 2008 triggered sweeping regulation reform for financial institutions globally. Concerns about the systemic risk that such institutions created for the wider economy, in addition to alleged abuses caused by a "too big to fail" culture, prompted regulators to impose multiple new obligations on the financial sector. These reforms, including the Dodd-Frank Act in the United States and the Markets in Financial Instruments Directive (MiFID II) in Europe, have fundamentally changed the regulatory landscape at a wholesale market level.

The resultant challenges that regulated institutions face are numerous. They must ensure that they're compliant with any new requirements, consider how to proactively respond to emerging risks from FinTech, and try not to let regulatory compliance restrict their innovation benefits.

This chapter looks at how financial institutions and FinTech companies are regulated. It looks at vendor risk — and why it matters — and introduces you to the major regulatory agencies in the United States and Europe. It also discusses what regulatory changes may be coming in the future and what opportunities we see in the regulatory technology (RegTech) industry.

Supervising FinTech

The increased requirements that financial institutions now face have had an unfortunate side effect of hindering innovation and new product development. But it hasn't been unfortunate for all. FinTech companies have received a boost from it, because they're cherry-picking the areas that have lighter or no regulatory requirements and can therefore be more competitive — for now, anyway. The danger for regulators is that regulation fails to keep pace with new technology and business models if not constantly reviewed and modified. Regulators are therefore trying to find ways to sufficiently regulate FinTech companies and level the playing field without unduly stifling innovation.

Understanding that location matters

Because they have lower costs and fewer barriers to entry, FinTech firms can now develop services that would have previously required more capital than they had available. It involves risks, though. With borderless platforms, like those provided as apps or via the cloud (see Chapter 6), it's sometimes not clear where they're legally domiciled, so it's hard to know where and by whom they should be regulated. This is particularly true where FinTech firms are developing business-to-consumer (B2C) services that aim to disrupt the existing financial institutions for services such as investment advice or retail payment facilities.

To avoid dealing with onerous regulations, FinTech firms sometimes establish themselves in a location with a favorable regulatory environment and rely on passporting (allowing firms regulatory freedom of movement across borders) into other jurisdictions. However, the United Kingdom's exit from the European Union (Brexit) and the removal of the cross-border regulatory equivalence rules for Switzerland have made it harder to passport regulated services from one jurisdiction to another in Europe. In addition, certain activities in the United States require regulatory oversight under individual state licenses, so FinTech firms need to be aware of potential barriers to entry.

As a reaction, many regulatory organizations, such as the Financial Conduct Authority (FCA) in the U.K., have established so-called *regulatory sandboxes.* These sandboxes aim to build rapport with both the traditional financial industry and fledgling FinTech companies, helping them better understand the changing landscape. It gives the companies an opportunity to discuss new business approaches from an early stage, and it enables regulators to explain how they believe the companies should meet the regulatory requirements.

REMEMBER

FinTech firms need to decide whether they're going to be pure technology companies that facilitate the financial activities of their clients or whether they're going to provide a regulated service themselves. When they've made that decision, they can explore what that means in terms of licenses and supervision.

NUMERIX: THE SECOND PIVOT

Reflecting on the five operating tenets of 2004, Numerix's choices and decisions led the company to unprecedented double-digit growth from 2004 to the end of 2008 when Lehman went into bankruptcy. Even after Lehman's bankruptcy, Numerix continued to grow.

The maturity of the pricing tools led Numerix to a new partnership with Bloomberg in July 2006. This was a remarkable deal because Numerix leveraged its analytics to create about 75 static derivative calculators that were mobilized within the Bloomberg Terminal. Each time Bloomberg users used one of its calculators, the displayed pricing results would show the Numerix logo along with the model that they used. Coupled with an enormous quantity of Bloomberg blasts (communication to all Bloomberg users about the offering), Numerix quickly became the recognized derivative pricing leader.

During 2008, Celent published a report on the state of the pricing market with Numerix listed as the leader in this space. Numerix was touted as the pioneer of multi-asset class pricing, something no other firm did at that time. The Bloomberg partnership also enabled Numerix to sell its Excel-based pricing tool to the Bloomberg user population. The product was dubbed the Numerix Bloomberg edition because Bloomberg data was linked directly to Numerix's offering inside the Bloomberg Terminal. What is significant about this is that it was the first time Bloomberg had entered into such a partnership that allowed direct access to a partner's offering.

By October 2008, Lehman collapsed and the market went into a tailspin. History reflects on this moment and days following as the beginning of the Great Recession. Numerix became the benefactor of this historic debacle by outselling 20 different data and/or valuation companies and becoming the partner to Lehman's creditors through the unwind. Numerix was awarded this business because of its pedigree in understanding its front-office requirements, its technology, and most important, its ability to price any derivative ever created. Lehman had more than 300,000 derivatives that needed to be priced, and Numerix was the only company capable of doing this work. From January 1, 2009, to December 31, 2018, Numerix provided valuations on every trade it ever did for the first 15 days after bankruptcy. These valuations were used by the estate as part of the unwind.

Recognizing that more regulations are coming

Some say that regulation has been unable to keep pace with the changing landscape that the rise of FinTech firms has created. FinTech companies have been allowed to swerve around conventional intermediation, and some say that their approaches to traditional banking, capital formation, and cryptocurrencies have changed the centralization of money itself.

Financial regulatory agencies must recognize the longer-term, collective, systemic risks of decentralized financial markets. They must then increase their regulation, in the same way that they have increased the oversight of "too big to fail" financial institutions since the financial crisis. FinTech may operate relatively under the radar today, but they can expect greater supervision as they continue to disrupt and disintermediate.

Originally, regulators handled FinTech with "light touch" rules that promoted the benefits of competition and diversification away from incumbent institutions. However, some fairly serious risks developed due to these policies. Regulators have become worried about the way consumers can now access financial services online from questionable providers in different jurisdictions. While several international standards have been published, their implementation has been inconsistent in some jurisdictions and too explicit in others. There has therefore been no mapping of responses to recognized risks.

Regulators have recently introduced international standards aimed at FinTech firms (see www.bis.org/speeches/sp191017a.htm) and have built international alliances between regulatory sandboxes (see www.thegfin.com), allowing information sharing between supervisory entities. These high-level principles cover areas such as anti-money laundering (AML), cybersecurity, data privacy, know your client (KYC), and risk governance. National implementation differs significantly across jurisdictions and financial sectors, but it's a good start.

Leveling the playing field

Regulators must create a level playing field for all providers, but some would argue that it's even more important to do so when some of those providers are BigTech players such as Facebook and Google. (*BigTech* refers to enormous tech companies that provide products and services across multiple industries.)

BigTech companies' balance sheets are more robust than those of many financial institutions, so financial stability isn't the major regulatory issue. The greater issue is fairness, making sure that BigTech companies don't have an unfair advantage and don't inappropriately leverage the vast amount of information they have collected. Given that a BigTech company's customer base is larger than that of most financial institutions, how do regulators limit access to information while also ensuring data protection?

The most high-profile example of BigTech challenging traditional financial services was the announcement of Facebook's Libra cryptocurrency/stable coin. Initially, this seemed like a plausible threat to fiat currencies (issued by governments) and payment services, because it was backed by a consortium that included traditional financial services providers. However, the project has been stalled until Facebook provides further proof that it will be safe and secure, according to a report produced by a G7 taskforce that included senior officials from the International Monetary Fund (IMF), central banks, and the Financial Stability Board. They warned that digital currencies such as Libra could present a systemic risk to the financial system. In the meantime, many of the traditional institutional backers of the project have pulled out due to regulatory uncertainty. Some argue that other BigTech firms have stayed away from financial services precisely because they don't need to deal with the regulatory requirements given the less onerous opportunities available to them elsewhere.

NUMERIX: LESSONS LEARNED FROM THE LEHMAN EXPERIENCE

The valuation of the Lehman unwind catapulted Numerix into being the primary authority on exotic derivatives pricing. The sub-prime debacle, however, singularly pointed out the limitation and loss of appetite in the market for such high-risk instruments. Numerix had been built to price the most complex offerings rapidly and flexibly. No other analytics company could make that claim. During the Lehman unwind, Numerix also employed more financial engineers and PhD mathematicians than some of the largest banks and financial institutions.

What became apparent to coauthor Steve O'Hanlon at this time was that due to regulations and tightened risk controls, Numerix had to change. The company had to adapt to the need for greater insight into the risk around companies' portfolios, the expanded government restrictions and oversight on risk handling, and the increased appetite for low margin but safer vanilla vehicles.

REMEMBER

FinTech firms need to be proactive and establish business models that fulfill the financial services regulatory requirements. Part of their competitive advantage should be to mitigate risks related to any supervisory requirements. Regulators will determine new rules that consider new or changing FinTech products and services and their related emerging technologies. Therefore, adopting a framework that focuses on aspects such as capital, controls, governance, liquidity, and operations will ensure that the company meets existing and future requirements. Many B2C FinTech firms are focusing on apps that handle payments, investment, crowdfunding, lending, or open banking opportunities, and their first research should be what regulatory approvals they may require for such activities.

Examining Vendor Risk Issues

While adoption of FinTech creates innovation potential, it also may increase exposure to unintended compliance risks for both the institution and the FinTech firm. It's important that financial institutions understand what that means for them.

REMEMBER

Financial institutions are adopting more third-party software technology to broaden their innovation, but they need to be aware how this exposes them to risks of cyberattacks and of client data privacy being compromised. Institutions need to undertake due diligence to research vendor relationships and ensure that their own systems safeguard client information. This is part of the reason information security and procurement checks are so stringent at most financial institutions. In addition, the introduction of the Senior Managers and Certification Regime (SMCR) in the U.K. puts an onus on senior management and the board of directors to be aware of and understand any FinTech applications licensed by their firms so that they can manage any risks effectively, even down to individual managers being allocated specific responsibilities.

Moreover, even FinTech firms that consider themselves as "just technology vendors that collaborate with financial institutions" are being reviewed. Depending on the services they provide, regulators are reviewing whether gray lines exist between providing services for a client and how involved they are in providing services for their end customers directly. Some institutions would also argue that if a technical problem occurs with the FinTech company's service that causes a regulatory breach, the FinTech should share in the consequences! Regulators will be quick to remind the institutions that *they* have the regulatory responsibility and that they can't pass the buck on such misdemeanors.

Introducing the Regulators

Who has the authority to regulate financial institutions and FinTech firms, and in what ways? It's important to know whether you're part of an organization that may potentially be subject to regulation.

In this section, we look primarily at regulatory agencies and regulations in the U.S. and Europe, because FinTech firms are more numerous in these jurisdictions, capital invested has been spread across more firms there, and those areas have experienced some of the biggest changes in regulation since the financial crisis in 2008.

TECHNICAL STUFF

Countries in the Asia Pacific region are more fragmented than the U.S. and Europe in terms of FinTech regulation. For example, China is adopting more region-specific and perfected rules, whereas some other countries are still at a basic level of regulation with aims to help their local FinTech companies grow while maintaining client interests. Countries in the Asia Pacific region tend to follow standards that their larger neighbors implement, so it's likely that they'll all move toward similar standards in the future. In the meantime, regulatory arbitrage at both domestic and jurisdictional levels is probable. Singapore has been particularly proactive in creating a positive environment for FinTech firms, with Australia and Japan also active.

The United States of America

Many countries have one or few major regulatory entities that have wide-ranging and sole oversight of their particular jurisdiction. The U.S. is a clear exception to this rule, having many federal regulators with coinciding jurisdictions. This can result in a more complicated environment for given transactions and where actions by a given regulator may be changeable.

The U.S. is known for being a rules-based regulatory jurisdiction, rather than a principles-based one like the U.K. The U.S.'s approach may have to change at some point in the future, because the speed of innovation and change won't keep pace with the implementation of specific rules.

Another issue is that activities such as nonbank lending have traditionally been regulated at a state level, but online markets naturally operate on an interstate level, so federal coverage may be required to ensure consistent regulation. For example, robo-advisor firms, which provide wealth management products solely online based on an algorithmic approach to investment strategies, have become popular. They incorporate information received from clients outlining their risk tolerance, time horizon, and existing investments to create an optimal strategy. Regulators have suggested that such services could create systemic risks as the managed assets grow, and so these services should be reviewed at an interstate level.

REMEMBER

The following are the most important financial regulatory bodies in the U.S.:

>> **The Federal Reserve:** The Federal Reserve ("the Fed") is the main supervisor of state-chartered banks that have elected to enter the Federal Reserve System. The Fed also supervises all bank holding companies, which tend to have subsidiaries that may be supervised by other agencies. In addition, the Federal Reserve promotes payment and settlement system efficiency and safety.

>> **The Financial Stability Oversight Council:** The Financial Stability Oversight Council has a defined constitutional mandate that establishes joint account-ability for recognizing risks and reacting to evolving threats to financial stability. The Council has powers to limit disproportionate risk in the financial system. For example, the Council can designate that a nonbank financial firm (such as a FinTech firm) is liable for supervision to reduce the risk that such a firm could threaten the strength of the financial system.

>> **The Consumer Financial Protection Bureau:** The Consumer Financial Protection Bureau (CFPB) is responsible for enforcing federal consumer laws and protecting consumers in the financial marketplace.

>> **The Federal Deposit Insurance Corporation:** The Federal Deposit Insurance Corporation (FDIC) insures bank deposits and acts as the primary safety and consumer protection regulator for institutions that aren't members of the Federal Reserve System.

>> **The Office of the Comptroller of the Currency:** The Office of the Comptroller of the Currency (OCC) licenses, regulates, and supervises all national banks and federal savings associations, including federal branches and agencies of foreign banks.

>> **The Commodity Futures Trading Commission:** The Commodity Futures Trading Commission (CFTC) regulates the futures and swaps markets, including various financial products. Its mission is to promote open, transparent, competitive, and financially sound markets. The CFTC isn't a banking regulator, but FinTech companies can correspond with the CFTC to receive help understanding their approach to supervision through the LabCFTC hub (www.cftc.gov/LabCFTC/index.htm).

NUMERIX: THE MOVE TO RISK

Steve O'Hanlon quickly realized that the financial crisis would immediately create opportunities in derivatives risk management, so he wasted no time in pivoting Numerix in that direction.

Between 2009 and 2012, as part of its pivot to risk, Numerix started developing one of the industry's most comprehensive risk-management tool kits. Financial institutions were increasingly selecting Numerix because of the value they saw in its wide range of asset-class-based analytic tools and models, as well as its ability to enable clients to generate risk information. In fact, Numerix's new and enhanced technology offerings encouraged financial institutions to reexamine the way they exercised proper risk control, from front office to back office, to maintain their competency in a market full of challenges.

One of Numerix's priorities was to continually enhance Numerix CrossAsset, one of the firm's flagship brands. Numerix CrossAsset evolved into offering the industry's most comprehensive collection of models and methods, enabling institutions to price any conceivable instrument using the most advanced calculations, in addition to a wide range of calibration options for generating market-consistent valuations. With an infinitely flexible architecture for defining custom deals — and the ability to integrate its own internal models — Numerix CrossAsset enabled users to deploy a unified pricing and risk solution for all their derivative and fixed income positions across all trade types.

The United Kingdom and Europe

REMEMBER

In principle, the regulatory situation in Europe is simpler than the setup in the U.S., with one major regulator in each country, such as the Financial Conduct Authority (FCA) in the U.K., the Autorité des Marchés Financiers (AMF) in France, Bundesanstalt für Finanzdienstleistungsaufsicht (BaFin) in Germany, and the Authority for the Financial Markets (AFM) in the Netherlands. However, these are overlaid by E.U. institutions, such as the European Commission, the European Central Bank, and the European Securities and Markets Authority (ESMA), all of which can feed regulations down to the local regulators to enforce. This has in the past been held together by passporting rules that allowed regulated firms from one jurisdiction to offer their services to customers in another.

However, the U.K.'s decision to leave the E.U. has raised questions as to how passporting will operate in the future, given London's preeminent position as a financial center in Europe and the number of FinTech firms that have formed in the U.K. A "hard" Brexit (where no agreement is reached on how trade and regulation will proceed after the U.K.'s exit) will bring much more regulatory uncertainty in the future, whereas a "soft" Brexit (in which new agreements are reached) will help.

The E.U. responded to the aftermath of the financial crisis in 2008 by producing and applying tougher financial regulations. The E.U. has implemented a significant regulatory framework that institutions are still adjusting to, which has created initial uncertainty until firms develop a better understanding of how to fully comply with the new rules.

The European System of Financial Supervision

The framework for financial supervision in the E.U., as proposed by the European Commission, sits under the European System of Financial Supervision (ESFS). The system is made up of the European Supervisory Authorities (ESAs), the European Systemic Risk Board, and the national supervisory entities in each E.U. member state. Three ESAs are accountable for micro-prudential (individual firm level) supervision at the European level: the European Banking Authority (EBA), the European Securities and Markets Authority (ESMA), and the European Insurance and Occupational Pensions Authority (EIOPA).

The ESAs' use of their heightened powers and the increased prospects for cooperation and information sharing between national competent authorities (NCAs) will probably result in strengthened procedures and further information requests for certified firms.

The European Systemic Risk Board

To supplement the ESFS authorities, the European Systemic Risk Board (ESRB) is responsible for macro-prudential (risk to the financial system as a whole) supervision across the E.U. It's made up of delegates from the European Central Bank, national central banks, and supervisory authorities of E.U. member states and the European Commission.

The Financial Conduct Authority

The Financial Conduct Authority (FCA) regulates the financial services industry in the U.K. Its responsibilities include safeguarding consumers, maintaining the industry stability, and encouraging strong competition between financial service suppliers. In particular, the latter objective empowers the FCA to identify and address competition problems and adopt a more pro-competition approach to regulation than many other regulators. This has encouraged the FCA to have a more proactive engagement with FinTech firms than some other regulators.

The structure of the FCA's regulatory authority encompasses the Bank of England's Prudential Regulatory Authority (PRA) and Financial Policy Committee. The PRA is the prudential regulator for approximately 1,500 banks, building societies, credit unions, insurers, and major investment firms. As a prudential regulator, it has an overall objective to encourage the safety and soundness of the firms regulated. The FCA also created a separate body, the Payment Systems Regulator (PSR), in 2013. The PSR's role is to promote competition and innovation in payment systems.

The FCA has been an authoritative voice within the group of national supervisory entities of each E.U. member state, largely because of London's position as a financial center for Europe. However, in a post-Brexit world with the U.K. separate from the E.U., it will be interesting to see how they maintain their influence and whether they'll move away from some of the collective decisions they previously made.

The Global Financial Innovation Network

To further promote the idea of harmonization and standardization among FinTech firms globally, the Global Financial Innovation Network (GFIN) was launched in January 2019 by an international group of financial regulators and related organizations. This further developed the FCA's proposal to create a global sandbox environment for emerging FinTech ideas and companies.

TIP

The GFIN has 50 organizations in its network that are committed to backing innovation in FinTech for the interests of consumers globally. Its goal is to offer a more effective way for FinTech firms to cooperate with regulators, helping them find the best route to gain regulatory approval across countries as they scale up new ideas. It runs a pilot program for firms looking to trial innovative services, products, or business models across multiple jurisdictions. It also looks to develop a new framework for collaboration between regulators on topics connected to innovation, sharing diverse experiences and practices. Its website (www.thegfin.com) delivers information on GFIN's membership, cross-border testing, and current publications.

NUMERIX: CHANGING SOFTWARE TO FIT THE MARKET

The first steps in the move toward providing seamless pricing to risk calculations was an evaluation of the way in which the existent technologies could be repurposed to be used for front- to middle-office processes. It was imperative that the same analytics and the same data were used for all functions across all departments. With this in mind, the stack of technologies was expanded to entail the following:

- The launch of Numerix Counterparty Risk, an integrated solution for calculating potential future exposure and credit valuation adjustment (CVA) for derivative portfolios using a high-performance Monte Carlo simulation engine.

- The Numerix CrossAsset XL and Numerix Portfolio Products solution, which enabled users to take advantage of the high-performance features of Windows HPC Server 2008 and HPC Services for Excel 2010 with the most powerful grid computing capabilities across the industry. When coupled with the value of an integrated HPC solution, Numerix CrossAsset XL and Numerix Portfolio provided Numerix's clients with the improved systems productivity, interoperability, and full transparency for deal definitions and accelerated real-time valuations and ability to run rapid unified risk calculations for complex derivative portfolios.

- The launch of Numerix LiquidAsset for pricing over-the-counter (OTC) derivatives and exchange-traded deals. Built on Numerix's market-leading CrossAsset analytics, LiquidAsset is a function-based Excel solution valuing the most common set of OTC derivative trade types. Focusing on the user experience, the Numerix LiquidAsset product provided an intuitive interface that harnessed the power of Numerix CrossAsset to price common trades quickly and accurately. These types of trades posed new and different pricing challenges, because the bid-ask spread had orders of magnitude smaller than their exotic counterparts. With Numerix LiquidAsset, users were able to take immediate advantage of built-in deal conventions that are prepackaged for pricing and trading all the major currencies and their markets globally.

- Expansion to products like Portfolio and Liquid Asset, which were pivotal early-stage offerings to nascent markets that enabled Numerix to evolve as a leading pricing and risk company. Today Portfolio and Liquid Asset have been collapsed inside of Numerix's new platform and the names retired.

Investigating Regulatory Changes

Quite a few regulatory changes have already taken place that have enabled FinTech firms to benefit from changes in consumer behavior. This section reviews some recent changes to the ways payment services and data requirements are regulated and explain the areas where regulatory change has initiated innovation and tangible consumer benefits.

Payment Services Directives

Some of the earliest examples of FinTech success have been in the payment space. The area was ripe for disintermediation and disruption, given the large margins that incumbents received for their services.

In the E.U., the first Payment Services Directive (PSD 1) in 2009 regulated the information conditions, rights, and responsibilities of payment services operators and the prudential requirements to be a payment service provider (PSP). Establishing consistent rules for the payment services delivery led to the creation of an E.U. internal payment market.

The second Payment Services Directive (PSD 2) in 2018 introduced a further step toward comprehensive harmonization of the E.U. payments market and introduced additional new features. PSD 2 meant that regulatory approval for money transfer in a single E.U. country could be passported across other E.U. countries. This capability inspired many cross-border payment FinTech firms, such as TransferWise and WorldRemit, to grow into neighboring European countries before expanding across the Atlantic. Separate U.S. states demand licenses for money transfer, making U.S. expansion burdensome and expensive for international operators. That licensing requirement also explains why money-transfer providers in the U.S. have been slower to expand into international markets.

Because PSD 2 regulation requires banks to share their data with qualified third parties, it has laid the foundation for open banking in Europe. As a result, FinTech firms, challenger banks, and some retail organizations can now compete with traditional banks, something that was previously impossible. The policies introduced under PSD 2 have led to an increase in innovative banking offerings, more rivalry in a market that was usually closed to competition, and disruption in the traditional banking scene in Europe.

The construction of this regulatory framework has brought three main benefits:

>> More transparency in pricing, including fair and equal pricing rules (prices need to be equal for consumers and third parties)

>> Security, promoting firmer regulations for client authentication and verification

>> Technological standards, forcing banks to use application programming interfaces (APIs) to enable customers to disclose their financial information with FinTech providers if they want (this has lowered the obstacles to switching banks and enabled consumers to use alternative financial services that traditional banks don't provide)

In China, regulation has long been more accommodating. As a result, BigTech firms like Ant Financial have built FinTech ecosystems in China, which have entered and are remodeling whole financial sectors. These include digital payments, wealth and asset management, and loans. The U.S. and Europe still have more rigorous regulatory requirements and entrenched banking franchises, so similar attempts have been more disjointed and technology firms have been restricted to payment and smaller scale lending offerings.

The General Data Protection Regulation

In a world where social media has become more intrusive and consumers are increasingly concerned about how providers use their personal information, it's critical to have rules that govern who can access data and in what ways. Some people say that "data is the new oil," a sentiment that highlights how valuable it is to providers.

The E.U. has established rules that control how providers may collect and process data about individuals living in the E.U. The General Data Protection Regulation (GDPR) was introduced across the E.U. on May 25, 2018. It supersedes the initial Data Protection Directive and attempts to standardize data privacy regulations across Europe.

GDPR's full effects aren't yet entirely understood, and compliance and enforcement practices are still being completely established. However, the most important elements of GDPR include

>> **Wider international scope:** The regulations relate to all companies managing personal data for people living within the E.U., irrespective of where the processing takes place.

>> **Consent:** The regulation provides for tougher consent requirements. Data requests must be easily available, comprehensible, and withdrawable and must include the reason for the data management.

>> **Improving individual's rights:** By enforcing the need to gain consent and stating the reasons for maintaining your data, people's data privacy rights are safeguarded.

>> **Right to retrieve:** People have the right to know whether their personal data is being processed and/or stored, where, and for what purpose.

>> **Right to erase:** People have the right to erase their personal data and/or stop their data from being processed. This may be because the use of data is no longer relevant to the original request or because the person has withdrawn his or her consent to process it.

>> **Right to modification:** Any erroneous data must be corrected.

>> **Right to data transferability:** Any information on personal data currently being processed must be provided, free of charge, to an individual upon request.

>> **Confidentiality by design:** Relevant encryption and monitoring procedures to safeguard any data must be integrated into the design of the systems. Data may be used only for the original purpose. Such data must be stored only when completely necessary, and additional data shouldn't be collected.

>> **Breach notification:** Data infringements must be reported within 72 hours.

>> **Data protection officers (DPOs):** Where data management requires regular observation of data subjects on a large scale, or data relating to criminal convictions and offenses, a DPO must be appointed to guarantee GDPR compliance.

>> **Fines:** Companies found to be noncompliant with GDPR can face fines of up to 4 percent of annual global turnover or €20 million (whichever is greater). This applies to both data controllers (the party that has collected and controls/owns the data) and processors (the party that processes data for the data controller), so no one is exempt from these guidelines.

REMEMBER

Global businesses need to be aware of these regulations because they apply to all data management of E.U. residents, irrespective of where an organization is located. Therefore, internationally located companies still need to be GDPR compliant if they process data from people located in the E.U. Moreover, FinTech advances are continuously unearthing new areas for consideration or where enhanced regulation may be needed. In the use of artificial intelligence and blockchain/distributed ledger technology, or in the broader trend to gather more financial and nonfinancial data, further analysis of the consequences is required.

NUMERIX: THE NEXT-GEN TECH VISION

Viewing the entry into risk as a defining opportunity, and to cement Numerix's position, coauthor Steve O'Hanlon moved forward quickly, establishing Numerix as a dynamic financial technology company that provided a next-generation risk platform. He also pivoted to rebranding Numerix as a FinTech company, thereby evolving Numerix's reputation in the market and changing perception in the marketplace of Numerix as just a pricing and risk calculations company to a provider of trading and risk managing systems that help capital markets firms transform. To date, Numerix's key differentiator continues to be its unrivaled analytics.

Steve's future vision became that of strategically placing Numerix as a transformative and disruptive company in the capital markets via next-generation, leading-edge technology to give clients a strategic advantage in their markets and enable them to make profitable shifts in business strategy. The tenets Numerix used to determine how to enter a completely new marketplace called Risk were as follows:

- **Determine the most important risk measure to start with.** Numerix picked the credit value adjustment, known as CVA. It built this first and quickly emerged as the recognized leader in CVA.

- **Prepare for cloud implementation.** The infrastructure was imperative to deliver a front-office Risk product. It needed to be scalable and to deal with all the front-office value adjustments (which eventually become known as XVA). It needed to be an enterprise-ready application, and not a software tool, capable of being deployed one day in a cloud environment. In those days, few companies even considered that financial institutions could be cloud-based, so this was a radical plan. Numerix built a Java-based platform on top of its industry standard pricing and risk analytics. This enabled Numerix to become cloud ready, which at that time meant that it lived in Azure. Fast-forward to today; its technology choices made it agnostic so it can live within any cloud environment, including AWS, Google, and Azure.

- **Build a new code stack.** Numerix knew that few companies had the ability to leverage pricing and risk analytics and built a purposeful, scalable, enterprise Risk application leveraging the analytics. Therefore, it built out an entirely new code stack, today called NX CORE (a platform), on top of its award-winning pricing and risk analytics. This accelerated its path as leader in Risk because it wasn't reliant on quants or the banks analytics to deliver a world-class application.

Flexibility is key to the success of this positioning to a FinTech company. The culture of Numerix, which was always entrepreneurial, went into hyperdrive, creating an environment where idea generation and implementation flourishes, where there's the constant pursuit of greater technology, and where there's continuous innovative thinking.

Today, the capital markets are at a pivotal point. Disruptive technological forces are challenging traditional financial services businesses. Consumer demands and priorities are changing; economic, political, and market shifts are squeezing revenues; and regulatory uncertainties are raising serious questions about long-standing operational and legacy technology models. Banks and other financial institutions need to find a way to move forward. Transformation isn't a choice for them. It's a mandate to survive.

The dramatic changes in capital markets since the collapse of Lehman has led financial institutions to drastically cut cost to stay ahead and remain competitive. Regulations such as the Fundamental Review of the Trading Book (FRTB) are driving rapid change for financial institutions, including the assessment to eliminate legacy trading and risk systems in favor of new technologically advanced offerings, something Numerix provides, that replace stand-alone trading and risk systems by each trading desk. For the first time, regulations demand this type of transparency to the C-suite executives above the leader of each desk. Today, it's more imperative than ever before to ensure that one system can handle each trading desk, thereby reducing the annual cost of technology ownership.

Highlighting RegTech Opportunities

GDPR compliance (covered in the preceding section) is an interesting example of the potential opportunities for FinTech firms, particularly a given subsector known as RegTech (regulatory technology) firms. Given that GDPR essentially requires that firms understand precisely where any personal data sits within their business, for what purpose it was collected, and what is being done to protect it, FinTech firms may have an advantage in providing services than more established players.

FinTech firms, by nature of their size and maturity, don't have legacy systems and data management issues to deal with. Their data sets are integrated, and they know how to compile specifically curated data sets. In contrast, many older firms have siloed or ad-hoc data systems containing disparate data collected gradually over time. This advantage enables FinTech firms to more cheaply and effectively ensure their own compliance but also to scale both their and their customers' costs in line with the growth of their businesses. This preferably happens in a cloud environment, which saves further costs (see Chapter 6 for more about cloud technology).

FinTech firms enable financial institutions to navigate their data lakes (a storage repository that can store large amounts of every type of data in the file format that the application is designed to work with) and make sense of data mapping solutions. This leads to enhancing the financial institution's ability to query and mine its data inventory. FinTech companies can also help institutions grow bilateral relationships with them and multilateral relationships with their customers.

The requirements for data due diligence and security will become only more stringent in the years to come. FinTech firms are developing the technology, with the appropriate levels of encryption, to ensure data privacy for larger firms and give them the ability to respond within the mandatory 72-hour notification period for any data breaches.

REMEMBER

All of that is just one example of how financial institutions should be embracing RegTech. Compliance is an ever-increasing cost, with many firms employing huge resources, both capital and employees, to meet their obligations. Partnering with a RegTech firm enables an institution to focus on its core business and meeting customer requirements in revenue-generating areas. The RegTech firms can also automate processes and optimize efficiencies and thereby help the client company reduce operating costs.

Table 3-1 lists some of the regulatory compliance challenges that financial institutions continue to face in 2020 and the types of technology required to meet the challenges.

TABLE 3-1   **RegTech Challenges and Required Technology**

RegTech Challenge	FinTech to Be Deployed
Anti-money laundering (AML) and financial crime	Big data, natural language processing, machine learning, robotic process automation, rule extraction
Know your customer (KYC)	Natural language processing, robotic process automation, rule extraction, semantic web, blockchain
Information/data governance	Natural language processing, robotic process automation, rule extraction
Regulatory change management	Big data, natural language processing, machine learning, robotic process automation, rule extraction, semantic web
Cybersecurity and technology risk	Big data, machine learning, rule extraction
Trade and transaction reporting	Big data, robotic process automation, rule extraction
Trade surveillance	Machine learning, rule extraction, semantic web, speech pattern recognition

2

Learning the Technology

Chapter **4**

Defining the Tech Underpinning FinTech

Most companies have a complex mix of internal and vendor applications, which require in-house and third-party support and have their own interoperability issues. Many of the applications aren't integrated and often don't work well with each other.

Large institutions often have hundreds of internally deployed systems, each of which requires specialized internal support and knowledge to maintain and run. These are siloed environments that produce operational risk for the company — as well as guaranteed high-salary employment for the subject matter experts (SMEs) who deliver support and maintenance. These siloed environments also produce different results for the same queries, which makes data integration problematic, increases corporate risk, and gets in the way of effectively analyzing that risk. Legacy systems are outdated, inefficient, and expensive, but modifying them can be difficult, costly, and time-consuming.

Enter *FinTech*, a group of companies that service the financial industry by stream-lining processes and systems in ways that reduce redundancy, eliminate legacy issues, and introduce new time- and labor-saving efficiencies. This chapter explains how FinTech comes to the rescue for companies stuck with outdated, poorly planned, and inconsistently administered systems. It outlines the key benefits of FinTech and explains some of the concepts and technologies that make them happen.

Finding a Fix in FinTech

As you find out in Chapter 2, FinTech has caused some major disruptions to the established banking/financial services norms. It's not a big surprise out of nowhere, though. The move toward FinTech has been gradually happening for many years, driven by the high costs of systems maintenance, slow delivery of new functionality, the high salaries and high turnover of developers and special-ists, and increased demand for real-time solutions. The following sections briefly review the problems companies are facing and why they are increasingly turning to FinTech to solve them.

What's the problem?

Many large corporations and megabanks waffle between building and buying their IT infrastructure, lacking a coherent long-term IT vision. Consequently, their IT landscapes are often a mix of band-aided systems and applications. Such kludged systems may have arisen out of a need to control costs, but they end up being dif-ficult and costly to deploy and maintain. Such customized systems are also more likely to depend on a few key experts in the organization who "own" the deploy-ment. If those people leave — or even hold the company hostage for their specific knowledge — the company is in serious trouble.

When no overarching vision for the IT plan exists, each division or department is typically free to cobble together its own custom solutions. That's fine in the short term, but one group's solutions are likely to overlap capabilities developed in another, creating unnecessary redundancy and complexity. Then when different groups need to share data, their systems may not play well together, necessitating yet another system just to help them communicate. The risks and complexity compound with each new project.

WARNING

The problem gets even worse over time, because many such systems don't age gracefully. Some of these old applications have been completely developed in-house and aren't interoperable with newer technologies like Software as a Service (SaaS), which is an application distribution model offered in third-party cloud environments discussed in Chapter 6, microservices (covered later in this chapter), and modern application programming interfaces (APIs), covered later in this chapter. The only way to maintain them is through custom point-to-point integrations, which are prone to failure over time. Diagnosing and fixing problems becomes a costly challenge.

The solution to these challenges can be found in FinTech, which brings the benefits of the latest digital technologies to the financial industry.

Why FinTech now?

The definition of FinTech has changed with time. It originally focused on back-office applications. Over the last ten years, this definition changed to include any company that provides financial services/software or technology to financial institutions delivered across an array of platforms and through different media.

REMEMBER

The need for fast development and innovation, as well as the need to correct some of those IT inefficiencies, have made it increasingly appealing to outsource IT functions to FinTech specialized companies. In the last several years, some quantum shifts have occurred in the use of new technologies across the financial industry:

>> The application development process has changed overall. The Agile development process (discussed later in this chapter) has altered how releases and programming methodologies are conceived. At Numerix, this new approach to streamlined programming of small release delivery methodologies has sped up the time to market of new functionality by a factor of three. New development languages, mounting in-house costs, microservices, APIs, and the need for more flexible frameworks have all driven many institutions to adopt FinTech that were initially afraid of it.

>> Customers and partners expect change to occur at a different speed. The demand for real-time processing and innovative change has altered the perspective of many bank executives toward "new technologies." The high cost of legacy systems that don't fulfill the needs of the industry has made a move toward FinTech more compelling.

>> Changing social demographics are an additional driver. Millennials have become the new influencers for greater use of technology and less reliance on human interaction. They prefer an electronic experience over one in person. They expect applications to provide the flexibility that enables them to personalize the way their interactions with systems and applications fit their needs. They don't need personal interaction as a part of a financial transaction, but they do demand immediacy and transparent access to data.

Many different technologies are driving the future of FinTech, including microservices, API strategies, real-time delivery, distributed ledger technologies (see Chapter 5), and cloud-based delivery systems (see Chapter 6). In the rest of this chapter, we explain several of these in more detail and their relevance to the industry.

Creating API Strategies

REMEMBER

An *application programming interface (API)* is a set of reusable functions, procedures, and other tools. An API enables a developer to rapidly construct functionality once and then reuse it in different ways across different applications. For example, an API can enable data transmission across applications in a standard way regardless of the language/media or application type. The efficiencies that APIs provide enable rapid development with low overhead costs.

APIs are an essential component in cost-effective application development. To stay ahead of the development curve, developers and senior management in large corporations must strategically plan API environment creation and maintenance. For example, megabanks, such as Deutsche, HSBC, and JPMorgan Chase, have developer portals and APIs to help customers and partners develop tools that interact seamlessly with their data and their workflow needs.

Any API strategy has associated development and maintenance costs. APIs take time and labor to create. However, that time and labor is generally made up — and then some — by the convenience and efficiency they provide to the programmers who use them. A side benefit of using APIs is that they allow systems/applications to be built by a third party, because they simplify the programming process. An enterprise should develop an API strategy that consists of public and private APIs and that is well documented and part of all release cycles.

Understanding the concept

To better understand APIs, imagine that you had friends over, and you wanted to serve an Italian dinner. You could assemble all the ingredients yourself and make it, but it would take an hour and a half, and you have only 30 minutes. What do you do? You pull out a jar of spaghetti sauce, boil some water for dried pasta, and buy a prepared loaf of garlic bread. And voilà! Dinner is served.

Having APIs in your programming pantry is like having premade spaghetti sauce, garlic bread, and pasta. The components/ingredients needed to prepare the program are all available in the source code. When bundled together, they make up the API.

REMEMBER

The beauty of APIs is that you can swap out components. If you don't like spaghetti, you can easily have corned beef instead. Or if a friend wanted something different, he could take the APIs available to everyone and make something out of the same underlying components/ingredients. Anyone using these APIs doesn't have to know anything about how to cook or assemble the ingredients; it's all preconfigured for him. Figure 4-1 illustrates the concept.

An Italian Dinner as an Application

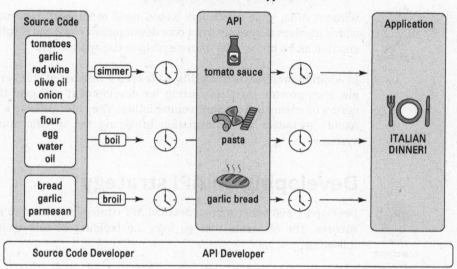

© John Wiley & Sons, Inc.

FIGURE 4-1:
Delivering dinner via APIs versus source code.

As you can see, having prepackaged elements already tested and ready to use speeds up the time to completion of any application. The providing company can choose what it wants to prepackage so the nature of the "secret sauce" (in other words, the underlying code) is never revealed — just the end product.

Looking at API benefits

REMEMBER

Providing APIs makes sense because they expand the reach of a company's core business through user-friendly interfaces and API tools. APIs provide for faster application development and integration, and they increase the ease with which partners and customers can use and develop custom work on the top of the application's code. Partners and customers can then own those components, which are specific to their corporate needs, and the company can retain and integrate those applications that have universal appeal into their master codebase. By providing easy access to API libraries internally, you can encourage employee innovation and ownership. APIs can also be used to modernize and replace legacy systems more efficiently.

APIs make modern digital ecosystems possible. An intelligent approach to creating and modifying APIs helps companies with both internal maintenance and customer and partner accessibility.

APIs assist in the integration of data and the streamlining of workflow. By exposing APIs, you can reveal important data to customers and partners without revealing proprietary code. APIs also speed up the development process and make development by external users possible without security risk.

WARNING

Without APIs, your developers would need to support application onboarding, which involves time away from core development work and results in less product creation and a higher cost of ownership to the application.

In addition to those core benefits, APIs offer a number of side benefits. For example, they provide clear formatting for development and give the developer the option of ensuring backward compatibility. They also provide a universal way to handle metadata and information brokering for specific applications and/or systems.

Developing an API strategy

REMEMBER

Developing and adhering to a detailed API strategy is critical to an organization's success. The elements that go into the building of this strategy include the following:

>> Defining the optimal outcomes for API usage both internally and externally

>> Publishing the expected outcomes and approaches to the target groups involved for feedback

>> Understanding and identifying the way your technical teams work

>> Understanding and identifying the systems that the organization, its customers, and its partners use

>> Developing a beta deployment process that includes an easy way to track and support internal and external beta users

>> Developing a feeder structure in which each iteration is first rolled out to "heavy" internal users and then to customers and partners who are committed to using the APIs and providing feedback

>> Assuring that support and maintenance personnel have been assigned and given clear key performance indicators (KPI) around the API framework

>> Tying the successful development and maintenance of this system to all new releases

- » Developing a user group philosophy where external users are encouraged to share and develop user groups and are rewarded and recognized for doing so

- » Establishing an API web portal that includes easy interfaces for gathering user feedback; a repository of new packages and libraries created by both employees and external users; easy access to all documentation; and rapid knowledge exchange

- » Developing a process for version control, tools, and documentation that provides and augments designing, testing, and developing in every release and every API package

- » Offering the ability to license the use of the APIs and to monitor the use against possible security intrusion via the web portal

REMEMBER

Any standardization practice is only as good as its users. The API strategy, once created, must be adhered to by all developers and participants.

Including REST and RAML

The API web portal (introduced in the preceding section) should house tools needed to develop and maintain the APIs. Having such tools available will permit fast development in RESTful API with documentation and an immediate feedback loop.

What do we mean by RESTful API? REST stands for REpresentational State Transfer. It is stateless — each action is treated uniquely, there is no record of previous interactions, and it enables plain-text exchanges, rather than HTML, which allows coders to use efficient configuration directives for start-up and saved settings. It also enables security policy inheritance, which allows for the inheritance of as well as adherence to security requirements. RAML (Restful API Modeling Language) allows REST APIs to be formally defined. RAML can define every resource and operation exposed by a microservice.

Both tools are scalable and secure components and include a mechanism for creating license agreements that stipulate how the APIs are used. Tools are also available for monitoring the use of third-party developers to guard against privacy and security violations. They also include provisioning tools for logging and updating issues.

Trying tips for API success

TIP

Here are some tips for making sure your API strategy is successful:

>> Recruit from the start. Get buy-in from senior management and appoint a project owner who is eager to evangelize about the benefits.

>> As with all development, it's important to keep an up-to-date library of use cases and terms so that instead of re-inventing the wheel, you're recycling and reusing whenever possible.

>> Don't get bogged down in the minutiae.

>> Build a flexible high-level plan that can be easily altered and expanded.

>> Revisit that plan on a scheduled basis. Each company should develop a calendar that meshes with its development cycles. In general, API strategies should be reviewed at least annually, though some are reviewed at the time of each release.

>> Develop a robust API portal to handle internal and external users — from licensing through downloads and support. Most API downloads are stored and updated on the general product download site.

>> Build a back-end management system.

Reviewing APIs and security vulnerabilities

REMEMBER

Some inevitable security risks come with implementing a flexible and accessible API strategy. Be sure to review the level of data vulnerability at each point in the process, looking at issues of data controls, movement, and encryption, and either accept or take steps to decrease the risks.

Some ways to make systems less vulnerable include the following:

>> Employ a comprehensive licensing mechanism.

>> Create clear requirements around authentication and event logging.

>> Test every release against clearly defined security standards.

>> Use multifactor authentication.

>> Establish clearly defined rules for data encryption.

Understanding Event-Driven Software

The earliest computer programs were procedural, as in Figure 4-2, which shows a simple workflow. They consisted of a set of instructions that were executed in order. The program ends when the instructions complete.

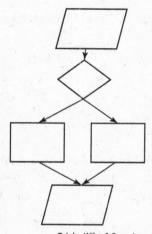

FIGURE 4-2:
A simple procedural workflow.

As program complexity increased, these instructions were separated into mini-programs known as procedures. Figure 4-3 shows a separation of tasks into segmented workflow.

However, interactive user interfaces don't work like this. They react to user actions, such as a key press or a mouse click. These actions are events that drive the software. These programs contain multiple sets of instructions, which are called when an event occurs. The procedures are called message handlers, and the main process, which orchestrates these handlers, is known as the event loop. See Figure 4-4, which shows a multifaceted event-driven dispersion of workflow managed by handlers.

Event-driven software is not only necessary for user interfaces but also useful for many other types of software. Applications must react to multiple events — those from users and those from other pieces of software: data arriving, connection requests, disconnections, and so on.

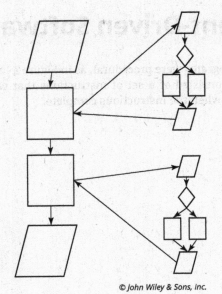

FIGURE 4-3:
The breakdown
of a simple
workflow into
mini-programs.

© John Wiley & Sons, Inc.

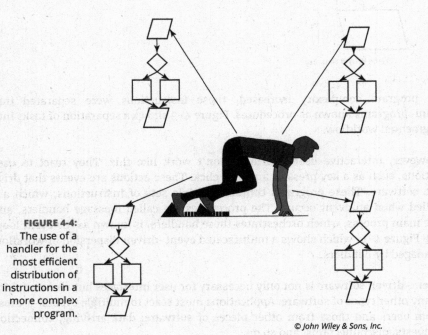

FIGURE 4-4:
The use of a
handler for the
most efficient
distribution of
instructions in a
more complex
program.

© John Wiley & Sons, Inc.

Event-driven software is part of the FinTech tool kit in that it allows the exchanges of data to flow between decoupled services, which is essential in the world of microservices (which are discussed later in this chapter.) The demand in the financial world is information anytime, anyplace, in any way. With the old procedural programs, all actions were linear and sequential in nature, which also made the decoupling of the structure they were housed in difficult. The demand for more immediate change is driving the banking industry away from its legacy systems and toward these non-serial, non-monolithic structures. FinTech facilitates the modernization of legacy systems.

Testing and implementation

TECHNICAL STUFF

Event-driven software is easier to write in many ways. The technical details of checking whether events have occurred are separate from the implementation of the business logic required when they occur. This technical event management may be handled by the operating system, the language, or a library, depending on the implementation choices.

If the event management is well implemented, the software will also be more efficient — it will wait until an event and use no (or limited) processing power as it waits. Poor implementations check periodically whether an event has occurred (polling), which is wasteful and delays the triggering of the next event until the next check.

However, although easier to write, event-driven software is often harder to test. With procedural software, you have an initial state and a path to a final state. You can check the code's validity by testing each procedure attached to an event. With event-driven code, the main difficulty is that events can occur in different orders, and even at the same time, producing different results for seemingly identical activities. If two events are being handled simultaneously that require the same resources (memory, disk), they may interact with each other and maybe even stop each other (for example, creating a deadlock).

The successor to event-driven software is *asynchronous software*. Asynchronous software uses parallel programming, running separately. In this paradigm, the event loop reacts to events. If the event handlers return results, the results are returned as other events. The results happen without the controlled response of the handler, so many events can be handled simultaneously. This behavior differs from traditional software, where the program will wait until the event handler has produced the answer.

Language support

A variety of programming languages enable developers to create event-driven software. Here's a rundown of some of the most popular choices:

» Because Visual Basic's roots are in user interface development, it isn't surprising that it not only supports event-driven software but also focuses on the paradigm. Objects (such as buttons, windows, and applications) are built as event handlers, which are called as the operating system responds to user-driven events.

» C# is the heir to Visual Basic but was designed to be much more multipurpose. Like Visual Basic, it supports event handling as an intrinsic part of the language.

» JavaScript is also a language for implementing graphical user interfaces (GUIs), which are the graphic components that are used to display designated information in an interactive way. Event handling is core to its design as well. Custom components present functions to the framework, which executes them as it reacts to events.

» Python's heritage is as a scripting language where small pieces of code were executed from within a (usually not Python) setting — sometimes by the user, sometimes by an orchestration framework. Therefore, Python has traditionally been the language used to implement the procedures called when an event occurred but not to call those procedures. However, Python's popularity as an easy development language has expanded its use case to include procedure calling.

TECHNICAL STUFF

Due to the GIL (global interpreter lock), Python apps can't respond to multiple events simultaneously, so the benefits aren't as great as in other languages. However, some recent enhancements to the language (such as async and await) have added support for event asynchronous programming.

» C++ is an object-oriented language; it's organized around "objects" and not actions. It's a much lower-level language than C# and Visual Basic and directly supports event handling. Various libraries are available. For example, Asio (which is a cross-platform C++ library for network and low-level I/O programming) executes functions when an event occurs.

C++ has evolved significantly over the last few years. It now supports multithreading rather than requiring an operating system–specific library, and new features (such as futures, promises, and asynchronous function calls) have meant that event-driven software no longer resorts to operating system calls.

>> Java's origins were as a "better C++," so it didn't provide out-of-the-box support for event-driven software. However, some Java libraries allow for event-driven software. For example, libraries provide support for queues (such as Kafka, which is an open source distributed streaming platform that allows simultaneous processing of transactions as they occur). Architectures like Swing (which handles data in real time with plug-and-play applications) provide interfaces for actions and handlers, leading directly to the asynchronous programming model.

Building on Agile: Microservices and More

The culture of "built here" that has permeated the financial and banking industry has made companies hesitant to ask for FinTech help. However, internal and external pushes for innovation and efficiency have pressured many senior managers in financial companies to take advantage of the new products and services that FinTech can provide.

Marketplace demand for more functionality and shorter development turnaround times has led to many application development innovations that are nothing less than a seismic shift. Agile development principles have served as the basis for these changes, which include things like rapid application development (RAD), incremental development, extreme programming, and microservices. You find out more about some of these in the upcoming sections. To understand these improvements, though, we need to start by looking at the traditional baseline we're comparing it to: waterfall development.

Waterfall development

The waterfall development process was created in 1970 and has been used extensively by large corporations. It's monolithic in its structure and methodology and provides for very stable but slow and methodic release cycles.

The stages

REMEMBER

Each stage of the waterfall process is clearly defined and linear, with clear deliverables and sign-off. As illustrated in Figure 4-5, the stages are

1. Gathering and documentation of requirements

2. Documenting of detailed specifications

3. Defining and documenting code and unit testing

4. Completing coding and unit testing

5. Testing the system

6. Performing user acceptance testing (UAT)

7. Performing quality assurance (QA) testing

8. Fixing any issues

9. Delivering the finished product

The waterfall release cycle is coordinated with the sales, marketing, and training components of a successful product launch.

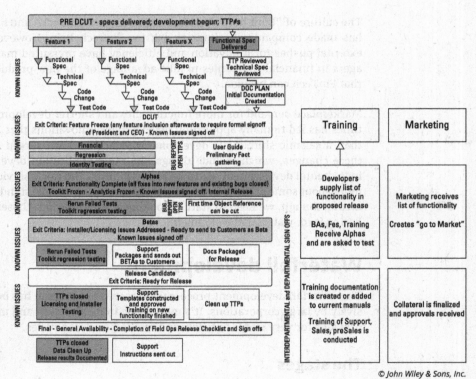

FIGURE 4-5: A waterfall development cycle with corollary marketing and training components.

© John Wiley & Sons, Inc.

The drawbacks

WARNING

Waterfall development has many drawbacks. Administratively, the projects tend to become unwieldy over time, with large teams and unrestricted growth of the codebase. Team coordination can be difficult, and often only one or two developers have complete oversight into the application and the code. Isolating functionality that needs to be changed is often difficult, and the lack of diagnostic tools impedes the ability to scale. In addition, change may rely on knowledge that's no longer available or available only in a restricted capacity. Because of this, applications created using the waterfall approach often don't age well, becoming old, brittle, monolithic structures with poor documentation.

Because of the large number of developers on the team, and the lack of coordination between them, there's a lot of duplication of effort in waterfall development, with limited code reuse across the application. This not only wastes developer time but also introduces operational risk, because the outputs for the same query may produce different results across the company.

Rolling out changes can also be difficult, because changes made must be committed to the whole stack. The software generally needs to be taken offline to update it, which can cause service interruptions with effects ranging from minor inconvenience to a near-crisis situation.

Waterfall development also depends on employees working under one roof. If a software development team is dispersed around the globe, people have trouble coordinating their efforts. That can be a problem in today's workforce because of the increasing employee focus on mobility, portability, and work-life balance.

Agile design

Software development methodology innovations in the last few decades have addressed many of the waterfall method's shortcomings. Incremental development, RAD, extreme programming, feature drive, test-driven, and Agile are all examples of how the industry has tried to fix waterfall's problems.

The Agile manifesto, written in 2001, revolutionized how people viewed software development. Agile techniques enabled software development to be focused on speed and frequency of releases. Unlike waterfall, the Agile process allows for discrete pieces of larger components to be developed in isolation, delivered separately, and integrated at a later point as part of a larger functionality.

Agile is a lightweight development methodology in which projects are built by small teams with interdepartmental disciplines — not just developers. Teams are self-organizing, self-testing, and jointly owned across departments. Teams build iteratively, deliver small releases, and measure their progress often.

The key differences to be understood between waterfall versus Agile development are in the way each is tested and spec'd. The Agile process has constant iterative developer testing transpiring from the initiation of the project. Waterfall testing begins when the code freeze is initiated after all the development has been completed. In waterfall, when the specs have been reviewed and accepted, they aren't changed. Agile doesn't develop granular specs but rather creates "stories" and use cases. The Agile product is iteratively changed, and the "stories" are enhanced with each iteration.

TIP

For more about Agile, check out the latest edition of *Agile Project Management For Dummies* by Mark C. Layton and Steven J. Ostermiller (Wiley).

Microservices

Microservices are a loosely coupled set of functions or modules with their own data store. In other words, as the name implies, they are small, reusable services that work together, like the APIs you find out about earlier in this chapter. Each microservice is independently maintained and represented by individual APIs. They adhere to three modes of scalability: load-balanced distribution; scaling by data partitioning; and scaling via functional decomposition — that is, creating a set of services that together represent the application.

Microservices are driven by business requirements and are composed of front-end services like an API gateway/REST APIs. They use a test-driven development method that features frequent small releases with highly planned test cases. And speaking of testing, microservices are highly tested by developers and stakeholders. Figure 4-6 summarizes some of the key points of microservices.

Moving to Microservices
"Small, loosely coupled autonomous services that can work together"

We take our traditional and existing centralized applications and decompose them into services that:
- Focus on one specific function or problem
- Provide APIs, event handling and notification for service functionality
- Own their data with separate storage and schema

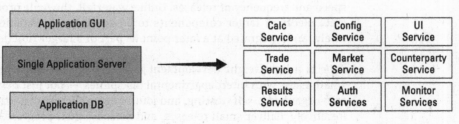

FIGURE 4-6:
The breakdown of large components into small, decoupled microservices.

© John Wiley & Sons, Inc.

REMEMBER

Here are some of the qualities of a microservice:

>> It's scalable and fault-tolerant.

>> It uses whatever technology is best suited to produce the expected outcome.

>> Each service is separable.

>> Each service can be upgraded independently.

>> It's extensible.

>> It's easy to deploy and test.

>> Development teams align with services.

>> Applications and solutions are created by choosing from appropriate sets of base services, optional services, and custom application services. (This is called *composability*.)

A microservices team is cross-departmental and driven by business process needs. It consists of a stakeholder, business analysts, developers, a developer head/code reviewer, and a QA/DevOps Team. Figure 4-7 illustrates how a microservices team may work.

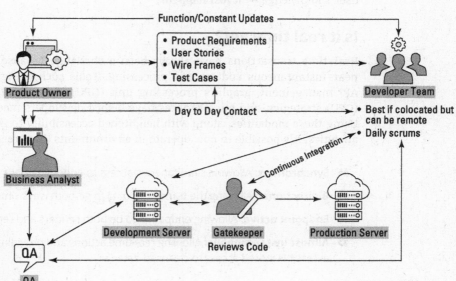

Microserving Team

Function/Constant Updates

- Product Requirements
- User Stories
- Wire Frames
- Test Cases

Product Owner

Developer Team

Day to Day Contact

- Best if colocated but can be remote
- Daily scrums

Business Analyst

Continuous Integration

Development Server

Gatekeeper
Reviews Code

Production Server

QA

QA

FIGURE 4-7: A typical microservices team and the functions they perform.

Why microservices?

Microservices incorporate many aspects of the new development processes. Through a change in development focus, they answer the call for speed of deployment and the ability to update functionality.

Organizations must be able to adapt to the needs of their customers quickly and create innovative solutions to remain competitive. Agile processes are well suited to meet these goals. Development begins with defining a business need or proposition and then determining how to assemble a system of services to meet those needs. Older development methodologies paid less attention to the real commercial drivers of change: the nonfunctional requirements or quality attributes.

REMEMBER

Customers today demand reusable components that can be swapped in and out of an application without disruption to the application, and microservices-based applications can meet that need. The financial industry's requirements for a better risk matrix and greater controls are driven not just by the markets but also by government regulations. Risk officers must be able to easily understand their positions and vulnerabilities in the area of liquidity, currency, credit, and equity risk, just to name a few. That's why risk systems for financial institutions should be based on a microservices architecture. The need for real-time capabilities inherently requires that systems should not have to go down to be upgraded. In the world of legacy risk systems, cost and time to upgrade are impediments; with microservice architecture, microservices can be deployed on the fly, without a user's knowledge — it just happens.

Is it real time yet?

Real-time transactions have always been a challenge because of the need for near-instantaneous updates and processing. Tools such as Agile development, API management, graphics processing unit (GPU) and central processing unit (CPU) strategies, and microservices have helped developers meet this challenge. Using these modalities, along with heightened accessibility to financial and data analytics, it's possible to now operate in environments that are

>> **Synchronous:** Allowing simultaneous access to endpoints/data

>> **Bidirectional:** Allowing the transfer of data to go both ways simultaneously

>> **Endpoint active:** Allowing endpoints to be both senders and receivers

>> **Almost instantaneous:** Allowing real-time actions and providing streamlined, accessible stored access to cleansed data

The still-outstanding hurdle is the need for computing environments to be flexible and large enough to handle volumes in constant flux. These environments and processes need to be both scalable and elastic. In other words, they must be able to scale up and scale down to accommodate the workload by adding resources and fit the resource need dynamically.

What are the benefits and challenges of microservices?

REMEMBER

Microservices offer many benefits, making them appealing to businesses struggling to overcome the problems with old development methods such as the waterfall approach. Here's a summary of some of the key benefits:

>> They have continuous delivery.

>> They have separate maintenance, deployment, and scaling of each service.

>> Small groups are needed who work autonomously.

>> They have continuous testing.

>> An error in one service is isolated to that service, making repairs easier to identify and fix.

>> Easy swapping engenders more experimentation on the part of the development team.

>> Speed of delivery reduces time to market.

WARNING

Some challenges are inevitable with any methodology, though. With microservices, it can often be difficult to

>> Define the microservices architectural structure.

>> Define the right set of functions in a service.

>> Coordinate the coupling of services to be delivered in one application.

>> Isolate the way in which the call requirements of the services are orchestrated in a "distributed" application.

>> Maintain data consistency across the individual data stores.

Rapid application development

RAD's process was developed because of the desire to shorten time-to-market through less-specific spec development, implement rapid review and continuous prototyping, and add business-driven functionality to the early stages of requirements development. The popularity of Agile development and microservices has created a demand for tools created specifically to support RAD. The concept of RAD was incorporated in the Agile development process and is utilized extensively in the microservices structure.

Microservices rely on tools like Git, a source control versioning development control system, and *containerization*. Containerization is the process by which the complete application is delivered with all its configuration files and dependencies in the cleanest and most efficient release process. Tools that developers commonly use to create this ecosystem include Docker, Mesosphere, and Kubernetes.

The end goals of RAD environments and process are

>> Uniform, consistent deployment where each service runs within a container and uses fewer resources than separate virtual machines would for each service

>> The ability to take advantage of automatic scale-out functions, including performance scaling, fault tolerance, and automated testing capabilities

>> Support within cloud environments

Continuous integration and composability

Continuous integration and releases are essential to microservice development success. Teams need to have environments that empower them to continuously submit code and to have it self-tested by the developer. All members of the team must have access to this environment so that stakeholders can verify, in real time, that what is being built conforms to the business needs. Continuous integration permits short release cycles and continuous QA.

The microservice architecture is built to incorporate not only code but also workflow and business processes. Adding workflow into the code enables speedy realignment when changes are required. Each service is separate and can be swapped out without reinstalling the entire application.

Microservices can communicate with each other natively by using industry-wide interoperability standards. These standards make it easy to combine "best-of-breed" code with custom processes or workflows without having to worry about compatibility. Some examples of these standards include the following:

>> The breakup of the code into multiple codebases called service-oriented architecture (SOA)

>> Polyglot persistence — multi data stores based on needs

>> Automated scaling and load balancing

>> Decentralization of the database

>> Optimistic replication

>> Cloud enabling and containerization

REMEMBER

Microservices development is a quantum leap from more traditional development approaches. Microservices development emphasizes business requirements and workflow. By understanding the business processes from start to finish across the corporation, teams can avoid reinventing services that perform the same function. The process becomes the building block on which all similar needs are called. Figure 4-8 shows a system built to utilize microservices.

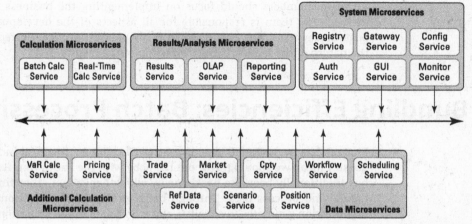

FIGURE 4-8:
A complex deployment of microservices.

© John Wiley & Sons, Inc.

The key to developing efficient microservice systems is for each microservice to have clearly defined REST APIs, an event manager, and a specific data store. A GUI may be designed to specifically call the end user's needs through Python scripts or wrappers. Microservices can also be called through a direct line call and doesn't have to use a GUI to display the results. Microservices can utilize RESTful APIs and business domain events, which can be published to a message broker or built within the microservice architecture. Although REST (covered earlier in this chapter) isn't a requirement of microservices, it's a useful protocol.

REMEMBER

When we speak about microservices, we're talking about a quality called composability. Microservices are highly composable. Each microservice is composed of components that can be used in various combinations to deliver different business needs.

Reusability is key to the cost-effectiveness and efficiency of a microservice. If architected correctly, the same service components serve multiple users in multiple business arenas. The delivery mechanism is built on the concept of "loose coupling." The services run autonomously, which increases scalability and availability. The services are fault-tolerant and can be automated to seamlessly swap out any failed services without disrupting or crashing any other microservices in use.

Assembling a microservices development team

TIP

Microservices development teams are based on Agile's small subset approach. These groups are cross-departmental and should include a project manager, development head, developers, QA resources, and business analysts. Domain experts are an absolute necessity. Local teams function the best because they can directly interact on a regular basis.

All team members should focus on implementing the business proposition as defined. The team is responsible for all aspects of the development as well as post-deployment. The cost of delivery should be significantly reduced based on the nature of the team and the ownership of the results.

Bundling Efficiencies: Batch Processing

FinTech has been viewed as a disruptive force in the financial industry, but that doesn't mean we should throw out the baby with the bathwater. Batch processing has traditionally been the backbone by which banks and other financial services handle and process data. Through batch processing, a traditionally structured organization generates, reconciles, and stores data for all operational areas: front, middle, and back-office. There is a reason for this method. It centralizes the data and allows accurate updates while alleviating the pressure of time constraints that exist during the business day.

While the modern push may be to real-time data processing and consumption (discussed earlier in this chapter), there still will be operations that are more intelligently delivered by batch mode at the close of a business day. Examples of some types of processing that should continue to be batch mode are historical data reports, billings reports, aggregated cost reports, and any reporting that doesn't frequently change over time, like end-of-month reconciliations or payroll. Batch processing will continue to be a key requirement for all organizations, although there may be portions of traditional end-of-day batch processes that can be handled in a more real-time fashion.

TIP

When considering which of the current batch processes should be handled by more expeditious API- and microservice-driven real-time computations, ask and answer these questions:

>> What is the cost benefit of converting this process?

>> Who consumes the data being generated?

>> Should this data be reconfigured and altered for different end users?

>> Must the data be continuously updated and reviewed?

>> Is the data generally run off a script that doesn't have to be altered frequently?

REMEMBER

If there is no pressing need for real-time analysis, if there is no time processing pressure, and if the data produced is stable and infrequently reviewed or changed, it won't be cost-effective to alter operations from batch to real-time compute.

Improving Data Management

Data is the lifeblood of any application. An often-repeated (but certainly true) cliché is "Data is the new oil." Most organizations, large or small, are constantly trying to become better at capturing all relevant data, making the right micro and macro decisions, and improving the speed at which data can be acquired and put to good use. As artificial intelligence and machine learning (AI/ML) and data science techniques become more commonplace, the importance of data is going to only increase.

Whether an application's focus is decision support, automation, or analytical processing, having timely, accurate, and complete data to feed these applications is a must.

Distinguishing the types of data

REMEMBER

The FinTech arena has great variety in data type and complexity. Data is often classified in the following major categories (listed here from slow-moving to fast-moving):

>> **Static data:** Doesn't change often and doesn't usually differ from one market participant to another. Examples include currencies, conventions, time zones, and calendars.

>> **Reference data:** Includes lists of permissible values and field descriptors used within transaction data. It changes regularly and is specific to an institution (as opposed to static data, which doesn't vary from one institution to another). Examples include product definitions, securities, corporate actions, counterparties, Credit Support Annexes (CSAs), netting/margin sets, legal entities, and books.

>> **Securities data:** This is a type of reference data. It's a set of records representing intangible financial assets denoting partial ownership in a corporate entity, or the right to future cash flows (such as for loans or bonds), with or without contingency clauses. Securities data is sold/bought in units and is

uniquely identified by values such as International Securities Identification Numbers (ISINs) and Committee on Uniform Securities Identification Procedures (CUSIP) numbers.

>> **Legal entity data:** Includes information about *legal entities,* as the name implies. A legal entity is an entity formed under applicable national or international laws that's permitted to trade and/or operate in certain financial markets. Counterparties and accounts are specific subtypes of legal entities, with which the entity has financial relationships.

>> **Trade data:** This is a set of records representing transactions between a buyer and seller of a security, or between two parties entering into an over-the-counter (OTC) derivative contract. Trade data can have many reference and static data attributes, such as legal, entity, book, counterparty, or currency.

>> **Position data:** A set of records representing the total number of securities held or the cash amounts held. Like trade data, position data can have many reference and static data attributes, such as legal, entity, book, counterparty, or currency.

>> **Market data/pricing feeds:** Data indicating the price at which securities or OTC trades were transacted or quoted. Market data can move very fast, at the rate of several ticks per second.

>> **Derived data/results data:** Derived from other data sets after a series of calculations or analytic processing.

The faster the data moves, the less reliable it is, because it's more constantly changing. Figure 4-9 illustrates the data speed versus data reliability tension that exists among these different types of data.

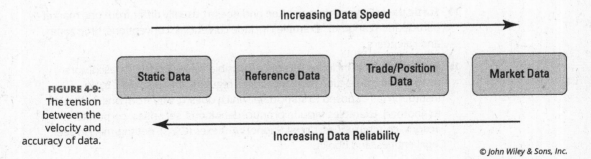

FIGURE 4-9: The tension between the velocity and accuracy of data.

© John Wiley & Sons, Inc.

Validating, enhancing, and cleansing data

REMEMBER

Data, particularly fast-moving market data, can often be noisy or corrupt due to the very nature of financial markets and the data capture mechanisms in place. It's imperative to plan and implement a holistic data validation, enhancement, and cleansing process to ensure that systems are operating smoothly and produce the desired results. Bad data can lead to incorrect results and even result in high operational risk if decisions are based on bad information.

The techniques commonly used for these purposes within the financial industry include

>> **Data validation:** This includes quality checks to ensure that data is accurate and timely. For example, data is assessed for missing data points, data outliers outside normal range, unsound financial data (end date of a trade before start data), and so on.

>> **Data cleansing and enhancement:** These are methods to fill in missing data via interpolation or extrapolation using averages or more advanced curve or surface fitting techniques. Often, data is also proxied using related securities or other related market information. In some cases, AI/ML techniques have also been used for multifactor, nonparametric data enhancement.

Note: The type of data cleansing and enhancement needed is directly driven by the time-to-market constraints and available data.

Making enterprise data management more efficient

Creating enterprise-wide data efficiencies is critically important. It not only helps ensure the smooth functioning for all existing applications, but it also enables more creative applications to be created in the future. The two major elements of creating an efficient data management approach for the enterprise are database management technology and database management processes.

Many data management technologies are available today. Some of the major ones include

>> **Relational databases:** Time-tested technology for storing data and ensuring data integrity, typically accessed via Structured Query Language (SQL)

>> **Big data technologies:** Hadoop and related technologies designed for massive scale but weaker integrity

>> **Time-series databases:** Technology for managing time-series data, typically fast-moving market data series

>> **Array databases:** Technology for managing large matrixes or arrays, used for managing result sets and counterparty exposures

>> **Object databases:** Systems for managing data at an abstract object-oriented level; suitability varies according to the specific need

>> **Document databases:** Technology specialized in storing large documents in XML, JSON, or text

REMEMBER

Because data is a huge asset for any institution, there must be an overall enterprise data architecture and strategy while allowing each application team the flexibility to quickly establish the data sets they require. This is where database management processes come into the picture. Often we see a hub-and-spoke architecture for managing data, as shown in Figure 4-10. Although centralizing this type of data architecture is essential, it's also important to make provisions for rapidly changing the hub. Otherwise, a heavy, enterprise data management strategy can impede experimentation and innovation.

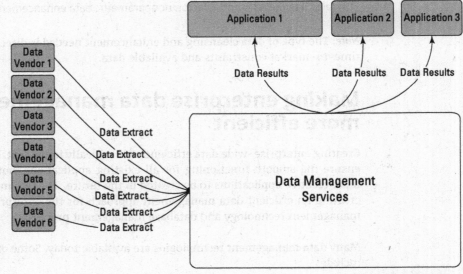

FIGURE 4-10: An example of data management services' input and output.

© John Wiley & Sons, Inc.

Working with CPUs and GPUs

Processing — that is, converting input to output — has traditionally been the job of the central processing unit (CPU), the main "brain" of a computer system. However, a recent trend in FinTech is to employ graphics processing unit (GPU) chips to help speed up calculations in computers that must process large amounts of data quickly. Systems can get better data processing performance by splitting a system's workload between CPUs and GPUs, allowing each to do the types of calculations that it does best.

The following sections compare and contrast CPUs and GPUs, provide tips on CPU and GPU success, and give an example of potential improvement.

Comparing CPUs and GPUs

CPUs and GPUs are built differently and designed for different tasks. A CPU converts input to output by performing math operations. It's the control center of a computer, running a variety of tasks that include analytics, mathematical logic, calculations, and image rendering. GPUs are more specialized processors that excel at simple repetitive tasks and were initially designed for the complex visual rendering in computer games.

A CPU can perform many different calculations to complete a task. Most CPUs have complex instruction sets, so programmers can call on the different math operations to perform a calculation. In contrast, a GPU has a reduced instruction set — fewer math operations it can do. However, partly because of that simplicity, a GPU can perform certain mathematical tasks more rapidly than a CPU can.

Both CPUs and GPUs operate on cores. A *core* is a single processor in a CPU or GPU. CPUs use to have only one core; today CPUs can use multiple cores, but only in series — not simultaneously. In contrast, a GPU uses all its compute cores simultaneously on one calculation, running thousands of processes in parallel, so it can render its output with incredible speed. Because the financial industry wants and needs parallel processing when handling big data, implementing a GPU strategy makes a lot of sense.

The power of a CPU can be enhanced by multiprocessing (adding more CPUs in series) or by multithreading (creating more threads on a single processor). In multiprocessing, the CPU switches between multiple programs, creating the illusion of running all the programs simultaneously. In multithreading, the CPU rapidly switches between threads and makes it appear like all threads are running simultaneously. Multithreading speeds up the CPU process because the memory used for all threads is all shared in one process. Multiprocessing allocates a separate store of memory to each process started.

CPUs have a stability advantage. CPU tasks are fairly stable, whereas a GPU will crash if taxed. CPUs also are more reliable and accurate in their calculations. In the financial arena, accuracy is important.

Determining the cost of CPUs versus GPUs in a system isn't necessarily like comparing apples to apples. CPUs are more expensive per core than GPUs, but fewer cores may be required to perform more complex tasks. The more complex financial computations when performed on a GPU require the more expensive GPU cards.

CPUs can rapidly pull data stored in the primary memory space (RAM). Virtual memory is a secondary space, which is less accessible but needed for storage of more complex computational operations. CPUs are optimized for integer calculations; floating point is much more compute intensive. The determination to use 32 versus 64 bit also can speed up or slow down CPU processing. The 64-bit systems are generally slower because they need more memory and they are recalled slower than the 32-bit. It takes more processing time to read a 64-bit pointer. With GPUs, all processing happens concurrently.

REMEMBER

Neither GPUs nor CPUs can at this time replace the other. Both types of processing units are needed for the most efficient output delivery. How exactly to best combine their capabilities will depend on the expected usage, and that's a determination best left to computing experts.

Planning for success

Maximizing computing performance isn't something that just happens because you throw a few extra CPUs or GPUs into a system. It has to be carefully planned and tested, beginning with defining a use case. The use case will drive the type of GPU card(s) to use, as well as the supporting hardware required.

In addition, the software has to be written to take advantage of the combination of CPU and GPU processing capability. Banks, hedge funds, and other financial institutions have all developed unique approaches for parsing their algorithms to perform more efficiently through accelerated GPU computing.

Performance enhancement is as much an art form as a science. Often code needs to be refactored to take advantage of the use of GPU. Many open source GPU-accelerated algorithms can be adapted to legacy code. Companies can use visualization tools to do the detailed use case and workflow planning that's required. The great advantage in finance for the use of GPUs is to speed up the compute-expensive financial algorithms.

Estimating the potential improvement

The GPU performance is highly nonlinear. A company must perform actual testing on the hardware to optimize performance and get real-time estimates. However, it's reasonable to look at other companies' data to get a rough estimate of what is possible.

Numerix, LLC, created and tested a use case, with the input and assistance of NVIDIA, to explore the computation speed improvements possible when using GPUs. The charts in Figures 4-11 and 4-12 summarize what they found. These charts show timing benchmarks for different financial instruments priced by various models. A typical speedup factor for pricing on one GPU device versus a single-threaded CPU pricing, which is one of the standard and popular metrics used for comparison of GPU speed versus CPU speed, is 20 times, up to 40 times at peak. (See the nearby sidebar "Using a Monte Carlo simulation" for the nitty-gritty on this testing.)

TIP

When considering a GPU strategy, note that it's still a relatively young technology, and advances are being made quarterly.

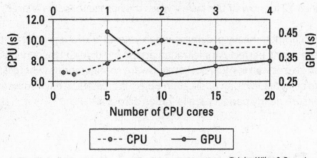

FIGURE 4-11: The speedup of a Monte Carlo simulation using CPU versus GPU.

© John Wiley & Sons, Inc.

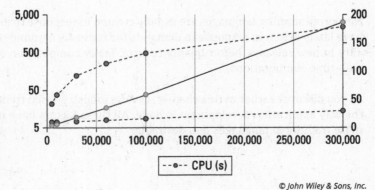

FIGURE 4-12: The accelerated speed of GPU over multiple paths.

© John Wiley & Sons, Inc.

USING A MONTE CARLO SIMULATION

To establish the inherent benefits of using GPU, a broad base of computations was tested from simple single transactions to multiple transactions of baskets of equities in multiple currencies. What was found was that the speedup across all types was uniform.

The GPUs were NVIDIA. CUDA is a parallel platform and programming discipline that NVIDIA has developed, which permits developers to maximize processing speeds through parallelization. It's a specialized discipline. With CUDA, the GPU is actually used as a coprocessor with CPU to parallelize the more computational intensive nature of the CPU.

The results were measured using NVIDIA Tesla V100, of the latest NVIDIA architecture Tesla for professional GPUs. The test was using a Monte Carlo (MC) simulation, which by its very nature requires many paths to assure better results. MC relies on hundreds of thousands of paths to across random samplings to assure accuracy. In typical numbers of Monte Carlo paths, they observed acceleration 20 times. At peak, they were able to achieve the speedup up to 120 times for a very large number of Monte Carlo paths: 300,000. The speedup factor grows with the number of Monte Carlo paths. Refer to Figure 4-11 for the efficacy of using GPU over CPU when the tasks have been simplified and optimized. And see Figure 4-12 for how GPU is fastest when the number of paths is large.

For highly compute-heavy programs, when your GPU strategy is set up correctly, you should see nearly perfect parallelization across multiple GPUs connected to the same CPU (a single socket). In multi-socket hardware configurations (where GPUs are connected to several CPUs), an application object is created on each socket in the application to ensure nearly perfect parallelization across all GPUs.

Choosing a Programming Language

New programming languages are usually created in response to unmet need. They have lately arisen in response to demands for faster turnaround of new functionality in new releases, better quality control, faster computation speeds, and near real-time computations.

As you discover earlier in this chapter, several industry-wide trends have changed the way application development is done. All these factors have made a lot of the more traditional languages less desirable:

>> API strategies have enabled development both internally and externally.

>> Microservices, with their small cross-functional teams, have changed who gets involved in the process and how the team members with differing skill sets communicate.

>> The demand for the processing of huge quantities of data in the shortest amount of time has caused developers to look at ways to involve GPUs.

Because financial engineers, scientific researchers, and business developers are now engaged directly with programmers, programming languages that are easy to write and easy to understand are coming to the forefront. Experts can use these new languages to write specifications and testing plans that everyone on the team can understand. The changing types of use has also driven language choices; Agile and RAD lend themselves much more easily to some languages than others. Not every project is best coded using one monolithic paradigm, so the ability to utilize multiple paradigms in a single language has led to more elegant software construction.

The following sections look at three modern, up-and-coming programming languages that the FinTech industry has embraced: Python, Julia, and R. Each has its place, and it's your job to understand the benefits of each so you can appropriately apply the correct language to solve your problem.

Python

According to the executive summary on Python's official website (www.python.org/doc/essays/blurb):

> Python is an interpreted, object-oriented, high-level programming language with dynamic semantics. Its high-level built-in data structures, combined with dynamic typing and dynamic binding, make it very attractive for Rapid Application Development, as well as for use as a scripting or glue language to connect existing components together. Python's simple, easy to learn syntax emphasizes readability and therefore reduces the cost of program maintenance. Python supports modules and packages, which encourages program modularity and code reuse. The Python interpreter and the extensive standard library are available in source or binary form without charge for all major platforms, and can be freely distributed.

Python was created in 1980, and since then it has become so widely used that it's now considered a "mainstream" language like Java, C#, or C++. What makes Python so appealing is that it doesn't require standard compiling, which makes debugging more straightforward and faster.

While the definition supplied by the Python website says that Python is an interpreted code, the reality is that it's really a hybrid. It's byte code interpreted that also requires some compiling. An interpreter is used to translate the code at runtime into executable code, thereby avoiding the need for traditional compiling. Because it isn't compiled in a standard way, the types aren't statically declared but rather are dynamic.

Python is open source (see Chapter 10), has an extensive user community, and has an active official website for support and development needs. The language is simple to use, easy to learn, and well supported. Python works in all standard operating systems. The following sections provide more details on Python.

Providing support for different programming styles

A *paradigm* is a classification of programming style that demonstrates the overall structure or focus of that language based on the features of the code structure. Python supports a variety of paradigms, either partially or completely, including:

» **Functional (mathematical):** The traditional linear type of programming, which sets forth the code in a mathematical linear series of functions

» **Imperative (best for ordering data structures):** A step-by-step or how-to approach

» **Object oriented (only partially available):** An approach that creates groupings that can be called in blocks

» **Procedural (iterative):** An approach that creates a list of instructions

One of the most redeeming aspects of Python is that it wasn't developed in a vacuum. It's delivered in a package that includes tools, libraries, and modules that the interpreter can access without additional importation.

Universities and new technologies have embraced Python as an instrument of change. It's used not only by coders but also casual developers, scientists, and subject matter experts (SMEs). Python has a specialized stack of tools and programs that have been created for the scientific community, called the "scientific stack." It can store and handle homogeneous or heterogeneous data. This stack is often the deciding factor for selecting Python over other types of new programming languages.

The finance industry uses Python because it comes closer to mathematical formulas and terms than any other programming language. Numerical algorithms are easily translated into Python. The fact that Python doesn't have to be compiled is an asset because the translation of the numerical construct to the Python code is nearly equivalent. Python is also deeply embedded in the programming used for artificial intelligence (AI) development, which is believed to be part of the FinTech future.

TIP

Python has an extensive library and packages that are tailored to the specialty of the developer. For examples, look at iPython (`https://ipython.org`) and Jupyter Notebook (`https://jupyter.org`).

Examining the pros and cons

Python has a lot of benefits to recommend it. It's easy to learn and use, even for noncoders. It has a robust ecosystem and user groups that support innovation and a robust interpreter. As we mention earlier, it has a scientific stack, and its language is close to numerical constructs, so it's a natural fit for the financial industry. In fact, Python has already been assimilated into many of the large banks. Add to that the multi-paradigm support, the built-in debugging tools, and the hundreds of preconfigured packages, and Python looks like a pretty good choice.

WARNING

Python isn't perfect, of course. It requires lots of memory to operate, and its database access layer isn't highly developed, so it doesn't interface well with more complex external data. It's also not very effective for creating mobile applications. In addition, the development process is different with Python because it's a dynamic language. Quality assurance isn't robust, and errors are often not anticipated until runtime.

Julia

Julia is a high-level, high-performance, dynamic, compiled programming language. Julia has been constructed to maximize speed, particularly for linear math computations and matrix simulations. It uses the Low Level Virtual Machine (LLVM) to compile code very quickly. The LLVM project is a compiler technology that utilizes reusable compilers and a set of specialized programming tools used to speed up compiling. Julia uses a dynamic type similar to scripting.

Like Python, Julia is open source, with an easily accessible language with libraries and tools that make it easy to use. It was created in 2009, so it's a relatively new language. It was specifically focused on the needs of the computational science and analytic community. Because it's still relatively new, it doesn't have the user community nor the user support network that Python has. It also hasn't matured sufficiently to have as rich an offering of libraries as Python does.

Code conversion in Julia is one-way only. You can move code from other languages into Julia, but trying to convert from Julia to another language isn't a simple task. Getting started with Julia may be easier than with Python (or R, discussed next), because the install is fully self-contained.

Julia is faster than Python. Its forte is in mathematical computations. Julia focuses only on core compute tasks and not on data quality/integration. Both Python and

Julia support parallelism and heterogeneous computing. Like Python, it was built for the future of AI learning. Like Python's scientific stack, Julia has been designed to be used for scientific and numerical computing. It has scientific tools and solvers built in and a framework to support simulations. It also has APIs that can be used for developing visualizations. In Julia, everything is written as an expression. The language is minimalistic but elegant, and it supports both distributed and parallel computing.

WARNING

The main drawback to Julia is its age — it's very young and doesn't have a robust user group. It's also mainly the domain of the single company that developed it and provides its support.

R

R was created in 1990 and differentiated from Python primarily by its focus on statistical and data mining computing. Like Python, it's an interpreted language. Like both Python and Julia, it's open source. Its adoption has lagged behind Python's acceptance because of the perception that its use case is limited to statistical and data programming.

R can be used to develop web applications. R libraries were designed to implement linear and nonlinear modeling. It's a highly extensible language and accessible through a myriad of scripting languages like Perl, Python, and Ruby. It can be linked to non-R code to run more computationally intensive functions. R objects can be called directly by almost any other first-tier code. It's most interesting because of its extensible nature. It's most often compared to commercial statistical packages like SAS and Stata.

R's data structures are different from those of Julia and Python. Derived from a language called Scheme developed in the MIT AI Labs in 1970, the R language is displayed as vectors, arrays, and data frames. Its limited design structure has made it of limited use, although it's considered elegant in its minimalistic design. It supports many paradigms. As a result, it's the user who extends and creates the packages that comprise the tools of the program. More than 16,000 packages are available for inclusion with the code. R has a substantial and active user group, which holds an annual event.

Because it was designed as a statistical tool, it handles the technical discipline requirements for big data computations very well, which makes it attractive to FinTech applications. It has been used in the research and scientific community for many years and has thousands of packages already developed and tested for use in that community. It was originally developed to run on GNU but can run on all the main operating systems.

IN THIS CHAPTER

» **Figuring out compute requirements**

» **Digging into decentralized applications (DApps)**

» **Considering quantum computing**

Chapter 5

Confronting the Compute Conundrum

Financial institutions face ever-increasing demands for real-time data processing and analysis. Along with the need to deal with "big data," there is growing concern around security and privacy as well as regulatory concerns around the processing and retention of that data. Through cutting-edge technologies, cloud-based delivery, and storage mechanisms, increased reliance on application programming interfaces (APIs) and new development processes, FinTech offers banks and financial institutions a road forward that more efficiently handles their performance demands.

This chapter looks at a variety of computing technologies that can be employed to meet those requirements. We look at in-memory computing, cloud computing, decentralized applications, and quantum computing.

Determining Compute Requirements

In FinTech, *capacity planning* refers to estimating the required hardware and software for a bank's processing needs. The new levels of data and transaction processing (often in real or near real time), the flexibility of cloud bursting, and regulatory requirements have all added levels of complexity to the process.

The concept of cloud bursting and its implications are further addressed in Chapter 6.

REMEMBER

For large computations and "big data" functions, four factors determine processing requirements:

>> **Volume:** How much data is collected and stored?

>> **Velocity:** How often is this data processed, and how often is it created?

>> **Veracity:** What is the quality of the data?

>> **Variety:** How different is the data being processed?

The answers to these questions directly impact the computational cost. You can use some general rules for rough estimates of computing needs, and most cloud providers have tools for determining costs based on proposed usage. However, the FinTech company has the in-house skill set for analyzing and determining the best configurations to reduce cost while maximizing performance.

A variety of innovative technologies are available to meet these requirements. The following sections discuss two technologies that do so: in-memory computing and virtualization. Some other up-and-coming technologies that assist in decreasing computational time include distributed ledgers (which you find out more about later in this chapter), expandable on-demand compute in the cloud (covered in Chapter 6), and artificial intelligence and machine learning (covered in Chapter 12).

In-memory computing

REMEMBER

In-memory computing stores data in random-access memory (RAM) across a network of computers that run processes in parallel. It's not a new concept, but lately it has been in higher demand because of the decreasing cost of RAM. For FinTech companies where processing power and speed are critical, a scalable in-memory computing network is a necessity. This network can be physically housed or available in the cloud.

An in-memory network consists of a distributed server farm that performs parallel processing of compute tasks. A memory cache, which interfaces between an application and a database, is replicated across the network, making services continuously available across nodes without being dependent on network performance. There is a persistent store, and workflows are customizable. The system can be extended to interoperate with other applications.

Virtualization

Virtualization, as the name implies, is the creation of a virtual environment on which to run one or many software-based virtual applications or systems. The major benefits of virtualization are in the reduction it provides in IT costs through the elimination of physical machines and in the efficiency it provides through increased scalability and efficiency. It also helps reduce processing costs and streamlines scheduling and utilization needs.

Virtualization has made cloud computing compelling because administrators can use hypervisors to scale virtual operating platforms at reduced costs while optimally allocating resources on the fly. Hypervisors are virtual technology that is used to create, run, and monitor virtual machines. Virtual machines act just like a physical machine, but they can be nested inside one server, and while they perform like hardware, they are composed only of computer files. A hypervisor can run multiple virtual machines off one server. The virtual platform enables resource provisioning for multiple concurrent use cases across all network arenas.

Virtualization can be used in different ways:

>> Hardware virtualization is used to monitor processes and hardware resources.

>> Storage virtualization pulls disparate storage devices together to function as a single logical unit. This is especially beneficial for disaster recovery and backup.

>> Server virtualization enables a single physical server to function as if it were many different servers.

>> Operating system virtualization enables multiple computing devices to scale and be reallocated on the fly.

Making Sense of DApps

A decentralized application (DApp) is peer-to-peer (P2P), open source technology, organized in blocks that are linked (a.k.a. *blockchains*) and identifiable through cryptographic verification. Not all distributed ledgers are blockchain, but the most well-known one is. Bitcoin is the best-known example of a DApp, but we look at some other examples in Chapter 7.

The term *peer-to-peer* means that there is no central store of data; each computer can act as a server for the others in use, and all have shared access.

DApps run on distributed networks. In a *distributed network*, there is no single location or entity that "owns" the data; the block houses the data. A node adds transactions to a *ledger*. Those transactions are visible to all the nodes on the network, but once added, they can never be removed.

Consensus protocol determines the creation of blocks, which are validated by each node. Each node is in a decentralized data network and is synchronized with the other nodes in that network. All nodes must agree on the data before it is added to a block in the blockchain.

Here are some things that all DApps have in common:

>> They were built on the philosophy behind open source, and the majority of all DApps currently available were built using open source frameworks.

>> They are decentralized. Being a distributed technology, DApps are, by their nature, extensible.

>> They require shared protocols. For example, Bitcoin requires a proof of work (PoW) protocol to operate. A PoW is a mechanism that validates the transaction using a difficult-to-produce, time-consuming operation that, once created, is easy to verify. For Bitcoin, the PoW is a series of hashes — alphanumeric strings — created by a "miner" (developer) to confirm the coin transactions on the blockchain. There is also a proof of stake (PoS) required; this is a protocol driven by a set of rules that are part of the transaction and confirmed by a "consensus" algorithm.

>> They reward good user action. For example, Bitcoin-type DApps rely on "mining" for the creation of hashes, which then validate a transaction. The "miner" may then receive a fee for the mining or creation of the hashes that are required for the transaction to be created and validated.

The following sections compare DApps built on public blockchain to traditional database structures and explain the role of DApps in FinTech. We also discuss permissioned blockchain.

Comparing DApps to traditional applications

Today, most financial institutions utilize traditional database structures. The structure in a traditional environment is that of a client–server network, which means there is a single centralized server functioning as the single source of truth for all data and transactions conducted on that network.

Only a user who has been granted permission, generally an administrator, can add or change data to that server. Any user who has permission to access data from that server receives an update every time there is an entry made into the master server, or any time the user queries that server.

WARNING

The security model around this type of configuration is also its weakness. Data is compromised when a breach of the "single source of truth" occurs. Also, because it is a centrally administered model, it is vulnerable to internal disruption through malicious or careless administrative actions and open to review of protected or personal data by those who should not have access.

A decentralized data structure (DDS) is revolutionary in that it operates without centralized data control and removes human administrative operations from the mix. A decentralized data app operates on a P2P structure. In this architecture/network, each compute node can act independently as both a data server and as a user. All nodes are connected through a consensus model, and they all work together to validate the data created and maintained. Figure 5-1 compares a DDS and a traditional structure.

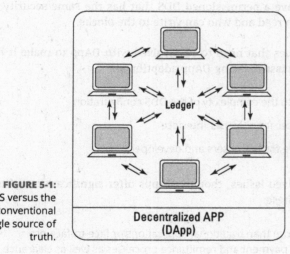
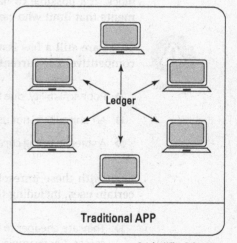

FIGURE 5-1:
A DDS versus the conventional single source of truth.

Decentralized APP
(DApp)

Traditional APP

TIP

The decentralized data model is best used when there is no trust among the event transactors and where having an administrator or record keeper isn't practical because all entries are created uniquely and simultaneously on separate nodes.

Most centralized databases don't make data available in real time. It's a snapshot of activities at a particular time. In contrast, a DDS makes information available in "now" time and keeps a chronological record of all activity held as an immutable instance. Because the history of a transaction is held randomly across a number of blocks, it's nearly impossible to alter it because of the high compute cost of such an action. There is no single record that can be easily altered. The record is therefore considered immutable. This immutability comes at a cost, making DDS an inappropriate methodology for items that require fast data processing and retrieval, such as e-commerce.

REMEMBER

When considering which of your operations should be on a DDS, keep in mind that each member of the network is both a server and a user. That means they all hold and process data independently and then compare their results collectively — "consensus." Such activity requires significant compute power. A DDS also relies heavily on cryptography to keep the data secure, which creates an additional processing burden. On the plus side, though, this methodology provides an almost unhackable environment.

Of course, if you choose to go with a permissioned or a private DApp, the structure of the network are different. The rules for validation and for transparency are also different.

Though a DDS is transparent, so any server can read to a block or write to a new block, it's possible to have a permissioned DDS that has the same security elements that limit who can read and who can write to the blocks.

WARNING

There are still a few issues that need to be resolved with DApp to make it more competitive. The current issues facing DApp adoption are

>> Poor scalability, due to the complexity of the DDS configuration

>> An unintuitive, not user-friendly user interface

>> A steep learning curve for both users and developers

Even with these unresolved issues, though, DApps offer significant benefits for certain uses, including these:

>> They are cheaper to run than traditional applications or face-to-face processes. For example, payment and remittance processes as well as clearance houses and regular online banking queries are recorded in fractions of seconds, and the transaction costs are minimal.

>> They are more secure. A distributed ledger is impenetrable to attack. It's also unchangeable. Many banks are already using DDS technology for secure, regulated operations.

>> The use of a distributed ledger assures transparency of records and automated enforcement of rules.

>> Data integrity is immutable.

Understanding blockchain

Blockchain is a DDS organized around a series of blocks. These blocks are comprised of time-dated data contained on a distributed network and connected in cryptographic chronological order. The first block in the series is the genesis block. A linkage exists from the first block to the next, and the next, and so on, creating a chain of blocks — better known as a blockchain. (We bet you saw that one coming!)

Blockchain is also a P2P distributed ledger. It has no central location and therefore carries no transaction cost. Each transaction is safe and automated. The initiation of a transaction creates a block. A network of servers verifies the integrity of the block. Because each server is part of the transaction, it's impossible to alter the record once it's created.

REMEMBER

Figure 5-2 shows the basic blockchain process for a Bitcoin transaction. (We discuss Bitcoin in more detail later in this chapter.) Here's a summary:

1. A transaction is created through proper protocols.

2. Multiple servers validate a transaction.

3. It's included in a block and confirmed.

4. This block is added to the ledger, and it's linked to the subsequent block. That link is hash pointed. When the hash point operation is completed, the transaction is considered to have achieved its second confirmation.

5. Transactions are confirmed each time a block is created.

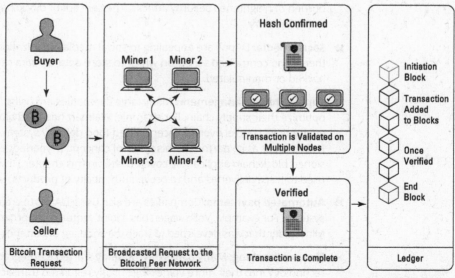

FIGURE 5-2: The workflow of a Bitcoin transaction.

© John Wiley & Sons, Inc.

The key benefits of blockchain are

» It is peer-to-peer. No third parties are involved.

» It is distributed.

» It is anonymous.

» It cannot be changed as data is added in sequence.

» Change can be made only in adherence to strict protocols.

» It is secure.

Knowing where to find DApps

DApps are beginning to gain traction in many different areas, including the following:

» **Decentralized exchanges:** You would think that this is the first area in which DApp technology would be imperative. However, currently, cryptocurrencies are being handled by hackable centralized exchanges, and only recently have DApps been seen in wide use.

» **Gaming:** The gaming industry has already succeeded in monetizing the use of DApps. It's also the one arena where funding for development has been relatively easy to obtain.

» **Gambling:** Though similar to the gaming industry, gambling does bear a great burden of heightened security attacks. The concept of blockchain is appealing to this industry.

» **Social media:** DApps are appealing to social media organizations because there is no centralized server on which to store data, so data cannot be hacked or manipulated.

» **Supply chain management:** Many large companies are using DApps to optimize their supply chain. For example, Walmart has used blockchain to augment its control over its decentralized food delivery system. It used Hyperledger as its partner in this proof of concept. (Hyperledger is a permissioned blockchain application, covered later in this chapter.) It was initially used to trace deliveries and to prove authenticity of products.

» **Automated payments:** Companies are also using DApps to create payment systems. For example, Volkswagen has a joint venture pilot program with Minespider that was developed to track the sourcing of batteries and battery parts.

» **Finance/banking:** Many banks have already started to integrate blockchain technology into their more vulnerable, highly regulated transactions.

These industries are primarily using DApps to handle high-volume exchanges that require transparency, accurate historical tracking of exchanges/interactions, and guarantee of privacy by large groups with low levels of trust or user identification. Some of them have chosen to go with permissioned blockchain applications or systems because of their need for more control on access and privacy. (Permissioned blockchain is covered later in this chapter.)

The following sections provide some company-specific examples.

Bitcoin

Bitcoin was created to be the only digital currency that provided a payment and transaction system, which was safe and transparent. It's a digital currency that isn't distributed or monitored by any bank. All transactions are P2P, the record of which is in a distributed (blockchain) ledger. A digital wallet holds the Bitcoins. Every transaction is recorded publicly and can be exchanged only if you have the code (a private key) to redeem it. A process called *mining* confirms any Bitcoin transaction. Any action in the blockchain requires that the transaction is packed into a block that is presented in proper chronological order across a distributed system.

The currency is entirely virtual. The value of the services or goods exchanged for that Bitcoin is the only intrinsic value assigned to that Bitcoin.

Circle

Founded in 2013, Circle is a relatively new DApp payments technology company. It was established as an alternative to traditional banks and financial institutions. It's now a platform for investment in crypto technologies. It currently offers an exchange where you can trade crypto assets, contribute seed money to crypto start-ups, buy a variety of cryptocurrencies, and research the crypto industry.

Circle is unique in that it accepts US dollars as well as cryptocurrencies and interfaces with credit card suppliers. Jeremy Allaire, the owner of Circle, wants to ensure that financial transactions on the Internet will be as simple and ubiquitous as email.

BitPay

BitPay, an automated payment processing system, is attempting to be the PayPal of cryptocurrency. Since 2011, BitPay's mission is to make the acceptance and exchange of goods and services with Bitcoin and Bitcoin Cash easy and seamless for merchants.

BitPay is aligned with Visa, and 20,000 merchants currently use BitPay's processing system. Its latest infusion of $40 million came as a Series B offering (the second round of funding for a business after the initial start-up phase). There is the potential for BitPay to revolutionize the financial industry, making payments faster, more secure, and less expensive on a global scale.

Ethereum

Ethereum is the first attempt at building a holistic DApps developer community. It's a generic blockchain platform that functions like an Infrastructure as a Service (IaaS). The Ethereum site provides tools, training programs, and user communities for blockchain developers.

Since 2015, Ethereum's mission has been to expand the use of blockchain to new applications that expose the commercial nature of the code. Its raison d'être was to fund itself through its cryptocurrency, called *ether,* so that it could provide an environment for developers to build and distribute DApps throughout the world.

Ethereum is also significant in that it introduced smart contracts, which are code-based, code-generated contracts. These contracts are anonymous, self-executing lines of code between two parties. While the contracts are visible and unalterable, they are also not centrally enforceable.

TECHNICAL STUFF

These smart contracts are built around the Turing complete language. Alan Turing, widely said to be the father of modern computer science, postulated a hypothetical machine that could manipulate symbols in a single line according to a set of rules. Though simple, this machine could create the most sophisticated algorithm. A Turing complete language can solve any reasonable problem on a computer given the right amount of time and memory. The Ethereum platform claims to be a Turing complete blockchain framework used in the creation of smart contracts.

Connecting DApps, Artificial Intelligence, and FinTech

The value proposition surrounding FinTech lies in its ability to take cutting-edge technologies and intelligently use them to streamline operations, security, and data analysis for the financial industry. Understanding which DApps should be applied to which use cases is a critical skill for any FinTech company.

There is no doubt that DApps will play a broad role in the future of banking. The use of DApps, in conjunction with artificial intelligence (AI), can further speed up operations while decreasing the need for human intervention and the risk of security breaches.

It is only a short matter of time before analytics and artificial intelligence are added to decentralized, end-to-end applications provided in blockchain. When this happens, the ability to use these transparent, immutable data ledgers with AI algorithms will result in automated and verifiable accounting in which all anomalies can be easily flagged and audited. AI finds discrepancies and identifies them, while blockchain retains the immutable record and all historical data around any transaction or event and provides an audit of those changes to all parties simultaneously.

This marriage of technologies will find application in credit modeling, end-to-end settlements, and high-frequency trading, and FinTech companies will utilize their expertise to deploy these changes to its clients seamlessly.

Looking at permissioned blockchain

In Chapter 7, we address some of the iterations that have come after Bitcoin. Permissioned blockchain is one of these iterative innovations. It's hard for a bank or a corporation to utilize blockchain as it's configured for the public. A *permissioned blockchain* has an administrative or control layer that dictates the operations of the blockchain stacked below it. This layer limits access and controls the permissioning process. The issue that arises with the introduction of these controls is that you have to be permissioned to join the network, which mitigates the desire for anonymity that drove part of the reason behind blockchain creation.

Needing to be permissioned also limits the manner in which a transaction is validated. Permissioned blockchain generally restricts or limits the consensus protocol and sets up an "authority" administration. The result of this change creates more efficient performance in that the consensus threshold can be much less, and the number of nodes required for transaction validation can be reduced, thereby increasing efficiency.

The introduction of an administrative layer is found to be somewhat more comforting to corporations overall. They can own the access and the level of visibility. And in general, because of the streamlining of the consensus and the number of nodes, updates and the processing of transactions are faster.

WARNING

There are, however, decided disadvantages to permissioned blockchains. The great advantages of public blockchains are mitigated by this layer of administration. For one thing, there is limited anonymity and limited transparency. The security can be compromised because with limited consensus or validation, the potential of data manipulation is increased. Blockchain was initially created to permit the transactors to control and determine the value of their event. In a permissioned network, the administrator can regulate the transactions in a profound way.

R3 (which sits on top of Corda), Hyperledger Fabric, and Quorum (which sits on top of Ethereum) are enterprise permissioned blockchains that fall into the category of permissioned blockchain consortiums.

Advantages of permissioned blockchain consortiums include the following:

>> The transaction times are faster than public blockchain.

>> The privacy is limited in a consortium and predefined.

>> They are more cost-effective than public blockchain.

Disadvantages of permissioned blockchain consortiums include the following:

>> They are not as transparent or open.

>> They are less secure.

>> They can be manipulated or controlled externally as well as through internal manipulation of the nodes.

>> Accessing information in a consortium can be slower because of the administrative layer and the change to protocols.

TIP

If you chose to go in the direction of permissioned blockchain, you should assess your need for data privacy, data access, and data storage to determine the best fit of the permissioned blockchain currently available. Keep in mind that you have added a layer of complexity on top of the blockchain, so deployment of one of these apps will be slower.

Understanding Quantum Computing

All classical computers, from servers to cellphones to smart appliances, operate fundamentally in the same way. They work with strings of conventional binary digits or *bits* — that is, 1s and 0s.

However, a *quantum computer* works differently. It operates on strings of quantum bits, called *qubits*. These qubits derive their properties from subatomic particles, which, as you see in the following sections, behave in ways that seem to defy common sense. Here, you also discover the disadvantages of quantum computing and how it works in the world of FinTech.

How quantum computing works

Consider electrons, which are the negatively charged particles responsible for voltages in wires, electronic circuits, and so on. Electrons have a property called *spin*. It's quantized, meaning spin can be clockwise or counterclockwise, one or the other. Clockwise spin and counterclockwise spin are the electron's *basis states* — that is, what you observe upon testing it. You can imagine how basis states might be used to encode digital information classically: Spin clockwise would represent 1 and spin counterclockwise would represent 0. In Figure 5-3, you see the electron spin of a qubit in the two basis states. The arrows point to the north direction of its magnetic field.

FIGURE 5-3:
In a qubit, the orbits can spin counterclockwise and clockwise simultaneously.

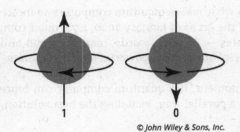

© John Wiley & Sons, Inc.

The behavior of qubits prior to observation is another matter. In this state, the electron doesn't have a definite spin. The spin is both clockwise *and* counterclockwise simultaneously.

In ordinary experience, that's impossible, right? How can a billiard ball spin clockwise *and* counterclockwise at the same time? Obviously, we aren't dealing with ordinary experience, and electrons aren't billiard balls. It's not that an electron has a definite spin and we just don't know what it is. No, quantum theory maintains that the spin exists only as a matter of possibility. In this case, the electron is said to be in a state of *superposition*.

REMEMBER

Although an electron in superposition does not have a definite spin, when the system reads out the qubit, there's a distinct probability of getting one of the basis states — that is, 1 or 0. Quantum theory predicts that when we measure the electron to report the result of a computation, we have an α chance, say 65%, of getting a 1 and a β chance, say 35%, of getting a 0 so that $\alpha + \beta = 100\%$.

You can see how superposition distinguishes classical and quantum computers. Superposition is also what gives quantum computers their unique advantages.

A single qubit contains two pieces of information: α and β. A bit usually contains only one piece of information, but here we're getting two pieces. It seems like we're getting something for nothing. However, this extra information from a qubit we get for "free" is offset by the lack of certainty, a notion that is integral to quantum physics — for example, Heisenberg's uncertainty principle.

This is only the start. Two qubits contain four numbers: α (the probability of observing the binary number 11), β (the probability of observing 10), χ (the probability of observing 01), and δ (the probability of observing 00). Therefore, $\alpha + \beta + \chi + \delta = 100\%$.

Three qubits have eight numbers. Four bits have 16 numbers, and so on. In other words, N qubits contain the equivalent of 2^N classical bits of information.

This idea is the key to what makes quantum computers so interesting and useful. In the current state of the art as of January 2020, a 72-qubit computer, as claimed by Google, has 2^{72} states — in other words, more than 100 billion *billion* states. This exceeds the capacity of the most powerful supercomputers.

Think about it for a moment. If a quantum computer can represent all possible states of a problem in a parallel way, including the best solution, we already have our answer.

Think about how a GPS, which is a classical computer, routes you to a destination. The device examines all paths, one after another in sequence, including ones no sensible person would consider. A quantum navigator would be different only that it would hold all routes in a state of superposition and examine them, not in sequence, but all in parallel. This is a much faster approach.

Imagine this same approach applied to Internet security. It depends on keeping secret the factors of very large numbers (for example, 2,048-bit prime numbers). The most powerful supercomputer today would take thousands of years to decrypt information protected by this means. It's the reason encryption as such is considered secure. A quantum computer, however, would have all the possible factors in superposition and, in a matter of minutes, test them all in parallel for the one that cracks the code. It has the potential to render Internet security as we know it today obsolete.

The drawbacks of quantum computing

However, don't make a run on the bank just yet. Quantum computers also have limits. They're not universally better than classical computers, only better for certain problems, like the ones described in the preceding section, that lend themselves to *quantum parallelism*. For anything other than that specific kind of problem, quantum computers offer no advantages and, in fact, have some disadvantages.

TECHNICAL
STUFF

For example, the hardware environment required for quantum computing is difficult and expensive to maintain. Quantum circuits must be submerged in a sealed cryogenic bath of liquid helium at a fraction of a degree above absolute zero to enable the superconducting circuits and to shield them from thermal and electromagnetic noise. In fact, quantum computers are so sensitive that they must be suspended on shock absorbers to avoid vibrational disturbances caused by seismic tremors, passersby, and so on. Absence of this shielding and stability gives rise to computing errors and limits the time a quantum computer can work on a problem. These complications mean that, at least for now, most potential irresponsible actors wouldn't have access to quantum computers.

WARNING

Even if the data center environment could be perfectly shielded and stabilized, there are still additional drawbacks. Note that quantum computers are unreliable by their very nature. Remember the α, β, and such probabilities we mention in the preceding section? These values fluctuate, causing the quantum computer to give different results at different times. It requires running the quantum app multiple times to get a statistically probable correct answer.

How quantum computing fits into FinTech

Consider quantum computing as an option for a FinTech use case. Entire classes of path-dependent derivatives have no known mathematical closed form, and for which Monte Carlo (MC) methodology, a type of simulation to obtain numerical results, has traditionally been used to price these options. The idea behind MC is simple: Simulate path by path and find the expected value of the payoffs.

Another use case is measuring value at risk (VaR) or conditional value at risk (CVaR; also called expected shortfall). Here, the approach is similar, except it is finding the worst-case scenario for a given confidence interval.

Among its upsides, MC is so-called "embarrassingly parallel," meaning that it naturally lends itself to parallelization — and it turns out, quantum parallelism in particular. In a certain sense, the application is like GPS navigation. The paths represent not turn-by-turn directions, but asset values that are held in quantum superposition and that can be evaluated all at once. There's empirical evidence that quantum speedup is not merely a theoretical potential.

One downside of MC is it gives approximate results. To decrease the potential for error, you have to run multiple simulations. Typically, to get one extra digit of accuracy, you need 100 times as many simulations. However, IBM researchers Stefan Woerner and Daniel J. Egger in 2019 showed that quantum computers need only 32 times as many simulations to get the same improvement, as shown in Figure 5-4, which illustrates the results of a MC risk assimilation on an IBM quantum computer. These kinds of speedup potential open the door to getting more accurate pricing, better risk assessment, and/or increased business revenue from larger volumes.

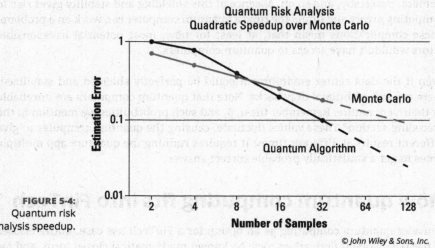

FIGURE 5-4: Quantum risk analysis speedup.

Chapter **6**

Calling Up the Cloud

The roles that cloud services, cloud storage, and cloud computing play in the financial arena have increased exponentially over the last five years. Two key motivators have driven this change: the need to speed up processing while reducing overhead, and the need to supply a seamless interface that permits users to define and control their level of interaction.

Only a few years ago, storing data outside the physical domain of any financial institution seemed an impossibility, completely anathema to the common understanding of the legal requirement to maintain data privacy and security. However, the popularity of the Internet and the wide acceptance of e-commerce, along with the coming of age of millennials, has sparked a reevaluation of conventional data management limitations. Trade-offs of risk versus expediency further forced open the door to the cloud.

In addition, the general costs for hosting, as well as greater oversight into cloud-based security and the need for greater work mobility, have lowered the barrier to entry for many corporations.

Nowadays, it's impossible to consider a FinTech strategy that doesn't also encompass the utilization of clouds — both public and private — for storage, computing, and/or analysis. The Internet has made the systems that deliver information to the end user much richer. You can be in contact with your fellow workers, customers, and data anywhere, anytime, and in any way.

As we explain throughout this book, FinTech doesn't thrive inside monolithic structures. The factors that differentiate FinTech companies from traditional ones are their speed to market/deployment and their ability to decompose functional needs in a way that allows small groups to be responsible for those deliverables. So it's not difficult to see why the cloud is consistent with new technologies used to deploy applications to the marketplace speedily. This chapter explains some basic cloud principles and how cloud technology can be employed in FinTech.

REMEMBER

As you go through this chapter, keep in mind that the cloud is not a monolithic thing any more than microservices or application programming interfaces (APIs) are. The cloud is a framework whereby specific services are automated and delivered in a seamless, scalable fashion. The cloud enables as close to real-time distribution as possible through microservices, APIs, and distributed ledger technologies (DLTs). Through the cloud, individual development teams, experts, and users can interface with the data and the technology as needed. The cloud provides the platform for plug-and-play functionality delivered in a fast, secure, and consistent fashion.

Getting to Know the Cloud

The demand for real-time access to processed data, consistently and immediately, has in the last two decades become critical to the financial industry, as it has to many industries. Further, the cost for banks and financial institutions to own and maintain their internal IT and development infrastructure has become such a burden, both financially and physically, that many institutions offload all or part of it to outside services. The best solution for many institutions has become on-demand cloud computing.

REMEMBER

The cloud can be loosely defined as a collection of servers that are available off premises and accessed on demand through private or public pipes and that function without direct end-user management. It is a means by which a corporation can have on-demand compute and storage inexpensively and seamlessly. The cloud can be used for data storage and/or computational processing, similar to on-premises servers. To meet regulatory requirements or mitigate potential data loss and downtime, cloud processes are often distributed so that they run at different locations.

The following sections provide the basics of cloud computing, including its key traits, benefits, and services.

Looking at the cloud's key traits

Some key characteristics of cloud computing include the following:

WARNING

>> It has the ability to deploy or change user experience rapidly and without disruption to the user. This can include cloud bursting compute processing and auto scaling, both of which are discussed in greater detail later in this chapter.

>> There is a cost decrease in capital expenditure but an increase in operational expenditure. It's important to monitor individual compute tasks carefully and select the correct pricing model for the use case to avoid paying too much.

>> There are in-house IT cost reductions due to outsourced IT functions. Fewer personnel will be required after setup, and there will be less day-to-day IT maintenance and user interactions.

>> A company can secure third-party support without the third party needing to have specialized knowledge of the company's IP (intellectual property).

>> Delivery is anytime/anywhere/any media.

>> It can be offered either as a single tenant or as multi-tenant.

>> There are guaranteed performance standards, driven by service level agreements (SLAs), which are auditable.

>> Public cloud multi-tenancy results in reduced processing costs.

>> The ability to provision on-demand cheap and low maintenance disaster recovery is available.

>> Provisioning is automated and dynamically provisioned.

>> Innovative new technologies like artificial intelligence (AI) can be deployed.

>> Designated experts can handle performance requirements.

>> Companies with heightened security concerns can improve security by centralizing and hiring experts to determine their best options.

Checking out the benefits of the cloud environment

The benefits in utilizing cloud environments over on-premises enterprises are numerous. The infrastructure is maintained by cloud service providers (CSPs), which are specialists in cloud delivery and performance. They continuously and seamlessly keep the underlying structure up to date. CSPs are also aware of the laws in the various countries and regions in which they operate, to ensure they conform to each country's regulatory requirements. They also constantly monitor the security landscape for breaches and vulnerabilities, so they can address any threats in real time.

TIP

The Center of Internet Security (CIS) has published a set of security standards and best practices to be used to ensure auditable controls against a cyberattack; visit www.cisecurity.org/cybersecurity-best-practices. CSPs provide CIS hardened images as part of their service offering and maintain the level of security necessary for regulatory compliance. Doing so relieves clients of the burden of having to think about these issues.

CSPs offer SLAs that guarantee a certain uptime percentage and disaster recovery speed. They orchestrate any updates and quality-control checks to minimize end-user disruption. Clients have access to state-of-the-art hardware and security measures, with support from highly trained specialists. The client can leave all these peripheral activities to the cloud supplier and focus on their core business.

Introducing types of cloud services

An organization can put anything in the cloud that it wants to. There are no limits except those the organization itself (or more likely its budget) imposes. The cloud infrastructure was built to be limitlessly expansive.

A CSP traditionally provides hosting, on-demand resourcing, data store, elasticity, network access interfaces, metered fee structures, and multi-tenancy. The big-name CSPs include Amazon Web, Microsoft Azure, and Google Cloud. These providers offer three basic types of services to customers, depending on what they want to do:

>> Infrastructure as a Service (IaaS)

>> Software as a Service (SaaS)

>> Platform as a Service (PaaS)

You find out more about each of those in the upcoming sections. Figure 6-1 provides a basic summary, as a preview.

While these three types of services are the most often deployed, and are potentially part of any FinTech solution, some new entries into the cloud-based arena may also prove viable, as the demands for faster, smaller, and easier solutions move to new delivery mechanisms. The following types may soon also gain traction, and we tell you more about them as well:

IaaS, PaaS, SaaS Explained
Summary of Key Differences

Software as a Service	Platform as a Service	Infrastructure as a Service	On-Premises
Networking	Networking	Networking	Networking
Storage	Storage	Storage	Storage
Servers	Servers	Servers	Servers
Virtualization	Virtualization	Virtualization	Virtualization
O/S	O/S	O/S	O/S
Middleware	Middleware	Middleware	Middleware
Runtime	Runtime	Runtime	Runtime
Data	Data	Data	Data
Applications	Applications	Applications	Applications

Key
Service Provider
Enterprise

Common Examples of SaaS, PaaS & Iaas

Platform Type	Common Examples
SaaS	CRM, Email, ERP, HRM, Payroll, Database management
PaaS	Collabration tools, Test environment, Storage, Persistence, Specialized developer environment, Programming language execution environment, Web servers
IaaS	Storage, Computer servers, VMs, Disk image library, File based storage, Fire walls, Load balancers

© John Wiley & Sons, Inc.

FIGURE 6-1: A summary of key differences and examples of each type of cloud service.

>> Mobile "Backend" as a Service (MbaaS)

>> Serverless computing (SC)

>> Function as a Service (FaaS)

>> Communications Platform as a Service (CPaaS)

Infrastructure as a Service (IaaS)

With IaaS, the tenant is responsible for building and maintaining many of the custom applications it deploys on its own private cloud network. The vendor provides APIs to be used to build structures on top of the cloud infrastructure it provides and maintains. This underlying infrastructure is similar to that provided in a SaaS environment (see the next section), but the maintenance and management are handled differently.

The vendor provides operating systems (OSs), execution environments, databases, and web servers but does not provide ongoing support for the way those items are maintained after provisioning. The provider may also offer the tenant a range of services, such as log access, monitoring, load-balancing, and encryption, as well as a virtualization and hypervisor layer. The vendor's data center still supplies and installs the tenant's environment. A wide area network (WAN) provides most of these services. The pricing model for this type of service is generally a monthly billing based on the resources used and allocated. This is a self-service model for the tenant.

The vendor delivers its infrastructure through virtualization tools. The tenant accesses the environment through dashboards or APIs. The tenant is responsible for maintaining all its customized work, and the provider is responsible for the underlying infrastructure, including virtualization tools, servers, and storage. This model closely aligns with FinTech needs.

Here are some IaaS characteristics:

>> It has rapid deployment of customized applications.

>> There is platform virtualization.

>> Scaling allocation is based on real-time needs.

>> Tenants maintain control over their custom applications and infrastructure.

>> Tenants retain control over access and security.

>> Resources are provided as a service.

>> Cost is directly tied to use.

>> Allocation is dynamic.

WARNING

IaaS is useful for companies that are growing but don't want to manage or purchase large network farms. IaaS may not be right for companies that have too many legacy systems to maintain without help, that don't have clear visibility into the costs for pay-as-you-go service, or that can't allocate IT resources to deploy and maintain customized applications.

Software as a Service (SaaS)

SaaS is the most common way for organizations to utilize cloud computing. The CSP provides applications for their tenants and stores data on a vendor-maintained cloud infrastructure. The applications are available primarily through a web-based thin client. The tenant doesn't have to maintain this infrastructure. The CSP coordinates and maintains all changes to the network, databases, servers, and interfaces.

End users are provisioned based on predefined profiles, with minimal customization. The tenant receives network-based access to a single copy of the application. The application is the same for all tenants, and upgrades apply unilaterally to all at the same time. The provider may make some APIs available for modifications to the application. The use of this service is "on demand" and is priced either as a pay-per-use system or by monthly subscription.

SaaS providers use virtual machines (VMs) — a simulation or copy of a physical computer system or network represented through computer files — that are provisioned as required for the workload. This workload is distributed across the total cloud environment and load-balanced to accommodate a multi-tenancy environment. The user is unaware of the provisioning and of any other tenants that may also be using the service. A public cloud of this nature enables small companies to use technologically advanced applications and to scale without having to invest in large network farms and IT personnel. This multi-tenancy approach is by its nature less secure than in a private cloud.

Here are some SaaS characteristics:

>> The provider maintains it.

>> It can be provisioned on the fly.

>> The provider manages it centrally.

>> It is hosted on the Internet.

>> The end user accesses it through the Internet.

>> The tenant has no maintenance responsibility.

SaaS is appropriate for short-term projects and for storage or disaster recovery preparation. It's also useful when you need fast deployment and for unified applications like customer relationship management (CRM), where a static and stable interface is required.

WARNING

SaaS may not be right if you have many unique applications to deploy or unique integration requirements. It's also not for those who need a lot of customization or complete control over data security and privacy.

Platform as a Service (PaaS)

PaaS is a platform in the clouds for application developers. The vendor supplies not only the same basic infrastructure supplied to tenants of SaaS and IaaS (described in the preceding sections) but also a framework in which developers can build their own customized applications.

In IaaS, the provider gives the tenant a database or a web server but doesn't manage it once it has been provisioned. In PaaS, however, the provider also maintains and manages all functions of the database. The same is true about encryption, web server, and container services. The vendor fully supports the underlying infrastructure, while the tenant manages and controls the upper layers through APIs and direct programming. The tenant also can set requirements for the custom hosted applications. The platform provided has tools, libraries, and an execution environment and recognizes multiple computer languages.

A PaaS provider may also provide Integration Platform as a Service (iPaaS) and Data Platform as a Service (dPaaS). Those services fully deliver new applications that the tenant can launch through this platform. Such cloud-based environments are great for FinTech development, deployment, and maintenance.

The main PaaS characteristics include

>> Built to support application development environments to disparate development teams

>> Scalable development

>> Reduction in new code creation

>> Easy migration tools

>> Easy virtualization tools

>> Ease of code versioning and synchronization

>> Lower cost overhead to development

PaaS is useful for development teams that aren't colocated, especially if developers need to be added dynamically, and for FinTech companies that support customer applications.

WARNING

PaaS may not be right if you have data security concerns, if you need to customize legacy systems, if the required development language or framework support isn't available, or if the cloud administration and automation tools don't provide sufficient flexibility.

PaaS is a popular choice for FinTech because it permits three modes of delivery:

>> Public cloud

>> Private cloud behind a firewall

>> As software deployed on a public version of IaaS

It also allows different developers and companies to deploy quickly, and it lowers operational costs. Replication is easy, and developer resources need not be spent on IT functions.

Other service models

This discussion wouldn't be complete without mentioning a few less common types of cloud services:

>> *Mobile Backend as a Service (MBaaS),* designed for developers and first offered in 2011, is a platform primarily for mobile and web-app developers. The problem these service providers solve is in the provisioning of a software development environment with a software development kit (SDK) that includes cloud storage and compute services as well as a robust offering of APIs. They also provide the libraries and tools needed for building and testing mobile and web-based apps.

>> The sole purpose of the *serverless computing (SC)* model is to manage VM provisioning. SC is not without servers; it's just an environment where the provider takes care of all the IT and operational needs of a network and allows the developers to focus only on building and running the services they are creating.

>> *Function as a Service (FaaS)* is aligned with SC in that it allows scripting of other functions that are called or are used to monitor VM processes. This type of cloud platform lends itself well to teams working on the development of microservices. It augments SC with on-demand functionality like batch processing.

>> *Communications Platform as a Service (CPaaS)* augments PaaS by providing real-time communication code and applications (video, voice, and messaging) into new applications under development.

Choosing between private and public clouds

REMEMBER

Cloud servers can be either public or private. How do they differ?

>> In a *private cloud,* the servers are discretely assigned (or owned) by only one tenant or owner. This tenant/owner may manage its own cloud internally, or it may outsource cloud management to a third party. Whichever approach the tenant/owner takes, the cloud is still secure and accessible only in accordance with tenant-created rules. The tenant or third-party agent is responsible for server maintenance, as well as the strategy, performance, and compute needs involved in delivering data to end users.

>> A *public cloud* is owned by a vendor who sells access and services to multiple tenants. The data available in a multi-tenant environment can be shared or separate. The cloud application service providers (CASPs) or FinTech service providers are responsible for all data management, repairs, and adherence to the contracted SLAs. The contract with the tenant dictates the minimum speed and capacity levels, but the provider is responsible for the actual delivery and support. Most cloud usage today is public.

Table 6-1 summarizes the differences between public and private clouds.

TABLE 6-1

Public Clouds versus Private Clouds

Public	Private
Multi-tenancy	Single tenant or owner
No hardware or capital costs	Can own servers or not
Off-premises/no operational overhead	Can be on or off premises
Low to no IT costs	Ongoing IT costs
Shared server/network	Private hosting
Scalable on demand	Scalable as contracted
Limited customizations	Built to customer specifications

Digging into a few details

WARNING

With a public cloud, the CSP controls the infrastructure. This means that the tenant has fewer options and less ability to customize the output. In contrast, a private cloud is constrained by the company's IT policies and procedures and is behind the corporate firewall. The infrastructure of a private cloud is the same as a public one, but because the company's IT department controls its privacy and security rules, some of the compliance hurdles go away. If a company has a highly regulated approach to privacy and data storage, the public cloud may raise issues as the location of the storage of its data isn't readily known by the owner.

TIP

Not sure which cloud type is right for your organization? Ask yourself these questions:

>> Is it important that nobody else has access to your data?

>> Do contracts or regulations dictate your security and privacy thresholds?

>> Is a dedicated data center required?

If you answered yes to any of these questions, either an on-premises or private cloud may be your only option.

TIP

Some public clouds now offer dedicated instances and/or dedicated hosting to mitigate some of the regulatory data concerns. A *dedicated instance* restricts the use of a server at runtime to only one tenant. A *dedicated host* always locks the use of a server to one tenant. Both these specifications come at additional financial costs but are significantly less expensive than a private or on-premises option.

Mixing it up with a hybrid strategy

For many companies, a hybrid strategy works. A hybrid strategy can be a mix of classic on-premises networks, private and public clouds, deployed to support specific use cases. You may use a hybrid cloud for compute services if you have dynamic or changeable workloads, if you need to do "big data" computing, or if you have varied demands for different levels of access and security across the organization. Figure 6-2 summarizes the differences among private, hybrid, and public clouds, and Figure 6-3 shows the layout of an example hybrid cloud environment.

Cloud Computing Deployment Models

PRIVATE	HYBRID	PUBLIC
Cloud computing is provisioned for a single and dedicated enterprise organization. The maintenance of this infrastructure is by the enterprise or a third party.	Can be a mix of any of the three possible models which are: - enterprise owned data center - publically hosted sites - private cloud	Third-party providers of hosting services. The providers maintain all aspects of the provided services
CHARACTERISTICS Single-tenant architecture On demand configurable pool of computing resources Enterprise tenant has full control of the configuration provided Direct control of underlying cloud infrastructure	**CHARACTERISTICS** Mix permits lower cost overall - a cheaper bursting environment on the public cloud - development structure on private cloud - end user interface on public cloud	**CHARACTERISTICS** Pay-as-you-consume multi-tenant Rigid and limited customization **TOP VENDORS** SAP, Google, Azure, AWS
TOP VENDORS Hewlett-Packard, VMware, Oracle, IBM, Cisco	**TOP VENDORS** Pocher, Amazon, Google, Red Hat, Kubernetes, VMware Cloud	

© *John Wiley & Sons, Inc.*

FIGURE 6-2: Cloud computing deployment models.

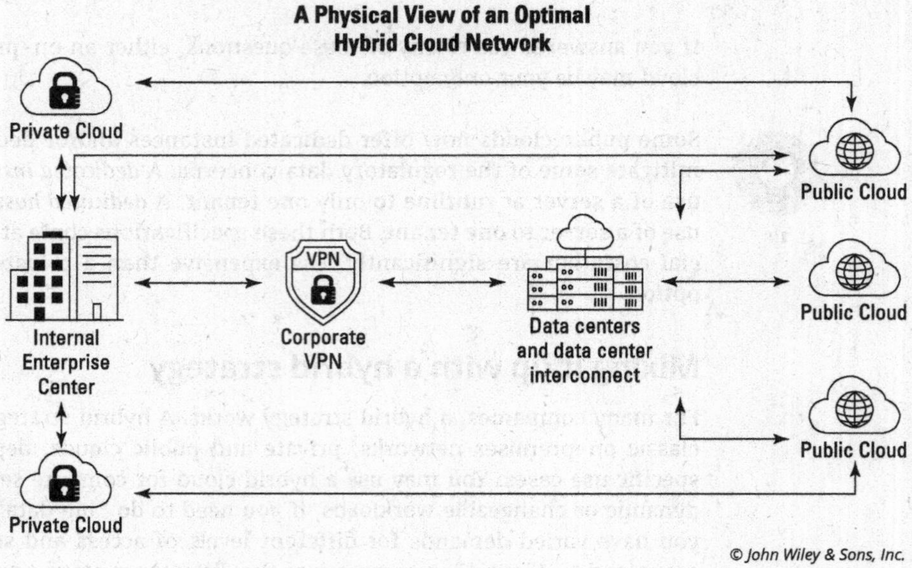

**A Physical View of an Optimal
Hybrid Cloud Network**

Private Cloud

Public Cloud

Internal
Enterprise
Center

Corporate
VPN

VPN

Data centers
and data center
interconnect

Public Cloud

FIGURE 6-3:
A hybrid cloud
network.

Private Cloud

Public Cloud

© John Wiley & Sons, Inc.

There are various ways in which a hybrid cloud strategy can be configured and deployed. A hybrid cloud can be

>> A mixture of traditional on-premises computing, private cloud, or public cloud

>> A mixture of different types of services that may be provided by any number of service providers over many geographic cloud locations

Cloud bursting

TIP

Cloud bursting is a cost-effective method by which companies can temporarily increase their capabilities to accommodate occasional spikes in compute needs without having to purchase hundreds of computer cores or a private cloud network. Access through the cloud allows an on-premises or private cloud to run computations on demand from a more cost-effective public cloud via bursts, which are short spikes in compute resources. Bursts occur only as needed, and the company is charged only when a burst occurs. Figure 6-4 shows an automated scaling listener scaling capacity on the fly.

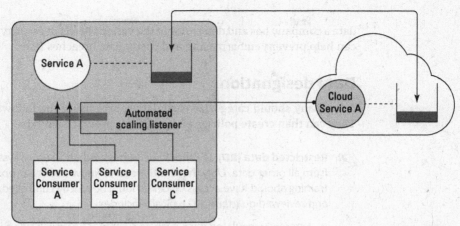

© John Wiley & Sons, Inc.

FIGURE 6-4: Scaling on the fly via an automated listener.

Developing an Optimal Cloud Strategy

To develop the best cloud strategy for your company's needs (with the help of this section), start out by reviewing your current network structure, your computation time requirements, and any legal or regulatory constraints that govern how you must maintain data. If you're dealing with legacy systems, you may have to do two lifts before you can launch on the cloud. Legacy systems may not be cloud-enabled, and you may have to refactor or rewrite the code to make it work. They may also require obsolete hardware that isn't cloud-compatible.

Next, define the use cases for your cloud deployment. You can take a number of approaches when considering a move to the cloud. You should categorize the different applications and databases the organization currently uses and determine which approach is best for each type. Define your end goals and determine the costs and cost savings.

Follow this up by developing a timeline with key ownership and dedicated resources. When your plan is ready for review, secure senior management and executive buy-in and get a budget commitment. As the plan firms up, make sure you set the priorities for application rollout and determine what issues and code changes are required.

Reviewing data security and encryption

Before deploying cloud services, a company should do a thorough security review of its data. Different data types require different levels of security. Analyzing the data a company has and determining the various levels of security/privacy required can help prevent embarrassing and costly data breaches later.

Data designations

A company should categorize each data source using the following designations. They can then create policies and processes around each type.

>> **Restricted data (RD):** RD should be segregated on a secure system or subnet from all other data. Only those with need-to-know and the proper security training should have access. Access should be strictly controlled, audited, and reviewed quarterly. RD typically includes

- Externally regulated data, such as customer personally identifiable information (PII)

- Customer information that contractually requires segregation

- Unfiltered customer databases

>> **Confidential data (CD):** CD is information that could seriously damage the company if breached. Access should be strictly controlled, logged, and reviewed quarterly. CD includes

- Proprietary source code

- The company's internal financial data

- Confidential business plans

- Customer contracts

>> **Private data (PD):** PD is data that should be safeguarded for individual privacy reasons, not for an overarching corporate reason. PD includes

- Corporate internal HR data

- Payroll data

>> **Sensitive data (SD):** SD is the standard classification for most data and includes

- Binaries

- Company information available to employees only

- Information that does not fall under another classification

>> **Public data (Pub):** Pub is data that has no restrictions on its distribution. It can include

- Public information

- Freely disseminated marketing information

Types of encryption

After a company has identified and categorized its data, it's ready to review the types of encryption mechanisms available on the cloud. A variety of encryption methodologies and types are available. The types offered should be consistent with the regulatory requirements for data storage. Any service provider should be able to provide written documentation around its level of encryption. That level may or may not be enough to meet the company's regulatory needs.

Encryption is the cloud's primary security control. To maintain security, companies must have well-defined procedures governing encryption key storage and use. If the company doesn't have a security expert on payroll, then it should engage third-party experts to help develop and manage its policies and encryption procedures.

For example, a cloud encryption service (CES) would be responsible for encryption key management, escrow, and security controls. A regimented life cycle for reviewing and removing data and its associated encrypted keys must be part of the process. The company's security expert or the third-party CES should maintain an on-premises enterprise key management system. For best security practices, the CES shouldn't be the CSP. The CSP must maintain complete separation of data and encryption keys from each of the tenants if the company is a part of a multi-tenancy.

End-to-end encryption should be a requirement for all sensitive data. This type of encryption requires encryption keys for decryption as well. At a minimum, all connections on the cloud should be HTTPS — that is, secure HTTP. With increasingly complex applications on the web, one of the simpler approaches to security may lie in FinTech developers directly inserting code in applications that will call crypto APIs and routines.

Encryption has associated costs. It requires additional bandwidth, it slows down the delivery process, and each aspect of security management increases the actual financial cost to the company. The company may eliminate some of this cost by doing its own encryption on premises before uploading it to the cloud.

The one prime objective for encryption is that the overhead must not prevent the users or the web-based development team from having full and immediate access to the data and results. A FinTech corporation removes some of the uncertainty around the decisions that will have to be made in the area of corporate security.

Because of the increase in protections around personal identifiable information (PII), most CSPs are now offering some standard level of encryption. But before entering into any cloud agreement, make sure you understand what level of encryption is available and what is needed. The company's auditors or regulators must review the encryption offering and augment it if it isn't sufficient. Whatever the ultimate decisions, the data encryption methodology needs to reflect the interoperability of that encryption and decryption, offering a speedy solution to the transfer of data.

Surveying data states

Data is vulnerable to intrusion at three common states:

>> *Data at rest* refers to data in storage. Protecting this data can be complicated because it typically involves a variety of databases, as well as one-off spreadsheets and reports. One of the easiest approaches is to split data into disparate data stores in different locations. Policies should exist that dictate the levels of access any individual has to data.

>> *Data in transit* refers to the time data is in transit. It can be from user to endpoint media; it can be data transported from machine to machine or through hybrid environments. Simple but tested encryption tools such as Transport Layer Security (TLS) or Secure Sockets Layer (SSL) can protect data in transit, and Internet Protocol Security (IPsec) can protect virtual private network (VPN) access. Rules should be in place that govern encryption key dissemination and destruction.

>> *Data in use* refers to data used in actual data processing. Protecting this data is tricky. Tokenization is currently being used to handle this need, but it isn't a complete or elegant solution. Tokenization replaces the actual data with a surrogate or token that can be used to redeem the original data from its secure location outside of the original environment.

REMEMBER

In multi-tenancy, the CSP must make sure data from one company is completely inaccessible to any other company or individual. End-of-life rules must exist for data and encryption removal. Encryption of the data shouldn't interfere with the end-user access to it.

REMEMBER

Whatever approach is selected for monitoring and encrypting data, the ultimate responsibility for the protection of this data is the company. A company must have a comprehensive and interoperable approach around security, including

>> Templates for the conversion of nonencrypted to encrypted data

>> Standards for determining the types of data and the level of security required for each type

>> Support of standard encryption algorithms

- » Incorporation of crypto APIs and routines in applications deployed on the web
- » Incorporation of encryption of information metadata (metadata provides information about the use or type of other data in a program)
- » Incorporation of built-in data compression
- » Creation of public and private keys

Considering cloud scalability

Scalability is the maintenance of a continuous level of stable performance during increased or diminished load requirements. One of the most compelling arguments for the use of cloud computing is its ability to deliver on-demand scalability.

The cloud offers a cheaper and faster solution to more stable compute performance than the traditional on-premises network farm. Also, the pricing model for this type of use is such that companies pay only for the time needed to complete the computations. Through the multi-tenancy model, servers don't sit idle, and the compute time provides economy of scale across multiple companies' needs. By dynamically provisioning through a scaling algorithm based on a threshold number of active sessions, VMs can be programmed to automatically scale to provide uninterrupted and speedy computations with near real-time results.

The cloud is also suited for asynchronous compute loads where redundant computations and/or user actions can be captured and reconsumed. *Asynchronous compute loads* are code blocks that enable disparate operations to be through timing control, triggered when another operation completes.

Scaling on the cloud can be done through various methods, depending on the work and programming required. For example, you can enhance user experience by increasing the number of available VMs to permit nearly unlimited web interface usage and faster compute times. Such speedups require only initial configuration and subsequently operate without further human interaction or monitoring.

TIP

Elasticity is similar to scalability. It refers to the ability to increase the total workload dynamically across an entire system. Think about a balloon growing larger as it expands equally in all directions — that's the basic idea of elasticity. With both elasticity and scalability, the tenant is billed only for the exact amount of usage.

Understanding cloud-based virtualization

Cloud computing exists because of virtualization, a technique for simulating a discrete hardware environment using software. Virtualization allows the same set of hardware (a single physical instance) to be shared on "virtual" devices to multiple users. For example, a single hardware server can host multiple virtual servers of different types, and even using different operating systems. Each of the virtual servers thinks it is the only server running on that hardware. From a cloud perspective, virtualization allows a single remote server to perform server services to multiple remote clients all over the world.

Four types of virtualization make cloud computing possible:

>> *Hardware virtualization* creates an intermediary software layer between the actual hardware and an OS that wants to use the hardware so that multiple OSs can timeshare the same hardware.

>> *Server virtualization* allocates the resources from one physical server to serve multiple virtual servers. This is basically the same thing as hardware virtualization except that it pertains specifically to servers.

>> *Storage virtualization* pulls disparate storage devices together to function logically as a single storage device.

>> *Operating system virtualization* enables system hardware to run multiple OSs concurrently.

One of the key components needed for successful scaling, elasticity, and virtualization is the hypervisor used to manage the process. A *hypervisor* is a virtual machine monitor (VMM) that is used to manage and run VMs. A VM functions just like a physical computer, but it shares the underlying hardware with other VMs. The hypervisor permits those VMs to work jointly or separately as needed. A hypervisor virtualizes hardware resources. It provides a virtual operating platform that permits the scaling and provisioning of services from the tenant across public/private and on-premises networks. It allows multiple operating systems to share the same hardware.

There are two different kinds of hypervisors: those that are embedded in the system hardware (also called Type 1, or bare metal), and those that run on the virtualizing operating system (also called Type 2). Type 1 is loaded directly on the hardware, usually used in a data center or network. The Type 2 is hosted in the OS and designed to run on desktop or laptop. Note that bare metal (Type 1) servers are single tenant only.

TECHNICAL STUFF

The most common Type 1 hypervisors are OracleVM, Microsoft Hyper-V, CITRIX XenServer, VMwareESX, and KVM. The most common Type 2 hypervisors are VMware Server, VMware Workstation, Oracle VM VirtualBox, Red Hat Enterprise Virtualization, Parallels, and VMware Fusion.

As you can see in Figure 6-5, without a hypervisor, each machine must retain its own unique setup of the application, OS, and database. When a hypervisor is used, the host machine deploys all those services to multiple VMs.

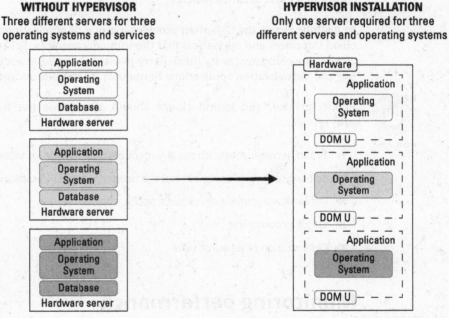

FIGURE 6-5: Efficiencies offered by the use of hypervisors.

© John Wiley & Sons, Inc.

Using self-service provisioning

CSPs eliminate much of a client's ongoing support and IT costs by providing easy self-service provisioning through an extensive back-end module. These administrative modules give end users control over their environments and over how they interact with their data. They can launch services and applications, and super admin controls can monitor and control their access. End users don't have to rely on in-house IT or support provided by the CSP using this model.

This self-provisioning is available to all cloud configurations, whether they are public, private, or hybrid. The service provider and its contract dictate the type and level of provisioning — that is, Infrastructure as a Service, Platform as a Service, or Software as a Service (all covered earlier in this chapter).

Through expanded administrative controls, a company can lock down what an end user can see or manipulate. It can also establish policies and create profiles for onboarding new users and for removing rights on the fly of those no longer privileged. A company might also use APIs to create environments that mirror the corporate IT and security policies.

In a public cloud, the CSP often provides a group of applications that support the cloud interfaces and operations that the company requires. For private and hybrid clouds, the company (or its third-party manager) can build additional provisioning and virtualization applications to monitor its procedures and users.

REMEMBER

Public, private, and hybrid clouds should all provide the following types of self-service:

>> Broad network access across any media (laptop, phone, or tablets)

>> Self-service provisioning without the need of human interaction

>> Dynamic assignment of resource pools

>> Elastic provisioning

>> Optimization of resource uses

Monitoring performance

REMEMBER

Performance monitoring is key to maximizing the efficiency and speed at which data is delivered to end users. Myriad out-of-the-box tools are available for monitoring an organization's cloud usage. However, to determine an organization's cloud configuration effectiveness, the organization must first understand the possible outcomes and have realistic expectations for the services they are deploying. They can use various metrics and methodologies to monitor performance after identification and benchmarking has taken place.

The standard monitoring needs include process speed when executing heavy data-intensive computations, site and application throughput and latency, and data integrity, encryption, and decryption.

Some key aspects to monitor to evaluate performance include the following:

>> End-to-end visibility into the applications used on the cloud

>> End-to-end visibility into the total site structure, including user interfaces, VMs, access controls, databases, third-party tools, and security/encryption

>> End-to-endpoint connectivity and response times

>> Interoperability and interdependencies across applications and services

>> Adherence to SLA commitments

>> Throughput speed of applications and services

>> Data security and speed of access

>> Surge reporting, which shows potential risk of outage or cyberattack

>> Network communication of the VMs

>> Storage analytics

REMEMBER

The most important qualities to look for in monitoring tools are good documentation, ease of installation and use, and availability across different media.

Evaluating potential security risk on the cloud

As with all things, there is often a trade-off between security and other attributes. In cloud computing, that trade-off is generally speed versus security.

As you discover earlier in this chapter, the least expensive approaches to cloud computing are deployed on a public cloud. Multi-tenancy, by its very nature, provides economy of scale. Multiple users share resources. They also share the cloud architecture whereby many customers share the same virtual experience and user-interface configuration. The CSP must be able to provide security measures that prevent one customer from accessing another customer's data.

WARNING

The central concern of any organization utilizing the cloud should always be whether its data is safe. Rules govern the public cloud's level of protection. It's the tenant's responsibility to understand and determine whether the level of protection is sufficient for its legal requirements. Read contracts carefully and question the terms around the CSP's security model.

TIP

Installing an identity management system (IMS) increases a company's control, enabling it to at least monitor and review security controls as needed. An IMS offers insight into who is accessing the systems, who is using data on the system, what type of data, and with what frequency.

Here are some important security-related questions to ask a provider:

>> Is my data partitioned and not available to any other customer?

>> Do your support personnel have access to my company's data?

>> Can your support team alter my database?

>> Do you have the right to grant access to my company's data without informing me?

>> How do you encrypt data at rest? And how do you encrypt data in transit?

>> Can I review all data logs and access records without exercising an audit clause?

>> Do you have an IMS associated with your cloud?

>> Do you adhere to a Service Organization Controls report (SOC), which is part of the Statement on Standards for Attestation Engagements (SSAE16) that is produced by the American Institute of Certified Public Accountants Auditing Standards Board, or any other audit standards? When was your last security audit?

>> How do you handle problems such as data loss or leakage and insecure APIs or user interfaces?

>> Do you adhere to the Gramm-Leach-Bliley Act (GLBA) and the General Data Protection Regulation (GDPR) about the handling of PII?

>> Do you separate administrative functions from security access?

REMEMBER

The safest approach to data security is to maintain your data on a private cloud or network. However, if your budget doesn't permit that, or it's simply not right for your needs, you may be able to utilize the public cloud with relatively good security by locking down some of the functionality through a dedicated instance or a dedicated host.

Understanding Privacy Compliance and Government Requirements

Developing an effective cloud strategy is impossible without first resolving the issues of government requirements and data privacy protections, which are the focus of this section. Over the last several years, the industry has placed great emphasis on the safe and private retention of data. Government regulations have sprung up in all regions and countries around the world.

Before a company can determine the best cloud solution, its corporate counsel must research and recommend policies regarding a cloud deployment's impact. This recommendation must take into consideration which countries will hold and process the data, what laws apply, and what the costs might be, both operationally and financially, when selecting specific providers. After such a review, the company can create a policy that follows a least risk approach toward compliance.

REMEMBER

Most privacy compliance laws focus on protecting and maintaining individuals' personal data in a specific region. Consent is the critical component in compliance. If a company understands what form the consent needs to take, it can easily put controls in place to protect itself from inadvertently violating an individual's rights.

In most data protection laws, codicils allow for data transfer with limited or no liability. Some such exceptions are

>> Consent has been requested and received from the end owner of the data.

>> The contractual process has been defined and documented, as have processes that specify the way data access can be stored and used.

>> The country where the data will ultimately reside has laws that protect that data.

>> There are preexisting contract requirements around access to the data.

Regulations differ on personal data storage and maintenance from country to country. However, because a cloud service is universal in its application, it may not be obvious what country the data will ultimately reside in physically, which makes it tough to know which government's regulations need to be considered. To further compound the complexity, the countries through which that data may pass may have different laws and regulations of their own. This presents a Gordian knot that may make some global use of cloud applications untenable. Only by understanding where and how the cloud service provider (CSP) conducts its business can a tenant develop a comprehensive strategy.

Almost every data protection law (DPL) includes a requirement that, in the event of a security breach, all concerned parties must be informed promptly and fully. The form that disclosure must take varies from country to country. If you follow the most stringent country's guidelines, you will cover the disclosure requirements of all the remaining countries.

Data protection laws

Data protection laws (DPLs) around the world were written to prohibit any person or entity from misusing an individual's private information. An entity or individual can't share information held about an individual without the individual's consent. The data holder must employ verifiable policies and procedures to protect against disclosure. In addition, any company engaged in online payment or payment processing needs to review the Data Security Standards under which their receiving entity is governed.

The following are a few of the national or regional laws that protect personally identifiable information (PII):

>> **CLOUD:** Clarifying Lawful Overseas Use of Data, United States

>> **GDPR:** General Data Protection Regulation, EU-wide regulation

>> **POPI Act:** Protection of Personal Information Act, South Africa

>> **GLBA:** Gramm-Leach-Bliley Act, United States

For a comprehensive list of data protection laws, see `www.dlapiperdatapro tection.com/`.

Data localization laws

Data localization laws (DLLs) require that all personal data that legal entities or citizens of a country use or own must be stored only in that country. To accommodate this law, storage and data computation providers must either be local or have local server farms that include auditable integrity, such that they must be able to produce logs indicating the location and access instructions for the data in the event of an audit.

The fines and penalties for noncompliance are punitive. When you're shopping for a CSP, make sure that it will attest in writing to its compliance with your company's regulatory requirements. If it isn't able to reach this threshold of accountability, don't engage with that CSP.

Data sovereignty laws

Data sovereignty laws predate the Internet. They essentially state that each country has the right to control all data collected and maintained in that country. Once it's collected in a country, it must reside within that country, and its use is dictated by the country's laws.

This is a double-edged sword for the consumer/individual:

>> On one hand, the laws provide the right of access to the consumer directly and the right of the consumer to object to the accuracy of what has been collected and to have it removed.

>> On the other hand, the government has rights to use the data for a variety of reasons, such as taxation, security, and legal processes. Through the laws that regulate the consumption and access to data, sovereign states can also use all data that is collected in a fashion that may be harmful to the individual.

Access to information laws

Ninety-five countries have entered into an agreement that gives their citizens the right to request and receive government-held information. Right to information (RTI) laws aren't new. Sweden passed its first such bill in 1766 — a bit ahead of its time. Such laws are designed to provide accountability to the citizen for the actions of the government.

Due to the borderless nature of the Internet and the jurisdictional scuffles over personal and corporate IP, governments now have flipped these information structures to allow access to information about individual citizens and corporations housed in specific countries. These new Internet-driven laws work via a mutual legal assistance treaty (MLAT). A MLAT enables a sovereign state to issue a warrant to secure personal data across multiple borders. CLOUD is an example of a law that provides the right of governments to access data transborder.

Seeing How FinTech Helps with Cloud Strategies

The process of selecting and implementing the best cloud services for a financial institution can be quite complex and may require specialized education or experience. FinTech companies can be of great assistance to businesses trying to develop long-term cloud and technology strategies. FinTech companies are generally well versed in the complexities of infrastructure analysis, banking and financial industry regulations, and legacy systems. FinTech aids in streamlining and evaluating all systems, whether they are administered in-house or by a third party. A subdivision of FinTech actually specializes in the area of regulations. It's called RegTech (regulatory technology), and many FinTech firms have in-house subject matter experts (SMEs) who deal in this area or have partner relationships with RegTech firms.

To review all applications that support an organization, evaluate the relevance and workflow of each application or tool within the context of the new technologies available in the FinTech suite of systems and services.

As you're reviewing each application, system, or tool, ask yourself whether it should be

>> **Kept in its current state with no change?** This option would retain the application and data in its current mode.

>> **Decommissioned?** Cloud strategy evaluation is a good time to retire outdated and unused technology.

>> **Refactored?** You should determine which applications are important to the organization and rebuild them to conform to the new flexible, lightweight FinTech structures.

>> **Replaced?** Determine whether it still meets the business's needs. If not, find and deploy new applications that meet those needs.

>> **Reconfigured?** Review applications for their benefits and reconfigure those aspects that would be more beneficial in a cloud environment.

>> **Repurposed and/or consolidated?** Review applications currently on the cloud and how they fit together. Develop a comprehensive approach to building a comprehensive cloud presence, rather than a piecemeal one.

"Lift and shift," a strategy that refers to moving an application from one environment to another without much review or testing, doesn't work well in a cloud environment. When moving applications or systems to the cloud, you must anticipate some operational change and downtime.

If nothing else, we hope you'll take this one point away from this chapter: It's generally a better policy to utilize third-party FinTech companies to handle new technologies and systems that aren't core to the corporation's growth and focus. FinTech companies make it their business to determine the best architecture, use cases, systems, and tools to implement when integrating a company's required functionality into the cloud. A third-party FinTech company can assist the corporation in determining the best strategy, as well as do the heavy technological lifting, for cost-effectively leading the company away from its legacy systems and into the cloud.

Chapter 7

Understanding Blockchain beyond Bitcoin

A s you find out in Chapter 5, *blockchain* is a new technology for securely storing and retrieving data in a decentralized environment. Blockchain technology is disrupting multiple industries, including finance and banking, so it's important to understand how it works and how companies are using it.

FinTech is poised to assist the banking industry with its integration of blockchain into those areas of banking that can benefit from an immutable, decentralized record system that can remove error and risk from daily operations.

In this chapter, we extend our discussion of blockchain beyond the basics in Chapter 5. You see how the technology works at a deeper level and how it plays a role in current and future FinTech operations.

Understanding the Basics of Blockchain

REMEMBER

Here, we recap what you find out about blockchain in Chapter 5. The following points are key:

>> Blockchain consists of a decentralized data structure (DDS) organized around a series of blocks that are connected and protected through unique hash encryption.

>> The data is time-dated and connected in a cryptographic, chronological order. The blocks are linearly linked to each other, thereby creating the blockchain.

>> A blockchain has no central database and no administrator. The decentralized database is validated via a concept called consensus.

>> Blockchain is a peer-to-peer (P2P) distributed ledger; each iteration is unique and must be verified by at least five other nodes to be validated. Each record is immutable.

>> Blockchain doesn't need the Internet to function; any network will do.

Blockchain is best known as the technology created to support the privacy, anonymity, and accuracy of cryptocurrency transactions. It has already gone through several iterations since its inception in 2009. A blockchain ecosystem now exists, and the use cases around its acceptance have grown.

The issues that blockchain faced in the finance sector, which kept it from early adoption, are the very reasons why blockchain was created initially. They are anonymity, transparency, and immutability. New iterations of blockchain have come to the market with technologies that their creators hope will sidestep the concerns of auditors and administrators. One of the more successful approaches created to mitigate the lack of controls has been that of creating permissioned blockchain. Permissioned blockchain adds a more traditional control layer that wraps the blockchain technology. This administrative layer can alter protocols, limit nodes, modify the need for consensus, and provide visibility as to the identity of the transactors. In essence, this layer, while speeding up the transaction process, co-opts the distributed components of the system through the introduction of a single point of control. The need for speed and auditability in the financial sector trumps the need for security and anonymity.

The following sections describe some blockchain basics used in public decentralized applications (DApps), like mining and consensus, smart contracts, and network types.

Mining and consensus

Mining is the method used to create consensus on a Bitcoin network, but there must be other ways to achieve consensus, or the DApps created will be limited to financial/payment-driven operations only.

On Bitcoin, miners are *compute nodes* (blockchain developers and node owners) that perform work to solve a computation, which then allows them to create or add to a block in a blockchain. These miners receive rewards for their success via Bitcoins or transaction fees. Miners create hash values encapsulated in the blocks that they create.

In this modality, consensus is achieved by adding all the hash values in the blockchain, using a proof of work (PoW). The PoW is automated so that miners/nodes on the network add up all transactions on linked blocks every ten minutes. Only a miner that solves the original computational problem can add to the block. A blockchain is only as strong as the size of its network (measured by the number of nodes engaged in validation). The reward scheme used in the PoW is an effective economic model that reinforces correct action on the part of the players.

In addition to PoW, other types of consensus include the following:

>> Ethereum, a blockchain platform, utilizes a form of consensus mechanism in their smart contracts called *proof of stake (PoS)*. In this environment, the miner contributes to the value of the transaction instead of receiving a reward for their work.

>> *Delegated proof of stake (DPoS)* is a variation on PoS. In this model, network users cede their rights and responsibilities to *supernodes.* These supernodes are elected or appointed by all the other network nodes, thereby eliminating the competition required in the solving of the mathematical problem. The supernodes become the de facto block producers. This model is the most efficient approach to consensus. The result is low latency and high efficiency. The issue here, however, is that it breaks the model of the DDS. It provides identifiable members rather than the collective anonymity of the decentralized network. It also creates a security risk in that the supernodes could, in theory, conspire to undermine the system.

>> Another recent iteration of the more traditional forms of consensus is the hybrid mechanism called *proof of activity (PoA),* where some of the miners perform the computational work while others approve the work by adding to the value of the transaction.

>> Newer forms of consensus have developed in anticipation of corporate adoption of blockchain as a valid tool in the corporate arsenal. One method uses groups that have a hierarchical structure around the reputation of a participant. Only those approved or authorized can participate in the consensus process.

WARNING

As you can see, the mechanics around the development of consensus in a public blockchain is compute labor-intensive, time restrictive, and cumbersome in form. Another drawback of the consensus model is that it is energy inefficient. After all, the premise it was built on entailed the nonproductive engagement in mathematical problem solving just to create hash links and new blocks. The fact that this computation can be conducted simultaneously by all the nodes on the network could well equal the needed electricity of a large city or small country over a year. It has been postulated that the power required to maintain the Bitcoin industry is equal to the power utilized by all of Finland. This model results in high transaction fees paid to miners and slow processing for the transaction initiators. The energy requirement of PoS is significantly lower than that of PoW. The process doesn't require that all the nodes are engaged in solving the mathematical problem.

Smart contracts and DApps

Ethereum has taken simple blockchain technology one step further by introducing *smart contracts* created without human intercession. These contracts are lines of code that can be fully automated, with complete rules-based structures that are executable programs written in blocks as part of the blockchain structure. This new usage extends blockchain from merely the storage and recording of data to the actual processing of it into immutable forms. The Ethereum platform offers a new richness to blockchain by making new economic models and payment processes available via DApps.

Ethereum states that its program is *Turing complete* code, which is a reference to a hypothetical machine proposed by Alan Turing that could manipulate symbols in a single line of code according to a set of rules. It is through this coding that smart contracts can be created and extended. When you create a block, deployed to the ledger, it cannot be altered. This immutability fosters public trust. Like all blockchain constructs, when the contract has been created and confirmed, it's published on distributed nodes across a decentralized network.

WARNING

Even though blockchain is a P2P network, the user still must run its program locally to create a smart contract. The localization of some of the process involved in the block creation can present privacy and security issues. The goal of the DApp technology is that all parts of any transaction take place entirely inside the P2P network. If created in this fashion, the integrity of the results is without question. Once created, the block should require no further maintenance or user interaction.

Some people hold that Ethereum's smart contracts and their subsequent settlements are at best "probabilistic" in that there is no control or curated list that would enable someone to know the percentage of consensus that has been achieved by a transaction, nor is there a way of knowing the number of actual individuals engaged in the validation of the transaction.

Smart contracts provide the settlement rules for transactions built automatically in code without human intervention. One of the ways it does this is by requiring secure online automated signatories. The signatures are segmented locks in which each node holds only a part of the key. The whole key must be reassembled to move the transaction forward.

As you find out in Chapter 5, DApps are a set of linked smart contracts that contain the sequencing of a transaction, the level of security and privacy around it, and the data to be shared. These transactions can be set up to require human participation or can be automated tasks, performed by autonomous agents. A whole series of these agents could be linked to perform a complete process on a distributed autonomous enterprise (DAE).

Once created, the ledger runs with completely automated oversight, determined by the rules established in the smart contract. This function is called decentralized autonomous organization (DAO).

All blockchain DApps adhere to the following standards:

>> They are open source.

>> They are structurally decentralized.

>> They operate on the concept of consensus validation or smart contracts.

>> They have no central point of failure.

Blockchain network types

You can implement a blockchain network in several ways: public, private, consortium, and hybrid. Each has its own unique combination of features and characteristics:

>> **Public blockchain** networks are centralized, open, and transparent to members and validated by consensus.

>> **Private blockchain** networks are different in that they have an administrative component. Participation is by invitation only, and a network owner (a single organization) controls participation and privileges. Transparency can be

limited based on established rules and profiles. Each transaction is based on an honor system, which removes the heavy overhead cost of consensus validation. Private blockchain networks are more efficient and scalable and have fewer latency issues than public ones. The protocol and security may be different from that of a public blockchain because there is already a level of trust among participants and external controls are in place.

>> **Consortium blockchain** networks exist where several organizations jointly control privileges and participation. Consensus resides in the hands of a preselected set of nodes, and a group of organizations determine the policy and rules around transaction workflow and validation. This makes it more efficient and scalable because it can compute data in parallel. It is otherwise similar to the private type.

>> **Hybrid blockchain** networks are a mix of open user access and restricted access, based on the network's use case. Transactions can be private but verifiable on the permission less block.

Table 7-1 summarizes these types and their characteristics.

TABLE 7-1   Blockchain Network Types

	Public	Private	Consortium
Network	Decentralized	Centralized through a permissioned layer	Centralized through a permissioned layer
Transactions per second (TPS)	Low: very high consensus overload	High: fast due to limited nodes and identified users	High: fast due to limited nodes and identified users
Visibility and Participation	Open	Restricted	Restricted
Security	Indeterminate	High: permissioned access	Medium: though permissioned, the level of users is still not completely known
System Governance	Difficult	Easy	Moderate

Discovering How Blockchain Technology Works

Blockchain technology centers around three basic principles: decentralization, security, and transparency. We look at each of these principles in greater detail in the following sections.

Decentralization

REMEMBER

As we point out earlier in this chapter, one strength of blockchain lies in its decentralization. Traditional databases are inferior in that they have single points of failure and are vulnerable to operator error. Decentralized systems are virtually bulletproof because of the number of systems that would have to fail, and the number of operator errors that would have to occur, to bring down the system.

Decentralized data storage can be prone to synchronization issues unless rigorous methods are in place for ensuring consistency. That's why consensus (covered earlier in this chapter) is important. Transaction completeness can be confirmed, verified, and published only if there is consensus.

In the most tolerant blockchain architecture, no more than 30 percent of the nodes exchanging information can disagree on the validity of the information shared; in a more restrictive model, the consensus must be unanimous. This concept of consensus is called a *Byzantine fault tolerance* (BFT), which means that two nodes or more can safely share information/data because it is the same data.

Another form of consensus that is being used by permissioned blockchain like Hyperledger Fabric is *crash fault tolerance* (CFT). CFT allows the system to reach consensus even if components fail. (BFT allows systems to reach consensus if there might be malicious actors.) Permissioned blockchain like Hyperledger Fabric utilizes a control layer to establish "ordered" service, which orders the transactions of each peer in the system and verifies they are the same through an endorsement policy and a validation process.

The fact that the definition of an acceptable level of consensus can vary introduces the possibility of a breach due to a Sybil attack. A Sybil attack is an attack on the reputation or trustworthiness of a network to prove it contains reliable and confirmed data. An attack can manipulate the consensus process by creating false identities that disagree with the consensus in a larger-than-permitted proportion. These attacks in *Bitcoin Cash* can result in *double spending*.

WARNING

Some technical concerns related to decentralization have not yet been solved by blockchain architects, including these:

>> **There is no easy approach for removing contested transactions.** The immutable nature of the distributed data structure makes it impossible to just "fix" a ledger entry. What is in a ledger stays in the ledger and cannot be removed. Instead of patches to remove data, there must be other forms of remediation. Writing new blocks across the entire network and extensive pretests must be in force.

>> **There is currently only one way to do an upgrade to a blockchain system through a hard fork.** A *hard fork* is a complete and systemic change of network protocol. This change can cause valid blocks to be invalidated and invalid ones to be valid. All nodes are changed when a *hard fork* is invoked. (We talk about forks in more detail later in this chapter.)

>> **There are interoperability issues.** Blockchain networks/systems/ledgers can talk to other nonrelated blockchain systems. There are currently no rules around the hierarchy of the blockchain process. Which system's rules and protocols take precedence?

>> **Overhead is high.** Because, in public blockchain, creating and accepting a block relies on the work of miners who create the hash link, and because you need a minimum of six miners to verify and validate the transaction before it's added to the blockchain, there is a very high overhead for the completion of a transaction. An average transaction time is approximately one hour from initiation to validation. This operational cost makes DApps less competitive than non-blockchain computes. (Find out more about mining earlier in this chapter.) As we mention in Chapter 5, permissioned blockchain and private chains are faster because the nodes and the number of users are limited.

>> **Public blockchain isn't currently designed to handle high throughput and large volume transactions.** With blockchain technology, the calls are handled as pending transactions until they are completed, which can create large backloads. The structure of permissioned and private blockchain is faster and more efficient because of the limitation of users and nodes.

>> **Blockchain does not perform well in series.** The concept of consensus requires that all nodes on a network respond before a transaction can be verified/executed.

TIP

Blockchain is new technology, and as you can see, making changes to it is not trivial. When selecting what public blockchain DApps to use, you should look to its history. How often has it been hard forked? How many users does it have? How many innovative projects have been started around the original release? Look at code commits and branches to determine its viability. When using permissioned or consortium blockchain, you should ask the same types of questions.

Security

REMEMBER

We shouldn't confuse security with anonymity or complexity. Blockchain is, to some degree, all three.

Its claim to security arises first from its anonymity and then from its complexity. Blockchain was started to hide the owner's identity around transactions taking place in public view. It was also set up to assure the immutable nature of that data because the owners of the data and the results didn't trust each other. There is no arbiter to oversee the outcome of these transactions. The immutability of a block comes from the fact that anyone can create a block, but no one can remove it. All similar blocks are linked. You cannot pull out a block and replace it because all blocks are time-stamped, uniquely hashed, chronologically linked, and cryptographically coded. This makes them unhackable by standard definition.

There are two levels of security in blockchain:

>> The security of the data and workflow associated with the blockchain, protected by hash links and through mining activities

>> The security associated with the owner of the transaction

The transaction owner's or recipient's access is governed by two keys:

>> A public key, which is viewable and associated to the transaction

>> A private key, which is encrypted and only the initiator or recipient knows

Since its inception, blockchain has evolved into several different types of use cases. Each of these use cases has different security protocols:

>> **Public:** All eyes can see the transaction, validate the data, and engage in the verification process.

>> **Consortium blockchains:** This is a semiprivate blockchain system with a specified user group that can span many organizations. This model has a concept of authority, which the initiator can establish. Business-to-business (B2B) systems utilize this type of use case.

>> **Private blockchain:** Access is restricted at the node level. Profiles can be created limiting access and visibility.

Though initially built on the premise of complete anonymity, some newer DApps, which are trying to monetize their offering, are attempting to create more flexibility in their security and access model to make it easier for large corporations and banks to use them. In some instances, there is a desire to hide the identity of users. In others, there is a desire to restrict access entirely.

There is also a move to build privacy and access applications on top of the blockchain model. The problem with this approach is that it takes the security offered by the blockchain decentralized data structure and puts a centralized database or a permissioning and administrative layer on top of it, rendering some of the protections ineffective.

REMEMBER

The security of blockchain lies in its cryptographic digital signature; the cryptographic hash functions that miners perform to validate the block transaction; the verification consensus that the miner and users perform; and the private key created at its inception. Smart contracts require a thorough and formal review of the code. Just because it is decentralized does not mean it is unhackable.

The following sections discuss forking and security concerns in more detail.

Forking

The concept of forking comes from open source development. In open source, a *fork* is a split in the code. It retains the majority of the functionality of the original source but may differ significantly from it. The fork doesn't create conflicts with the original code.

In blockchain, a *soft fork* can be used to create new assets. A soft fork is a fork that can add or tighten existing protocols and can exist with old nodes. The old nodes accept the changes made by the new fork. A new node, however, won't accept an old node because it doesn't have the same protocols. A miner will soon recognize that a new version has been created and upgrade to the newer protocol. Eventually, by attrition, only the new fork will remain.

WARNING

Unintentional or viral forks can sometimes cause data to become corrupted. Forks in blockchain can be very dangerous because they can cause disputes in data integrity. Luckily, because no record can ever be removed, a fork can be verified by a review of all preceding history.

Hard forks are more disruptive, in that they indicate a fundamental change to the protocols and can render older versions invalid. Hard forks are currently the only way to upgrade the blockchain. When a hard fork takes place, it can invalidate whole blocks in a ledger. If both the new and old versions can exist, the rules that govern the blockchain can be different between new nodes and old nodes; this can cause the data to vary. If a hard fork takes place, one branch must be rendered obsolete and retired, and the assets on it must be reallocated to the new version.

Figure 7-1 summarizes the difference between a hard fork and a soft fork.

REMEMBER

Testing is a critical component of the whole blockchain transaction. Before any transactions should take place, the business needs to thoroughly understand their use case. Further, they need to create security/risk scenarios and test them end-to-end.

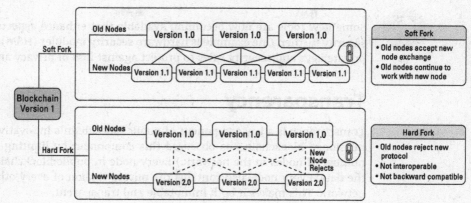

FIGURE 7-1:
Differences between hard and soft forking.

© John Wiley & Sons, Inc.

Security concerns

WARNING

One important security concern is the potential for consensus protocol manipulation. Because nothing is added to the ledger without consensus, members of the network can add false identities or nodes to take over the system and manipulate the consensus outcome to their advantage. Because blockchain operates on the premise of total anonymity for its members, hackers can become members and hide their identities while performing malicious acts. The only way the transaction outcome can be retrieved is through a private key. Hackers can gain access through cryptographic key theft. When hackers have obtained a private key, they can make fraudulent entries.

Another concern is with sloppy coding. Even with blockchain, a lack of proper development processes and complete end-to-end testing can result in poor results and code vulnerabilities.

In addition, there can be issues in complying with regulations. Personal data protection levels may be regulated differently in different jurisdictions. Through its very architecture, the possibility of a personal data breach is minor. However, most privacy laws include a stipulation that the personal information a company holds must be removable upon individual request, and as we note earlier, blockchain blocks cannot be removed.

With public blockchain, every block on a network is transparent to every node. If the actual information is written into the block, by the very nature of immutability, the data cannot be removed, and by the very openness of the system, it can be viewed by all nodes. Therefore, all personal data needs to be added to the block only by link. This provides an area of vulnerability around the data store's security.

TIP

Some new tools are now becoming available that enhance aspects of blockchain security further. One example is hardware security modules (HSM), which provide private keys and security rules to protect against loss of privacy and security.

Transparency

Transparency is a key component of public blockchain's innovative nature. (Permissioned blockchain has obscured this component by limiting access and the number of nodes in the network.) Every node in public blockchain has access to the data. Every node also contains the mirror version of every other node on the network. This makes it both immutable and transparent.

Transparency and immutability equal trust for individuals engaged in anonymous transactions. Any user or node operator can access the ledger and all information in a public blockchain. This doesn't mean that any viewer will know the identity of the transactor, however. The hash links that individual nodes create all trace back to the Genesis block, which holds the first record created for an individual transaction.

This transparency, married to the immutable nature of the data, makes it a very interesting option in the financial sector for the following use cases:

>> Processes that require validation of accuracy for review — that is, audits, payroll, and tax reviews

>> Receptacles for verifiable record keeping like voting and 401(k) processing

>> Stock processing and controls

>> Inventory controls and verification

>> General ledger

Note: The need for auditable process and review is provided more robustly in a permissioned or private blockchain.

Wherever you have anonymous interaction with definable workflow and payment exchanges, you have an opportunity to use blockchain and smart contracts. Here are some example use cases:

>> **Smart hardware:** Smart contracts allow contract processes to be automated so they happen without human intervention, enabling the hardware to be smart, too. *Smart hardware* brings the real-time improvements of artificial intelligence to the smart contract. When the hardware recognizes a positive

change, it adds the result to the contract. The smart hardware automation is then recorded and memorialized as part of the product function and is driven by smart contracts through all subsequent iterations.

» **Supply chain management:** Efficient and comprehensive real-time management and logistics within a supply chain greatly decreases overall product cost. Though it appears that the process of getting an item from its inception to its consumption should be fairly simple, in reality there are many points of failure. Complexity is compounded by governance rules, data integrity, real-time logistics, and third-party coordination.

Introducing blockchain and smart contracts helps remove some of the overhead through automation and real-time scheduling. The supply chain function starts by procuring and delivering raw materials and ends with product delivery to retail stores or end-user purchasers. The many steps in between include certifications, multiple and complex delivery schedules, resource allocations, and mechanism coordination that now can be more effectively handled by smart contracts and blockchain. Blockchain retains all the time schedules, assets involved in the logistics, and transaction elements. It introduces transparency to the process and creates an immutable record should shipments be lost or delayed.

» **Scheduled payment for goods or services:** Though not yet in full production, blockchain is being viewed as the next great thing in payment processing and real-time bank-to-bank international transfers. The use of a distributed ledger and smart contracts provide for a fully automated real-time transaction history. Blockchain B2B payment processing started prior to 2017 and was driven by the advance of cryptocurrencies. These payment processing services are being directly tied to the use of supply chain management.

Looking at Blockchain's Role in FinTech

Blockchain is one of the tools that FinTech uses in transforming and redesigning banking business processes. As you discover in this chapter, it offers a decentralized data structure with an immutable source of truth that is traceable, tractable, and auditable across the complete history of a transaction or an event. Through automation, it minimizes the potential of human error or malicious activities while reducing costs.

Because of all those benefits, blockchain has the potential to disrupt the financial industry. Financial, banking, and insurance companies considering implementing blockchain must understand its value and strategically position it in their digital infrastructure. FinTech fills a knowledge void that enable banks and financial companies to advance a well-planned approach that focuses on needed applications and technologies but does not disrupt the banks or financial companies' focus on their core businesses.

Blockchain will provide benefits most readily to currency funds, capital markets, secondary market trading, and post-trade settlement processors. It will also help eliminate logjams, audit issues, and security concerns in payment and remittance streams, regulatory compliance requirements, securitization, and personal data and identity management. The greatest benefits across all the use cases in the future of blockchain lies in its transparency and its immutable architecture that eliminates manual processes and automates repetitive functions.

TIP

When considering partnering with a FinTech company to develop a strategic blockchain and DApp plan, some important questions to ask and answer include these:

>> Is there any component in your business that would benefit from a decentralized data structure?

>> What are the benefits for your business?

>> What are the costs and potential risks?

>> How will blockchain disrupt your business processes, both internally and externally?

>> How does blockchain fit within the bank's risk management system?

>> Are there any early adopters in your sector that are successfully utilizing this technology?

>> What are the long-term objectives for deploying blockchain technology?

>> Is there a way blockchain will expand the organization's reach to new markets?

>> What are the short-term wins?

>> How does blockchain fit with other technologies the organization currently needs, such as cloud, microservices, and application programming interfaces (APIs)?

REMEMBER

A FinTech company should do a current, complete assessment of the state of the organization. After that analysis, it should be able to produce a phased plan for rolling out the needed technologies that demonstrates an understanding of the company's strategic needs. The plan should offer a holistic approach to replacing and integrating current systems and should present significant use cases for future enhancements. The plan should include steps for addressing legal concerns and regional governance issues and should provide a transition and support plan for making changes to the blockchain network.

REMEMBER

In some instances, the banking industry has been racing to advance or adopt some cryptocurrency strategy. Because no regulatory agency governs these currencies, banks have an opportunity to engage and set their standards and their own financial regulatory controls. Cryptocurrencies offer many benefits to the banking industry, like lower transaction costs.

Chapter **8**

Acclimating to the App Mentality

T *here's an app for that.*

In 2008, when Apple released the iPhone 3G, a technological evolution occurred as people started seeing smartphones as more than just phone call and text message tools. The idea that you could extend a smartphone's functionality by installing apps from an App Store was a game changer. Apps gave consumers more choices. For simple computing tasks, they no longer needed traditional PCs, because they could use their phones instead.

As smartphones began to represent larger and larger shares of the personal computing device market, programmers started developing with a *mobile first mentality*, also known as an *app mentality*. In other words, when they planned new software, they began to first consider how it would work on mobile devices, because that was the kind of device that the largest segment of their target audience would be using.

This app mentality has been a significant driver behind the disruptive nature of FinTech. Companies that hope to reach consumers must develop software that goes where they are — and where they are is online, on their smartphones, and connected to the cloud. This chapter looks at the various types of FinTech apps that consumers want today and provides some tips for planning and building such apps.

Introducing Types of FinTech Apps

App is a shortened form of *application*. An app is software designed for end users that enables them to do a certain specific task or a group of netted tasks easily. Though apps were initially supposed to be platform and media agnostic, the term has come to refer specifically to applications built for mobile devices. However, the concept of small, task-focused applications targeted to specific types of end users is becoming more pervasive throughout all of modern software design.

REMEMBER

Here are some specific types of apps that you may encounter in the world of FinTech:

>> **Web apps:** Web apps are stored on and run from web servers. Users don't have to download anything to run them. A web app delivers a consistent user experience through its interface, regardless of the platform being used to access the server. A web app differs from a regular web page in that it's interactive and can be user defined.

>> **Native apps:** A native app has been developed to run on only one kind of device or platform, such as only iOS or only Android. A native app typically requires you to download and install it on the device. It's called a native app because it's written not only for a specific platform but also generally in a language that's specific for that platform.

>> **Mobile apps:** As the name implies, these run on mobile devices such as smartphones or tablets. They're usually native apps designed for a specific mobile operating system (OS).

>> **Hybrid apps:** A hybrid app acts like a native app, in that it must be downloaded, but it's written in standard development language like HTML or Java. This makes it easier to develop, maintain, and use.

>> **Killer apps:** Killer apps are native apps that are so compelling and unique that they drive users to become loyal to the specific platform on which they run. For example, if the app is available only for Android, some people may switch from iOS to Android just to be able to use it.

>> **Legacy apps:** In technology, *legacy* is just another word for "old and out of date." Legacy apps are past their prime; they may no longer be supported or may be built in obsolete languages or for obsolete platforms. They continue to exist because they serve a specific function that either is not easily replaced or would be too expensive to re-create in a modern version.

Surveying the FinTech App Landscape

To understand how the app mentality is driving development in all areas of the capital markets, it's important to look at some of the first mover sectors that defined the rise of FinTech in the past ten years.

Digital banking

Digital banking is one of the largest areas in FinTech, with challenger banks having raised more than $3 billion in 2019 according to research firm CB Insights. FinTech is attacking every core banking operation, offering focused services for savings, student loans, small business services, and credit cards.

Traditional retail banking is under attack due to the rise of Internet banks that can handle all transactions through apps and anonymously advise customers. Users can open savings, checking, and credit card accounts via an app and can interconnect all accounts without any human intercession required. These banking apps track each transaction and auto-generate transaction and payment statuses daily. Through machine learning and artificial intelligence (AI; see Chapter 12), the apps can also develop a sense of the user's fiscal patterns and spending requirements and offer banking assistance tailored to those patterns.

TIP

Some key disrupters in digital banking include Chime (www.chime.com), Aspiration (www.aspiration.com), Varo (www.varomoney.com), and Simple (www.simple.com).

Wealth management

One of the more visible areas in FinTech has been in wealth management app development. These apps and their associated banks have opened the market to a new group of investors and have challenged traditional wealth management institutions. They offer benefits such as robo-advisors (algorithmic trading) for individual investors, low minimum balance requirements, and the ability to open accounts with very little investment.

If you use Merrill Lynch, TD Ameritrade, E*Trade, Schwab, or Stash Wealth, you're already receiving advice that has been generated by AI apps. Some apps now will automatically invest your "free" money using algorithms you've enabled.

Some key disrupters in wealth management include Betterment (www.betterment.com), Robinhood (https://robinhood.com/us/en), Nutmeg (www.nutmeg.com), Raisin (www.raisin.com), and MoneyLion (www.moneylion.com).

Payments and peer-to-peer money transfer

The payments sector is hot because it has such a large potential user base. Nearly everyone wants to be able to pay for small purchases more conveniently. Being able to simply tap your phone to pay for a cup of coffee or transfer money to a friend has had a profound impact on banking. The loss of transaction fees has driven many financial institutions to partner with FinTechs or even develop competing offerings.

E-payment systems now enable completely electronic transactions. Cash is rapidly becoming an anachronism. Many of the Scandinavian countries have moved off cash and into plastic and electronic payments. This trend is very appealing to governments because it makes it more difficult for people to bury money or to create underground economies.

Peer-to-peer (P2P) payment apps can provide near to real-time transactions. It's now all about immediacy and seamless user-friendly experiences. Using blockchain validation ensures security and immutability (see Chapter 7 for more about blockchain).

Some key disrupters in payments include Stripe (https://stripe.com), Venmo (https://venmo.com), TransferWise (https://transferwise.com), and Square (https://squareup.com/us/en).

Lending

While the alternative lending market isn't new, FinTech apps have extended credit availability to a much larger pool of individuals and small businesses. The innovation in this sector is less the apps themselves and more about the disruptive business model these companies are utilizing. AI and Internet data mining make it possible for first-time borrowers to meet the criteria to secure loans without any significant credit history. Specially developed algorithms are able to consider social media and other history stored on the Internet to advance new credit recipients.

Service to the small-to-medium enterprise (SME) market has been greatly enhanced through the introduction of AI into organizations like OakNorth (a U.K. online lending firm) that utilize AI to build smart apps for the SME lending business.

TIP

Some key disrupters in lending include SoFi (www.sofi.com), Credible (www.credible.com), Zopa (https://zopa.com), Funding Circle (www.fundingcircle.com), Banking Circle (www.bankingcircle.com), Credit Karma (www.creditkarma.com), and Upgrade (www.upgrade.com).

Looking at the Nonretail Side of FinTech Apps

As we indicate in previous chapters, FinTech has driven disruptive changes in the banking industry. Those changes have been motivated by disgruntled customers and by innovation attempts that have taken too long to get to the marketplace. FinTech apps offer speed to market, ease of use and simplicity of design, customer empowerment, and workflow and functionality modification to meet end-user desires. The following sections discuss some ways outside of the mainstream financial services that FinTech apps empower their internal users.

RegTech

The primary role of regulation in financial services is to protect the consumer, but regulations also protect the entirety of the financial system and the economy of a country. In response to the financial crash of 2008, many new regulatory regimes were created, affecting the entire financial services industry.

Regulatory requirements have become more complex and numerous over the last decade, especially for international enterprises, and companies are understandably nervous about them. Nobody wants to pay more taxes or be exposed to fines and penalties because they failed to comply with a regulation they weren't even aware existed. Regulation frequently introduces new costs, and businesses look for ways to minimize those costs. As a result, a new industry sector has arisen, RegTech (regulatory technology), to assist institutions with regulatory compliance. Institutions are looking externally for FinTech companies to provide solutions to help comply with regulations, shore up workflows and compliance gaps, and do those things more cheaply than they could with in-house builds. RegTech helps manage a business's regulatory compliance via technologies such as big data analytics, AI, machine learning, and blockchain.

This developing industry is not yet driven by the need to deploy mobile apps. They are building their base by catering to the more traditional client application approach, though some have been adding mobile capabilities to their infrastructures.

TIP

Some key disrupters in RegTech include Trulioo (www.trulioo.com), Convercent (www.convercent.com), and Palantir Technologies (www.palantir.com).

Capital markets trading

Capital markets functions such as trading have long been a profitable part of many financial institutions' offerings. However, increased regulatory burdens have decreased the return on equity for trading operations, and financial institutions are lately looking for ways to cut costs and increase automation.

Driven by the app mentality, end users demand the information they need to make trading decisions when they want it. Many of these decisions require sophisticated analytics and significant compute resources. Legacy systems have been deficient in meeting end-user requirements due to a reliance on batch processing.

Cloud services (see Chapter 6), real-time processing, and artificial intelligence (AI) and machine learning (see Chapter 12) have all opened the door for FinTech in this segment of financial services. New, modern architectures explicitly designed to take advantage of the cloud's scalability have empowered new players to enter the market. And many financial institutions are glad to have their help instead of trying to build their own technology solutions in-house.

TECHNICAL STUFF

Although AI is still very much a nascent industry, it's quickly gaining traction in the capital markets space. According to October 2019 data from Greenwich Associates, 44 percent of capital markets professionals globally say their firms are already using AI in their trading processes. (See www.greenwich.com/press-release/artificial-intelligence-permeating-global-capital-markets for more information.)

AI promises to provide numerous benefits to any financial services firm that embraces it. The potential advantages include improved operational and cost efficiencies, enhanced client services, improved data and analytics, as well as increased profit and revenue generation. For portfolio managers, adding AI's high level of computational and algorithmic complexity to portfolio management, including for trade decision-making and execution, means they may ultimately use AI to find alpha, build custom portfolios, improve portfolio allocation, rebalance portfolios, and mitigate risk.

The most important application of AI in the financial services sector may be risk management. AI could be a game changer for risk management. The capital markets have been hammered with a regulatory tsunami since the financial crisis of 2008, and as a result, a more stringent and prescriptive regulatory environment is having a significant impact on front-office risk-management technology. Today, some institutions are putting AI to work to augment their current front-office risk-management processes.

This is where machine learning, a type of AI, comes into play. Machine learning models have the ability to crunch enormous calculations and analyze huge amounts of data with more granularity and deeper analysis. Doing so can potentially greatly improve analytical capabilities in risk management and compliance. It can help traders make more informed decisions not only at a securities level but also across their entire derivatives book of business. By incorporating a broader set of financial and nonfinancial data, AI applications in risk management could include specific functions, such as identifying the right counterparty with whom to trade, discovering potential counterparty risks, unveiling additional costs within a portfolio, or identifying new trading patterns that could be used to adjust trading strategies — all in more efficient and automated ways.

TIP

Some key disrupters in capital markets trading include Numerix (www.numerix.com), Halo (www.haloinvesting.com), and CloudMargin (https://cloudmargin.com).

Building a GUI Framework

The most successful FinTech apps are intuitive to use. Successful apps tend to be graphical in nature and present a dashboard view of the most critical information the user needs when first opening the app. That's important because most apps don't include detailed documentation — and if they did, users probably wouldn't read it anyway. Even complex apps should be able to effectively communicate their use within five or six tutorial screens.

The importance of a good user interface (UI) drives the way developers create apps. In many cases, app development starts in Adobe Photoshop or even in Microsoft PowerPoint before a single line of code is written. In other words, developers first think about how the screen will *look* and only later think about how it will behave.

Another important element of a successful app is that it usually addresses a single use case. The app's purpose is clearly defined, and users tend not to expect more from the app outside of that narrow scope.

In the following sections, we explain how a graphical user interface (GUI) provides a good user experience (UX) and how to create a successful GUI framework.

Introducing the GUI

Companies pay a lot to protect their brand. They do so by creating a good user experience (UX). The UX is the overall design of the software, with the main goal of solving the user's problems via an intuitive experience.

Every interaction a consumer has on the Internet is logged somewhere. Business intelligence tools (see Chapter 9) can mine that data to tell a company how successful it is at giving the customer a good experience. In the olden days, companies used efficiency experts to determine the best set of commands needed to make a customer happy. Today, they use metadata, user logs, AI, and machine learning to hone the look and feel of their software. With website development, the rule of thumb is that a user should never be more than four clicks away from a resolution.

A *graphical user interface (GUI)* is a user interface based on pictures rather than text. Most modern end-user operating systems are GUI-based, such as Windows, macOS, iOS, and Android. Before there were GUIs, developers and users navigated operating systems and applications via command lines. Some of the text commands are still there, but with a GUI, they are behind-the-scenes. Thank goodness we don't have to type HTTP or Python commands at a prompt to surf the web!

A GUI is based on the integration of the user experience with the following tools and basic components:

» **Icons:** Small clickable pictures that serve as shortcuts to files or addresses.

» **Desktop:** The background behind the active application, or the background behind the icons on the main screen (for example, on a mobile device).

» **Windows:** Rectangular areas that define a particular application or dialog box within a larger area such as a desktop. On mobile apps, you don't usually have windows because apps run full-screen.

» **Menus and toolbars:** A list of commands or options you can select. A menu is usually text-based; a toolbar is usually icon-based.

» **Widgets:** Can be any element of interaction like a scroll bar or a drop-down menu.

» **Pointer:** The arrow or other marker that represents the mouse or trackball's control. On a mobile device, you typically use your finger or a stylus as a pointer so there's no onscreen pointer.

Everything that you can do using a GUI has associated code. For example, when you click or tap an icon to run an app, the command for starting that app executes.

The code behind every GUI is created in standard formats and can resolve to text or graphic. The uniformity of these standards permits data sharing.

Getting the GUI right

Underpinning the GUI is the GUI framework. The *GUI framework* is a set of software tools utilized to provide developers a faster and more consistent way to deliver GUI-based applications. A GUI framework has many components and many choices of solutions that can be utilized and customized to an institution's requirements. Using standardized GUI frameworks can save developers months of work and allow the development of new user experiences in a matter of weeks.

GUIs are built in many languages and out of the box. Open source libraries exist to make the creation of a GUI framework easy. Python alone has four basic technologies that it uses as "bindings" across its interfaces: Gtk, Qt, Tk, and wxWidgets. (Flip to Chapter 10 for more information on open source.)

A GUI framework standardizes the objects taken from other more standard programs found in operating systems (like fonts and jpgs) and wraps them in an agnostic form (like classes or handles) making them universal. Figure 8-1 provides a basic look at how a GUI framework may operate.

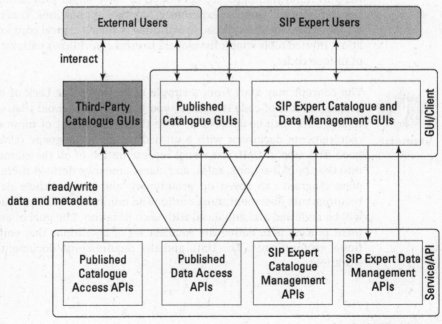

FIGURE 8-1:
The relationship between the user, the user interface, and the APIs that call the functions and data.

© John Wiley & Sons, Inc.

Each browser has its own set of metadata that affects the way the user sees and accesses information. Application programming interfaces (APIs) are used to translate between the way a specific GUI has been coded and a nonnative environment you want to run it under. The API defines the way the components interact in a nonnative environment. The API provides a consistent GUI experience across the different browsers or media. As we note in Chapter 4, the API provides the building blocks that create a consistent user experience in different environments.

Establishing the Requirements Needed in the Development of an App

As we say earlier, there has lately been a shift in the way applications and systems are developed. In the past, the focus was on the programming, and the business drivers were often lost in the process. Business drivers came at the end instead of at the beginning of the requirements gathering. Nowadays, though, business requirements drive the development process, and the workflow can make or break any app's value.

Keep in mind that apps are developed to solve small programmatic needs with small-footprint, singular experience/function applications. Essentially, an app is all about the workflow. Because workflow is such a critical component of app creation, myriad tools enable developers to create workflows without writing one line of unique code.

REMEMBER

The concept may start from a simple sentence on the back of an envelope, but before one line of code is written, you need to understand that specific steps are required for it to be successful. With the development of more complex apps, a requirements document with a unified modeling language (UML) diagram is a good first step. A UML is a visual representation of all the elements that will go into the app. All actions, roles, and classes must be defined there. Having a complete diagram can speed up prototyping and the workflow development. The requirements document must outline the minimum viable product (MVP), which will be reviewed and enhanced with each iteration. The goal of an app's development process is to define the smallest set of operations that complete the functional requirements. The UML and the requirements document will define the workflow.

Because of the heightened importance of business needs, a *workflow engine* has become essential to developing a successful app. A workflow engine is software that is designed to manage business processes. These applications have three main functions: determining the validity of executing a task, checking the permissioning of the user who is doing a task, then executing that task.

For example: When you invest money via your favorite wealth management app, it initiates a workflow engine involving security selection, order selection and execution, confirmations, and portfolio rebalancing. It's the workflow engine that's moving one stage to another.

Chapter **9**

Breaking Down BI Tools

N
early all companies and industries have a tremendous amount of data available, but mounds of information without context is useless. *Business intelligence (BI)* is the coordinated use of technologies, processes, and architectures used to mine, transform, and analyze raw business data to help make intelligent business decisions. BI takes raw data and structures it in a manner that provides meaningful intel. Some of the tools that it can employ include reports and dashboards, real-time analysis, and forecasting.

FinTech is often brought into financial and insurance institutions by C-level management because they are unclear of the actual state of their business. They aren't receiving data that is reliable or consumable in a fashion that assists them in making business decisions for their organizations. FinTech, through the use of BI, helps make the data at hand understandable through near real-time solutions.

This chapter explains how businesses can use BI as part of their overall strategic plan, and it reviews some of the most popular and effective BI features.

Taking a Strategic Approach to BI

The first step in developing a BI strategy is to assess how the company currently uses data and how the lack of visibility into that data causes disruptions and potential monetary loss.

A company needs to accelerate its reaction times and anticipate disruptive technologies. It can do so by facilitating data usage in logical, consistent ways through a well-developed business intelligence and information management strategy that includes a *management information system (MIS)*. An MIS is an IT system that aggregates, processes, analyzes, and organizes data across an entire company and a larger industrial base, directly improving operational and financial outcomes.

REMEMBER

A business intelligence strategy provides the whole organization as well as the individual end user with benefits, including

>> Trusted, real-time data

>> End-user-specific delivery mechanisms (such as providing mobile delivery for sales and server-based delivery for finance) with configurable dashboards

>> Alert mechanisms that drive productivity and financial analysis

>> Flexible storage and access (cloud-based where possible; see Chapter 6 for more about cloud computing)

>> Scalable systems that can handle changing data-processing activity

For several decades, technology has been a core component in the successful operations of the finance industry, and its importance increases each year. As the use of technology in finance has increased, so too has the amount of *structured data* — that is, any data that has been mined and resides in a fixed field within a record, file, or database, like an Excel spreadsheet or a SQL database. (SQL stands for structured query language.)

FinTech solutions have astronomically increased the amount of structured data available and the uses that companies can make of it. Recently, vast amounts of *unstructured data* have also been added to the mix. Unstructured data is, as the name implies, unformatted and not easily differentiated or stored. It could be manifested as images, files, web-based metadata, or handwritten notes. By its nature, unstructured data is hard to analyze and collate into interactional information; it must be transformed into more rationalized forms through natural language processing (NLP), pattern review, and text mining. Machine learning tools are now used to help unearth the value of unstructured data. The more complex analytic tools used on unstructured data are applications that deal with more subjective analysis.

Now more than ever, BI comes into play both upstream and downstream of FinTech:

>> Data that comes in upstream can originate from artificial intelligence (AI), blockchain (see Chapter 7), and data science.

>> Downstream can come from decision tools that navigate the universe of data derived from FinTech solutions for banking, investment, and insurance.

REMEMBER

BI usage is critical to any organization's FinTech strategy. A FinTech solution must include processing real-time information that is relevant to the end user and the company at large. The areas requiring FinTech oversight and integration include

>> Analytic computing

>> Complex event processing

>> Data mining

>> Process regimes

>> Visibility and insight into all operations and delivery mechanisms of data used by the company

>> Testing and accuracy of data provided

Exploring BI Tools

With a world full of data, it isn't so odd that a great array of BI tools exist. These tools are designed to handle large amounts of unstructured data in an integrated way, in conjunction with the more regimented and flexible business analytics systems.

BI tools help format and make the data available to end users through reports, dashboards, or any other visualization representation. Homogenizing this data and integrating it with traditional data stores results in accelerated and more accurate decision-making. The following sections explain some of the technologies involved in BI tools.

Online analytical processing

Online analytical processing (OLAP) is the database technology that transforms raw data into an architecture that business analysts can readily consume. OLAP tools organize large data sets into logical components for intelligent querying and reporting.

In a nutshell, here's how it works: Data analysts ask questions of data. Those questions are divided into sets of measures and dimensions. Measures and dimensions are structured into multidimensional data cubes. Data cubes are designed by data scientists with the intent of speeding up the querying of specific measures across known dimensions.

REMEMBER

Here are a few basic definitions to understand when thinking about OLAP:

>> **Measures:** A *measure* is typically what a data or business analyst seeks, the basis of most reports. OLAP measures are quantifiable, preprocessed, and one-dimensional data, such as credit risk exposure or expected profit and loss (PnL). PnL is the total profit and loss experienced by a company over a specific period of time. In an OLAP cube, measures are grouped into basic fact tables.

>> **Dimensions:** A *dimension* is a hierarchy in a data cube by which nested sets of measures are organized. For example, you can organize expected PnL measures into time period hierarchies such as days, weeks, months, and years; counterparty hierarchies; trade type hierarchies; asset classes; and so on. Dimensions are the basis for analysis and reporting. Dimensions require knowledge about how the analysis of the measures takes place.

>> **Cubes:** A *cube* is a multidimensional data structure for organizing and storing measures aggregated across several dimensions, like the one in Figure 9-1. Cubes are the basis for rapid analytical processing as individual cubes are designed from preconceived business analysis goals.

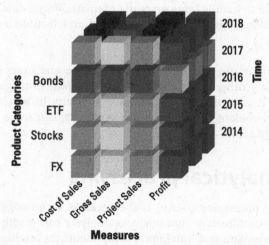

FIGURE 9-1:
An example of an
OLAP cube.

© John Wiley & Sons, Inc.

Querying and reporting

To build reports that can be presented to business leaders, data analysts must first retrieve the desired data from the database. With an understanding of what data is available and how it is formatted, a data analyst can ask the right questions. Analysts ask questions via database queries.

To begin the process of creating meaningful BI representations for the end user, an analyst engages in mining and retrieving the data from a variety of databases or stores. She does so by creating queries in a structured query language that the database engine understands. An accurate query retrieves precise data from the database. The format and amount of data returned from a query depends on the query. Results can range from a single-digit measure to several thousand rows of data. The data analyst's job is to write queries that retrieve the exact data needed for the specific report that is to be designed. Queries returning more data than is needed require more filtering at the reporting level.

Ideally, queries automatically retrieve and update reports based on a schedule. Query design can also incorporate real-time data retrieval from the database to update a report based on a change of a measure.

WARNING

Some systems limit the number of application programming interface (API) calls to BI solutions. The system providers usually want you to utilize their own analytic packages. Exceeding API calls to a system can either impede performance or potentially drive up costs from the vendor.

Data mining

FinTech systems utilize large sets of structured and unstructured data stored in many data repositories, including data warehouses. *Data mining* is the process of discovering what is in the data and what the data can do for you — in other words, what *has* happened and what *might* happen. Data mining has two main functions: to discover actionable trends and to make predictions.

Data mining starts with complete data. In the case where data is incomplete, data mining tools can apply algorithms that identify patterns and gaps to fit missing data. Data mining tools may also build additional projected data for input into predictive data models. *Predictive data models* act on sets of structured data to identify trends and behaviors in data. Such models may range from basic regression models to complex, machine learning algorithms that analyze unstructured data. The outcome of data mining is the creation of actionable trends and patterns and predictions relevant to business users.

Figure 9-2 shows the steps involved in processing data from its source, through ETL engines (ETL stands for extract, transform, load), into data stores from which the end user can access it via various media and visualizations.

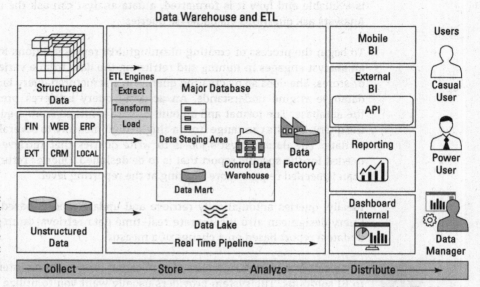

FIGURE 9-2:
An example of what a data storage environment looks like and how it's used.

Data visualization

Over the past five years, end users have pushed intensely for more graphic representations of their data. Many new tools have sprung up in the marketplace for gathering, storing, and mining that data. The result is more data than can easily be consumed. As the adage states, a picture is worth a thousand words — and no one has the time to read a thousand words. End users want to be spoon-fed data in forms that they can consume effortlessly. This desire drives the industry's need for configurable interactive dashboards.

Data visualization is the term used for graphic representation of structured data. As we mention in the earlier section "Taking a Strategic Approach to BI," structured data is any data that has been mined and resides in a fixed field within a record, file, or database. Data visualization takes disparate points of data, such as data from multiple spreadsheets or presentations, and represents them in a more visual, cohesive, and relational way. Visualization assists the end user in identifying trends and in visually showing past performance and future projections.

TIP

How the end user interacts with the presented data is important in refining the efficacy of what is being presented. A dialogue should exist between the end user and the creator of the BI output.

Figure 9-3 illustrates how data sources provide input for a data warehouse, which feeds into a BI application, which in turn feeds a dashboard that delivers charts and reports to end users.

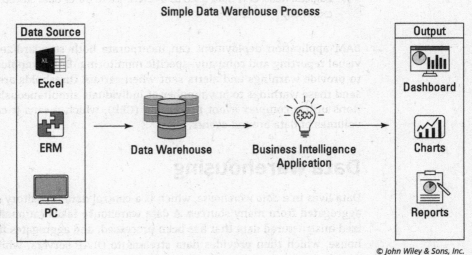

Simple Data Warehouse Process

© John Wiley & Sons, Inc.

FIGURE 9-3: A simple data warehouse process.

Business activity monitoring

Business activity monitoring (BAM) is a type of software that can illustrate and report on a business's or industry's overall health. It shows trends, key performance indicators (KPIs), and operational/business risks, usually in real time. BAM is a critical element in providing an organization with operational metrics. It does so by interpreting *business activity* in real time. Business activity can be any activity a company undertakes that affects its bottom line. Business activity can also include production workflows and sales initiatives.

Dashboards have always been part of the IT monitoring world, but only recently have nontechnical people such as sales and operations managers begun using dashboards to inform their business decisions. Upper management can also use customized dashboards for high-level oversight.

BAM data is constantly refreshing, so it's critical to make smart choices about which data is important to display and update in real time. The data types available in BAM are VARCHAR, DATETIME, INT, DECIMAL, and FLOAT. BAM data can be found in a table or a database. It can be streamed or static, and it can be retrieved by automated queries. The data used can be

>> **Simple:** Index or hierarchical

>> **Derived:** Inherits from other columns and adds to another column

>> **External:** The data persists outside the database

>> **Logical:** Read-only data used as a reference to other data stored inside or externally

BAM application deployment can incorporate both standardized templates for visual reporting and company-specific monitoring. BAM graphics can also be set to provide warnings and alerts sent when certain thresholds are crossed. It can send these warnings to any number of individuals simultaneously. BAM applications utilize complex event processing (CEP), which means it can process high volumes of data around events.

Data warehousing

Data lives in a *data warehouse,* which is a central data repository of cleansed data aggregated from many sources. A data warehouse takes rationalized or normalized unstructured data that has been processed, and aggregates it into one warehouse, which then provides data streams to OLAP servers, which then provide data for business applications like BI and BAM. A data warehouse makes it easy for data scientists and analysts to query data from several disparate sources without the need to configure connectivity to several other sources. (OLAP, BAM, and querying are all covered earlier in this chapter.)

A data warehouse is a *relational database,* meaning it contains multiple sets of data and joins them by their related fields. Sources may include in-house systems, cloud-based systems, mobile FinTech systems, local user systems, and so on.

It's essential that a data warehouse be able to synchronize data and maintain data integrity. There are different structures for maintaining data integrity. For example, ETL operates by porting batch mode data into the pre-architected data warehouse. A data warehouse also utilizes OLAP for handling multilevel inquiries. Various high-level BI and BAM tools pull data directly through the OLAP to provide business intelligence to different strata of the company as needed. Figure 9-4 shows how data is transformed, housed, and used throughout the data stack.

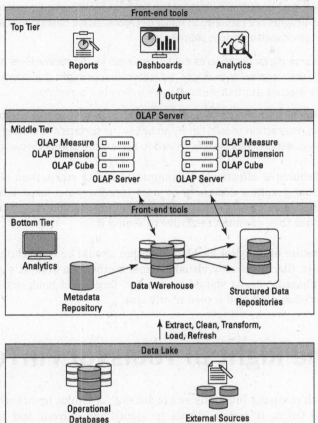

Complex Data Warehouse Structure

FIGURE 9-4:
A complex data
warehouse
structure with
workflows.

© John Wiley & Sons, Inc.

Digital dashboards

Digital dashboards supply attractive, available, and accessible visuals that enable business leaders to make intelligent decisions. A *digital dashboard* is a presentation of relevant insights derived from business data.

There are two main types of digital dashboards: static and dynamic.

>> A *static digital dashboard* presents a predefined set of business intelligence insights via noninteractive visuals. A business leader makes decisions from insights displayed at a point in time. Data analysts design such dashboards to answer specific predefined business questions, such as *What is my expected shortfall at a specific point in time?* A business leader should be able to find the answer to such questions by glancing at a static digital dashboard.

Static dashboards are ideal for the decision-maker who knows what measures and insights are required to make decisions. Static dashboards are designed for quick and intelligent snapshots.

>> *Dynamic digital dashboards* enable business leaders some level of interaction with the visuals. For example, a decision-maker might drill down to examine an expected shortfall measurement in another dimension.

Dynamic dashboards should avoid requiring their end users to reanalyze the data. Interaction should barely go below the surface and should aim to answer only questions very closely related to what is the primary visual required.

TIP

Good dashboards effectively communicate a data story. Data analysts can work with visual graphics designers or user interface/user experience specialists to ensure that data clearly communicates the information end users want to see in the manner they are most receptive to seeing it.

TIP

A key feature of a digital dashboard design should be the richness and impact of its visuals. Glance-worthy visuals should be the data analyst's goal in designing the dashboard. Visuals should be concise, large, and bold, with actionable data that users can read on a screen of any size.

Choosing the Right BI Tools for FinTech

A FinTech company functions as a facilitator for banks, insurance companies, and financial firms. It assists clients in identifying current and future needs and selecting the best strategies and tools to keep their businesses current and viable in a dynamically changing environment.

A FinTech company performs a detailed assessment of a company's landscape before recommending a software product by analyzing the client's needs and goals in relation to the products available. It's therefore imperative that the FinTech company has a good working knowledge of the best applications/tools available. The FinTech company should also have preconfigured infrastructure frameworks, APIs, and prebuilt connectors to the best of third-party breed software that the customer may elect to use.

REMEMBER

When determining the best BI software options, interoperability of the different requirements across the whole organization should be emphasized. It's also important to understand the client's current data model and to have viable options to suggest in consolidating that data in the future. To determine the best BI tools, the FinTech company must understand the applications and data stores used to retrieve the consolidated representations that a BI tool offers.

General BI applications

The available BI applications are quite numerous, and there is no one "best" solution across the board. Table 9-1 lists some of the most popular general BI applications and provides some quick notes on each one.

TABLE 9-1   General BI Applications

Product	Notes
Tableau (www.tableau.com)	No technical skills required to use prepackaged tools
Microsoft Power BI (https://powerbi.microsoft.com/en-us/)	The leader in decentralized analytics
ThoughtSpot (www.thoughtspot.com)	Search-based interface
Qlik (www.qlik.com/us)	Analytics and a strong road map
Sisense (www.sisense.com)	Focused on small to midsize companies; does data mash-ups
Salesforce Einstein Analytics (www.salesforce.com/einstein-analytics)	Point-and-click inside salesforce.com; AI-augmented
TIBCO Spotfire (www.tibco.com)	Very extensible; a complete package; an innovator in the field
SAS Viya (www.sas.com/en_us/software/viya.html)	Prebuilt analytics package; all standard visualizations
SAP Analytics Cloud (www.sap.com)	Prepackaged analytic content
Cognos (www.ibm.com/products/cognos-analytics)	AI-driven business visualization platform
Chartio (www.chartio.com)	On-the-fly dashboard collaborative tool
MicroStrategy (www.microstrategy.com)	Crowdsourcing and semantic graphic approach

TIP

Tools such as Microsoft Power Bi, Sisense, Chartio, Looker (see the next section), and Tableau offer rich sets of features for building simple to very complex dashboards with dynamic and interactive visuals. In designing with these tools, the data analyst should be very familiar with the target audience to avoid overcomplicated dashboards that may be overwhelming.

Good applications should support the following:

>> Separation of the analytics from their usage

>> A robust workflow process

» Multilevel provisioning of applications and data

» Cloud-based delivery (Platform as a Service [PaaS]; see Chapter 6 for details)

» Easy delivery, management, and auditing capabilities

» Drag-and-drop interfaces

» Ease of metadata management

» Scalability

» Advanced visualization tools

» Multipublishing capabilities

» Secure multifactor access to data

TIP

Many BI solutions come with prebuilt connectors to market leading solutions. Be sure to understand your system's architecture in evaluating BI solutions. Having access to prebuilt connectors will save time and frustration of moving data in and out of other systems.

Niche BI applications

In addition to general-purpose BI tools, many products fill specific niches in the market. Table 9-2 summarizes these.

TABLE 9-2   Niche BI Applications

Product	Notes
Looker (www.looker.com)	Permits data modeling as well as standard visualization on the cloud
Domo (www.domo.com)	Senior-level intelligence
GoodData (www.gooddata.com)	Cloud-based hosted data management
Yellowfin (www.yellowfinbi.com)	A new offering that has innovated a "storytelling" component; has great individual personalization of the analytics functionality
Oracle Cloud (www.oracle.com/index.html)	Emphasizes analytics and mobile apps
Infor Birst (www.birst.com)	End-to-end warehousing
Pyramid Analytics (www.pyramidanalytics.com)	A new entry; good workflows; platform agnostic

Chapter **10**

Reviewing the Role of Open Source

Five years ago, using open source in licensed proprietary software was practically unheard of in the financial industry. It was viewed as a risky approach, and in many organizations, it clouded the question of ownership and increased the concern over security breaches and bugs. Financial institutions were wary of any software they couldn't own or license in its entirety.

Fast forward to today, and you find that the complexity of the banking industry's needs and the need for real-time speed have driven many companies to adopt what was once considered a radical innovation. The loosening of controls around open source code has enhanced the ability of FinTech to solve problems and to replace the lumbering archaic monolithic systems that surround this industry.

A popular point of view among banks and financial institutions nowadays is that they should be directly engaged in the core aspects of their business that are key to their profitability and should rely on FinTech companies to build and deploy the support systems that contribute to those core aspects.

Several specific changes in the financial industry (and the business world as a whole) have opened the door to open source. For example:

>> The Agile development process is now the development process of choice, as opposed to the waterfall methodology, and with it comes cloud delivery and storage, the use of microservices, more seamless and continuous integration, and the desire for rapid application development. (See Chapter 4 for more details.)

>> Companies want to avoid being locked into a specific product or vendor. They want to be free to choose the best and fastest solutions at any given time.

>> Through the expansion of FinTech, large companies and banks are no longer tied to old technologies.

>> Large companies and banks are assembling smaller, more geographically divided teams around the globe to work together, and these teams are increasingly composed of millennials, who have different attitudes about security and ownership.

All these things add up to a much larger market for open source products and code. This chapter explores this burgeoning software sector, evaluating the pros and cons and looking at some attractive open source solutions.

Defining Open Source

REMEMBER

As the name implies, the source code for open source software is available for free to any developers, who then can use, share, and alter that code and in turn share their own modifications with others. Nobody creating or modifying the code receives any direct compensation. Programmers are motivated by a desire to improve and augment the initial package, and the result is a better functioning and more highly interactive software.

The following sections describe the open source community and compare open source software to free software.

The open source community

When an organization adopts open source, it embraces a community of users who enhance, revise, and drive the creation of that code. By its very nature, the output of this community isn't specific to the needs of one company but rather to industries at large and individual contributors. This approach to development demands collaboration, controls, and continued revision and testing. The created code is flexible in its construction and able to reflect a myriad of different types of use cases across multiple industries.

To assure the success of an open source project, individuals and companies that utilize open source code are often motivated to contribute resources and revenue to offset the benefits they receive. Most of the more successful projects have communities and user groups that enhance and support the packages as they're modified.

Free versus open source

Some people use the term *open source* interchangeably with *free software,* but they're not the same thing. Free software is a philosophical position around the use and ownership of code, whereas open source is a methodology around the use of public code.

Free software

Programmer Richard Stallman coined the phrase "free software" in 1982 to indicate a process by which developers could freely use specific code without any use restrictions. It was essentially permission that the code's creator granted to permit other users the right to use, modify, copy, and redistribute anything as part of that software package.

The use of the word *free* in this term is more about freedom of usage than it is about lack of payment received. Free software, according to the "Four Pillars of Freedom" that were codified in 1986, meant there were no constraints on the time the code could be used or the type or quality of the modifications that could be developed. There was also no need to acquire permission to redistribute that code, whether original or modified, and no restriction on who can receive that code or its modification. These freedoms also extended to the use of the source code inside any proprietary code.

REMEMBER

However, this freedom doesn't necessarily mean that no licensing is required. Free software can be licensed in any of these ways:

>> **A copyleft license:** Copyleft continues the copyright permission and doesn't permit anyone to add any restrictions that would alter the free rights of redistribution or lay claims to ownership of the original code or its augmentation.

>> **A permissive license:** Two types of permissive license exist. There is a permissive license with limited or no restrictions on the way the code can be changed. There is also a permissive license that requires that a notice of copyright and a disclaimer against liability be included in the package.

>> **A non-copyleft license:** This type has minimal to no restrictions.

A permissive open source license is non-copyleft, which means it does allow for the copyrighting of derivative works made off open source code.

Open source software

REMEMBER

On the other hand, the term *open source* refers to the methodology surrounding the use of the free code once it's modified, used, copied, or distributed. Open source commits to providing these rights:

>> Public use and reuse of the code is permitted.

>> Modifications can be created and redistributed without permission.

>> All iterations of the code can be freely distributed.

>> Any quality enhancements, documentation, or testing based on the use cases of a large testing audience of developers and end users will be available as part of the code.

>> This code can be used in conjunction with other codes.

The motivation for the use of open source rather than free software arose from a commercial desire for collaborative approaches focused on improving open software development across companies and industries. Such development would enable companies to benefit from the expertise of developers outside their organizations for functionality not core to their product or needs. Open source is a commercial approach for code collaboration and development across industries for generalized applications and needs. Agile development and speed to the marketplace were made possible through the development of flexible open platforms and functional business process-oriented developer languages.

Other types of software

WARNING

Neither open source nor free software should be confused with *freeware*, which is computer software that is owned and copyrighted but made available to the end user with usage restrictions. This type of ownership permits developers to control, distribute, and sell their work effort at any point. It often restricts any modification to the code offered and rarely offers source code. It also offers support at a cost as well as enhancements at a cost.

Another term sometimes thrown into this mix is *shareware*, which isn't free. Although initially offered for free, generally it's positioned as an evaluation copy with specific time-to-review constraints, after which there may be a fee for continued use.

Looking at Open Source Development Processes

By its nature, the development process for open source must be different from the more traditional models. The determination to even start an open source project is different. There isn't necessarily any business sector driving development. It may start from the curiosity of the developer, from a need to enhance some existing code, or to solve a problem for a large user base. Because individuals freely contribute to the code's development, more opinion and more discussion occurs about the nature of what gets developed. Open source develops in a democracy, which can make it more difficult to control.

Beginning a project

A project may begin as a snippet of code, as a distribution of similar software collections, or for the more ambitious, as the development of a complete system. Each type of open source code project has its own accepted form.

REMEMBER

The first step when starting an open source project is to gather and collect all the operations needed to maintain the code. Important elements to consider when setting up a project include the following:

>> Do you have a license template that all those who engage in the project should use?

>> Do you have a project website for collecting software versions and associated data? Have you selected the development and support tools to be used and made them available on the project site?

>> Have you created a written summary of the project that includes its purpose, scope, and success criteria?

>> Do you have a process outline that describes the code and documentation collection and review processes?

>> Do you have a project owner?

Discussing and documenting

Open source development doesn't lend itself to the waterfall development process. Requirements are rarely captured before the start of a project. When a release occurs, volunteers may begin writing the documentation and detailing the requirements and expected outcomes. Subversion (SVN; `https://subversion.apache.org`), Concurrent Version System (CVS; `www.akadia.com/services/cvs_howto.html`), and Distributed Revision Control (DRC; `https://en.wikipedia.org/wiki/Distributed_version_control`) are commonly used as versioning tools. Documentation publishing tools like Docusaurus (`https://docusaurus.io/`) provide a collaborative documentation website that developers and end users alike can use.

Most open source software (OSS) projects maintain a trusted repository that collects all the documentation, packages, bug reports, and developer spaces. Only the maintainers (the code reviewers and overseers of the project) can modify repository content. Developers use open standards and agreed-upon development conventions for all open source projects.

The process of collaboration and debugging is very loosely organized. No real standards or controls are in place. The users and community at large test the code and decide the direction of revisions and fixes.

The open source development process is closely aligned with the Agile/microservices approach that many FinTech organizations have adopted (see Chapter 4). The assumptions around open source development follow the microservices distributed model, with small teams in disparate locations working on small pieces of functionality and with code going through continuous integration. Maintainers review code constantly. Every release incorporates user feedback and bug fixes.

Developers and users submit feature requests. The code contributors directly discuss and prioritize each request for inclusion. This consensus approach can slow down feature selection, and there are no real throttles on what's included in any package.

TIP

OSS that is part of a proprietary software solution that a company is developing should be updated within the open source project repository when new functionalities are added. If this is done, the company won't have to monitor and incorporate its internal changes with each corporate release. Changes will be automatically updated with each open source release.

Transparency is key to the development of OSS. The architecture and design development process is transparent to all the developers and users and is open to discussion. The complete process relies extensively on peer review.

The open source development process utilizes the concept of "release early and often." Figure 10-1 illustrates the general process of open source development. Note that every step leads to the next in a circle around the outside, but every step also leads to the center component: discussion and documentation.

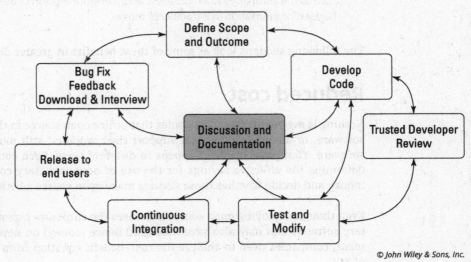

FIGURE 10-1: An open source nonlinear development process.

© John Wiley & Sons, Inc.

Perusing the Pros of Open Source

REMEMBER

The benefits of open source to a corporation are numerous, including these:

>> Decreased hardware and software cost, including an overall decrease in the total cost of ownership (TCO) due to lower setup costs and operational costs.

>> Increased employee utilization. In-house developers deal with company-specific high-value work while utilizing the already vetted general application or code available from open source repositories for noncore development.

>> No reinvention of the wheel. Companies build only the intellectual property (IP), which is unique to their organization.

>> An increase in the specific developer knowledge base without an increase in the number of employees.

>> As with cloud deployments (see Chapter 6), you pay for the open source development teams only as they're needed, not as full-time employees.

>> Better testing and product control. The code is constantly tested by a large user group for a wide assortment of use cases. This results in better code.

>> Increase in speed of development and more frequent releases. Open source utilizes the same development process as microservices development and Agile processes (see Chapter 4), including continuous integration and testing.

>> Cutting-edge technology can be cost-effectively delivered in areas that aren't core to the company's main business and therefore wouldn't have a large budget for innovation in a traditional model.

The following sections look at some of these benefits in greater detail.

Reduced cost

Nothing is ever really free. Companies that utilize open source in their proprietary software, or as applications that support their workers, still must pay for that software. That payment just happens in different ways. Each company needs to determine the effective savings for the use of nonproprietary code in time and money and decide whether those savings make open source a better choice.

Even though deploying open source decreases the corporate expense for proprietary software and may also save time (and hence money) on new code development, companies need to analyze the cost-benefit equation from the framework of TCO.

Open source is operationally efficient, in that you deploy/create only the functionality you need for the task at hand. It's also a more generic approach to deployment, support, and maintenance. Generalized functionality is known and shared across industries and corporations, making support cheaper and less proprietary in nature. There is no price lockup or extensive negotiation, because the talent is swappable.

TIP

One of the easiest tests for determining the value of open source versus proprietary software has to do with the longevity and robustness of the open source. If the software has been around for several years, has a strong user base, and has a good web portal with written documentation and many iterations, and if consultants or service companies have built businesses around its customization and/or maintenance, then it's probably a safe bet.

Community focus collaboration is a key concept that drives open source. For a piece of open source code to be accepted and supported, it must have a community that embraces and enhances it. Some of the new coding languages, which are more extensible and can support a larger user group, are used to build core functionality.

The nature of these users and developers is fluid. They're often innovators who are looking for new technologies and ways to improve their skills. Generally, any open source offering works because of a tacit agreement to adhere to best practices and universally agreed-upon software development standards.

Another consideration when choosing open source should be whether the development is part of the company's core business. Don't skimp on the critical components of the core business. However, for side functions, open source makes a lot of sense, especially in cases where the functions are fairly standard. The more generic the application or code, the more it should be open source.

For a large project or an internal supporting application, another key consideration is the length and complexity of the learning curve for integrating the open source code. When a project is complex, the company should consider hiring experts who have long-term experience with the open source projects. You may have to pay for the reengineering of parts of the code that don't work for your specific needs. If you choose to bring the expertise in-house, you must accept that there will be downtime to train the individuals on the applications and software already in place.

REMEMBER

Open source may not come with the best documentation nor with the best test methodologies. Research and full integration testing will be required.

Flexibility

Open source is flexible because it wasn't built from a single frame of reference. Many use cases drive its creation. No profit-making machine is behind it and therefore no incentive for anyone to cling rigidly to a proprietary standard that may not be the best performer. Most open source code is platform-agnostic and, in some cases, also media-agnostic. Using open source tools and components removes barriers to customization.

TIP

FinTech has taken advantage of the nature of open source to enhance deployment and integration speed. The tools that open source developers use are essentially the same tools utilized in FinTech development. Just like FinTech, open source embraces

>> Microservices and Agile development (see Chapter 4)

>> Application programming interface (API) strategies (see Chapter 4)

>> Speedy processing with central processing unit/graphics processing unit (CPU/GPU) compute modes (see Chapter 4)

>> Cloud/web-based delivery systems (see Chapter 6)

>> Artificial intelligence and machine learning (AI/ML; see Chapter 12)

Freedom

As you discover earlier in this chapter, free software is a statement about freedom around the development, distribution, replication, and modification of software. It's a movement rather than a process.

As reflected in the Free Software Foundation (FSF; www.fsf.org) principles, the "Four Pillars of Freedom" are

The freedom to run the program as you wish, for any purpose.

The freedom to study how the program works and to change it, so it does your computing as you wish. Access to the source code is a precondition for this.

The freedom to redistribute copies so you can help your neighbor.

The freedom to distribute copies of your modified versions to others. By doing this, you can give the whole community a chance to benefit from your changes. Access to the source code is a precondition for this.

Development speed

Open source utilizes development principles similar to those of microservices (see Chapter 4) and cloud deployment (see Chapter 6). Because of the highly complex interplay of all the moving parts in a free development environment, providing a project management and DevOps framework at the onset of an OSS project is critical. Economies of scale and development speedups can't happen unless a project manager owns the process. In open source, this person is often referred to as a *maintainer*. Including subject matter experts (SMEs) as reviewers and testers is also essential.

Open source development makes a developer more efficient. Sharing code to open source projects makes support and maintenance of systems or software, which relies on that code, more supportable.

Many large corporations are now opening their source code to external developers. Apple, IBM, SAP, and Microsoft are a few of the tech giants that have gotten on the open source bandwagon. They have done so to increase their product reach and to increase innovation of their products both inside and outside of the organization. GM, Ford, and Google all have open platforms that they're hoping will speed up development and innovation in the area of new technologies and AI integration. By older companies opening their development framework to outsiders, fresher and more dynamic standards will be codified and utilized in a fashion that will make reuse and innovation of open source code speedier and better.

Figure 10-2 shows how a simple open source project can morph into a larger system. The three sections demonstrate the additional structure that must be maintained as a project is transformed. More oversight is required as the complexity of the offering grows.

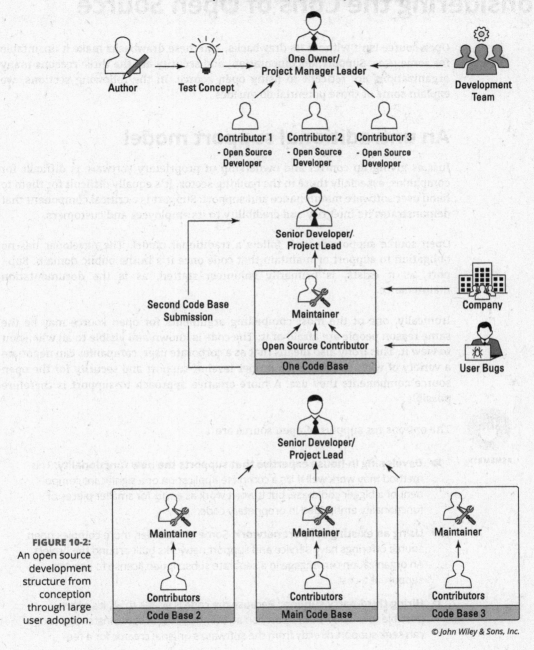

Open Source Project Development Structure

Author → Test Concept → One Owner/ Project Manager Leader ← Development Team

Contributor 1 - Open Source Developer
Contributor 2 - Open Source Developer
Contributor 3 - Open Source Developer

Senior Developer/ Project Lead

Second Code Base Submission

Maintainer
Open Source Contributor
One Code Base

Company

User Bugs

Senior Developer/ Project Lead

Maintainer
Contributors
Code Base 2

Maintainer
Contributors
Main Code Base

Maintainer
Contributors
Code Base 3

© John Wiley & Sons, Inc.

FIGURE 10-2:
An open source development structure from conception through large user adoption.

Considering the Cons of Open Source

Open source isn't without its drawbacks, and these drawbacks make it unsuitable for some uses. Support, documentation, and security are the three reasons many organizations are reticent to using open source. In the following sections, we explain some of those potential downsides.

An untraditional support model

Just as giving up control and ownership of proprietary software is difficult for companies, especially those in the banking sector, it's equally difficult for them to hand over software maintenance and support. Support is a critical component that demonstrates its integrity and credibility to its employees and customers.

Open source support doesn't follow a traditional model. The developer has no obligation to support or maintain that code once it's in the public domain. Support, as it exists, is primarily volunteer-staffed, as is the documentation maintenance.

Ironically, one of the most compelling arguments for open source may be the same reason people are afraid of it: The code is known and visible to all who want to view it. This irony also means that as a corporate user, companies can negotiate a variety of ways to ensure the proper level of support and security for the open source components they use. A more creative approach to support is therefore possible.

REMEMBER

The options for support of open source are

>> **Developing in-house expertise that supports the new functionality:** This method may work well if it's a complete application or a significant component of a bigger codebase, but it won't work as easily for smaller pieces of functionality embedded in proprietary code.

>> **Using an existing support network:** Some of the older, more complex open source offerings have service and support networks built around the project. An organization can engage in a separate subscription license to provide support at a cost.

>> **Hiring third-party support:** Because the code is visible to all, it's often possible to employ a third party on an ad-hoc basis. In some instances, you can seek support directly from the software's original creator for a fee.

>> **Adding on open source support to an existing support contract:** Some large support companies will take on the open source component support at an additional cost. They're traditional support companies with call centers and 24/7 hotlines.

>> **Using support tools:** As part of deploying code using open source, organizations can use several tools in a continuous monitoring fashion to handle potential bug issues. These tools do come at a cost and will require someone to be trained in their use.

Time and resources for maintenance

When software is purchased, it generally comes with a warranty and the guarantee of a certain level of maintenance and support. Vendors selling that maintenance also often have an interest in keeping customers apprised of the changes to the product so that they get new service contracts and revenue from upgrades.

With open source, however, there's no impetus to upgrade and no customer representative to remind the organization's stakeholders of the potential risk of using out-of-date products. When people hear "free" or "open source," they assume there's no cost. But as we indicate throughout this chapter, nothing is free. One of open source's costs comes when you must allocate resources and time to version upgrades. Failure to do so can result in serious downtime and backward compatibility issues.

It becomes the burden of the IT department or the DevOps team to build in timelines for updates and reviews of new open source network offerings. The installation of tools doesn't guarantee updates to open source software.

A secondary industry has arisen from the growing open source community that supports the more successful initiatives like Linux. These commercialized offshoots provide support and enterprise-level software for open source applications and platforms.

The possibility of uneven documentation

Documentation is another critical but voluntary component of the open source package. It's critical that the open source project site includes tools that enable developers and users to add documentation to the package on the fly. If the project has been well defined and a maintainer is responsible for the integrity of the code and the package, the docs should (at least theoretically) be of proper quality.

Supporting and providing reasonable documentation is in the developers' best interest. Developers want others to use and enhance their code. People can't do that if the documents are unclear or unavailable. Because no single department or individual oversees documentation, the documentation quality may be very uneven. One of the standard complaints about open source development is that the documentation is often confusing or lacking.

The main reason that documentation is often problematic for open source code is that developers underestimate its value and don't spend the time they should on it. They're not writers, so they don't know what's required, and they don't want to take the time away from coding to learn that new skill set. They wrongly assume users will take responsibility for completing the documentation. A related problem is that because documentation isn't prioritized, developers don't provide or explain style sheets and templates, so the documentation ends up being inconsistent.

TIP

When evaluating open source code, documentation quality and quantity should be a primary concern. To spot-check documentation, look first to the README file and then the error and help text statements and commands. You should also see how frequently the documentation is updated or rewritten.

Documentation generators (autodocs) programmatically include some specific documentation on the fly. Most of this type of documentation focuses on the developer and implementer's needs. Some auto generators will provide end-user quality docs.

TIP

The project should capture documentation from a variety of points of view:

>> One set should be from the end-user perspective and should provide basic how-to instruction.

>> Another set of documentation should focus on the software itself and the developer's needs.

>> A third set should be for implementors and should focus on the third-party deployment and code maintenance.

Security risks

The same openness that provides open source such flexibility is often also a legitimate reason to avoid it. The use of open source presents three types of security risks: legal, operational, and viral.

REMEMBER

The key security questions around the use of any open source software are as follows:

>> Is it really safe?

>> If everyone has access to the source code, why can't they use that to hack into my proprietary software or network?

>> What do I need to know about the software to make the use of it safer?

>> How do I know whether the code is well written?

>> How do I know it won't plant a virus in my healthy code?

To answer these concerns, you need to do your homework. Many sites advertise open source, and there are many repositories. To protect the organization, someone needs to own the process of vetting and reviewing each use case and solution. The following sections give more details on some of these questions.

TIP

Before you use open source software, establish what you're trying to accomplish. Here are some tips:

>> Create clear rules around who in your organization can do what.

>> Put processes around the vetting of code and software.

>> Assign an owner who is responsible for reviewing the selections.

>> Make sure the legal department reviews all written documents around the code or software before it's agreed to or installed.

How do I know my code is secure?

On its face, proprietary software appears to be more secure than open source, but that isn't necessarily true. The very aspect that concerns people about open source is the aspect that may make it *more* secure.

Any code, proprietary or public, has some level of vulnerability to a hack. A hack is the result of poor coding or sloppy process. The difference is in the level of control you have over that:

>> Proprietary software is essentially a black box. You must take the vendor's word that it's safe and has been tested.

>> Open source is tested, viewed, reviewed, and modified daily, making the probability of a vulnerability being discovered much higher. If a vulnerability is found, it's in the interest of the team that built it to fix it quickly, because their reputation is directly linked to the product.

That's not to say that open source isn't a hacker's playground. The moment a vulnerability is announced, the probability of it being exploited jumps. The end user may not be aware of the jeopardy, and the burden for security is on the IT department or the head developers. Companies can programmatically handle the security notices, provided they take on the added expense of tools or manpower to do so. Open source usage will require putting new tools in place for alert and fix notifications. The IT department must be diligent in the managing of these vulnerability warnings and fixes. Unfortunately, at this time, there's no centralized vulnerability database, so the users of open source need to have suitable internal alert mechanism handled by both developers and IT.

How do I know whether the code is well written?

As we state earlier, due diligence is required when installing or using *any* software. Open source is no exception. Proprietary software generally has a rigorous time-proven set of operations surrounding the release of any software package, and those processes include quality assurance. In contrast, the programming principles used in open source aren't standardized, and there's no established level or norm around the quality aspects of the code.

Having so many eyes on the code is a type of safety net. However, quality control isn't normally a developer's strong suit, and the fact that no regimented approach to acceptance exists makes the quality issue an ongoing concern. More mature code is often less of a concern because there has been time to get the bugs out. The number of users, the number of product reviews and updates, and the number and type of bugs found and fixed are all indicators of the product quality and the level of user acceptance.

When selecting open source, it's essential to review the usage data and the case logs, which is generally robust because of the commitment by the community of users to transparency.

How do I know it won't plant a virus in my healthy code?

Only policies and procedures that ensure full code review before any release can give you any level of confidence around the open source code. As part of any company's due diligence, version history and bug fixes should be the norm.

To help reduce the risk, consider aligning your teams with the user groups for the open source and having them regularly review the vulnerability alerts and the tools in use in your industry.

Sustainability issues

For corporations to commit to open source, they need to be confident that the open source marketplace is viable and won't disintegrate over time. Unfortunately, there's no clear understanding of how open source will be monetized in the future.

Within the software user market, a free model isn't completely understood. While end users accept that the code is open source, they still expect that it will work seamlessly and without issue. Because no ownership exists, there's no one on staff to handle issues. Those issues are all done by volunteers. Many end users don't understand this model and expect that the code is supported like proprietary software.

One of the ways open source generates revenue is through the sale of support and maintenance. This is a sustainable way to maintain the products. However, most open source users don't and won't pay for support. So how can the free model be sustained?

If indeed the model is that there's no charge for the open source software, then there should be some way to have large reusers, who are benefitting financially from the code, pay. For example, it seems reasonable that a company that's selling products with components of open source in them should be taxed somehow for the use of that open source.

Licensing issues

Potential types of licensing issues include

>> **Infringement:** Open source software (OSS) has a higher possibility of infringement than proprietary software. Because no legal organization supports open source, and anyone can commit any source to an open project, it's possible that infringement of some proprietary code could take place. Also, no warranty provisions are provided to the users of open source code, so they could inadvertently infringe with no recourse to the code supplier. In such a case, the end user would have to bear the complete burden of the penalties incurred.

>> **License restriction:** The complex requirements of open source licensing are the more dangerous potential burden for a corporation. If the corporation comingles its proprietary code with that of the open source in a way that obscures the ownership of the proprietary code, it could be deemed as part of the OSS.

>> **Licensing compliance:** When you use open source, every component, snippet, and application comes with its own license. These licenses need to be reviewed and adhered to independently.

Other concerns to consider

REMEMBER

Open source attracts innovative developers. They don't hold a lot of stock in the more traditional approaches to sustainable, supported development. Speed and new technologies are their forte. Their predilections present certain challenges to the needs of the more stable long-term marketplace. Some issues around the process of developing in an open market have yet to be fully articulated or resolved, including these:

>> **If everyone has a voice, what takes precedence when disagreements arise? Is there a common vision?** The very flexibility of the way the code morphs makes consensus harder to achieve.

>> **Are there common standards?** When building quality code, there needs to be agreement on what is standard.

>> **How do the products get more production proof?** More open source code is getting dropped into proprietary code, but the tools to help make this easy don't exist. The project plans need to include a plan for extending the open source code within the proprietary software.

>> **What about legacy systems?** The move to open source as a foundation for corporate development may be extremely disruptive. New skill sets may be required.

>> **How do you marry best of breed, legacy systems, and open source?** The integration of old and new isn't an easy fit. Integrators may be required to make the extraction seamless.

>> **How will old open source data processing be handled to accommodate microservices and the cloud?** What was new is already old; the data structures of open source may require rewrites that may be difficult.

>> **Do we have the expertise to handle the technology changes and demands for more fluid couplings?** The emphasis in development now needs to be on business outcomes and workflows. There may not be the personnel to handle it.

Evaluating Open Source Solutions

As you discover earlier in this chapter, open source solutions are reconsumable, reusable blocks of code with standardized interfaces and specified dependencies. They can range in complexity from snippets of code to entire systems. They are extensible and easily insertable into other applications or code. These solutions may also take on the appearance of microservices (see Chapter 4).

The following sections discuss developing your own solution, finding help, and considering open innovation.

Developing your own solution

REMEMBER

If you're developing an open source program, you must first create an open source project and house it on an Internet site. If you're developing or using open source within proprietary code, you must take precautions to

» Clearly mark the source.

» Make sure licensing is compatible with the use case.

» Stay vigilant in upgrading and testing the open source code as it evolves.

» Fix bugs and republish as soon as possible.

» Keep accurate versioning and inventory lists of all open source used and how and where it's domiciled.

Open source asset management programs can assist in maintaining and updating the code. When developing an open source code, you should maintain a repository of both the original code and the versioning.

The company has an obligation to adhere to the license terms of each piece of open code used. That means rules must be in place to rehydrate the original project code at its source with any changes made, not just within the company's proprietary code.

TIP

You should invest in software that will automatically search for updates to the open source code you're using and test for vulnerabilities and security issues. These run in the background and protect against viruses and conflicts.

For open source development to be successful, the initiator/designer/architect of the product must be willing to spend time creating a well-thought-out, tool-supported, easy-to-use, open, Internet-accessible, viable development environment.

REMEMBER

When utilizing open source, an organization must establish an owner of the maintenance and review of all open source components that are used by the company, and it must establish policy around the vetting and deployment of any open source component used. The owner of the open source process must make sure that within the process, there are controls around new versioning, testing, and bug fixes. The rules around the use of open source must be articulated and reviewed regularly with all developers and new hires. This must be done to avoid licensing conflicts, potential infringement issues and restrictions conflicts, misuse of the code, and redundant use of the code.

WARNING

The company is obligated to adhere to the licensing terms of all the open source code used. Failure to do so may result in legal action.

REMEMBER

There's no designated policy in open source around quality. Anyone who uses open source code assumes that a minimum standard has been applied to the available product.

The open source development process should reflect the Agile process (see Chapter 4) and should follow the same code review procedures as for proprietary code. Developers should employ the same tools used in the Agile or microservices process for open source integration, use, and maintenance. To ensure consistency across the open source code, they should record all bugs found and fixed and update the open source project.

The greatest asset in the use of open source is the level of community user involvement. Only code that has an active community of users will grow and become better over time.

REMEMBER

Traditional code development, where each group develops only for itself, often results in duplication of effort. Open source eliminates this problem by permitting developers to use generalized code developed outside the organization and maintained and revised across industries. To avoid the possibility of continuation of bad habits in new software, developers must follow an airtight, highly visible, highly integrated review and maintenance process for the open source code the organization consumes. This includes frequently sharing a list of all components with developers.

Finding help for the right open source solution

As we state earlier in this chapter, open source comes in many forms, from snippets to applications to complete systems. Websites are available that can help find the best code for an organization's needs. These websites are often sponsored by companies that sell services or products that support open source code or its communities.

TIP

The following is a list of some sites that offer download capability for open source access:

>> Bitbucket (https://bitbucket.org/) hosts projects.

>> BLACKDUCK (www.blackducksoftware.com) is an organizational site used as a repository of both projects and nondeveloper data (such as licenses, user ratings, and download stats).

>> Tigris (www.tigris.org) is focused on building collaborative software to support developers. It's an app development site.

>> SourceForge (https://sourceforge.net/) provides project sites with tools that aid rapid open source development and maintenance.

>> OSDN (https://osdn.net) is a collaborative, open source web platform that provides some free services to developers such as CVS repositories, bug tracking systems, and forums.

>> FossHub (www.fosshub.com) is a web portal that provides direct download links to open source software.

>> GitHub (https://github.com) claims to be the most used, most scalable, and most secure open source developers' platform. It hosts projects for more than 2.1 million users.

>> LaunchPad (https://launchpad.net) is an open source platform that provides tools and collaboration interfaces for developers and users.

>> Open Source Software Directory (https://opensourcesoftwaredirectory.com) is a web-based open source project management system. It's also probably the most complete directory for "mom and pop" organizations, and it has a good search mechanism.

TIP

In addition to the websites that provide access to downloads, there are organizations that have been pivotal to the development of the open source philosophy. The largest and most pervasive organizations have been built around operating systems. Some such organizations are

>> **Open Virtualization Alliance (OVA; www.linuxfoundation.org):** In 2013, OVA became a Linux Foundation Collaborative Project. Its mission is to "assure the expansion of the concept of free and open source software through education and technical advice."

>> **OpenStack (www.openstack.org):** OpenStack is offered as a free open source cloud computing infrastructure and was a joint project of NASA and Rackspace, a hosting company. This project was started to establish a standardized approach to cloud-based infrastructure that was easy to deploy and infinitely scalable.

>> **OpenPOWER Foundation (https://openpowerfoundation.org):** A collaboration between IBM, Google, Mellanox, Tyan, NVIDIA, and Microsoft, OpenPOWER is really a collaboration around POWER ISA driven by IBM. This foundation is an example of large corporations like IBM opening their code to the development community to increase adoption of their Power products and architecture. OpenPOWER has become a part of the Linux Foundation Collaborative. It's a good example of the expansion of private growth through open source collaboration. It's unique, however, in that the licenses offered are more restrictive than a true "open source" model.

Introducing open innovation

One of the major benefits of open source is that it builds innovation across companies and industries. Developers aren't locked into the constraints of working for one company with one set of use cases. Larger companies are now looking at a new concept that extends this innovation, called *open innovation*.

REMEMBER

Conceptually, open innovation is a shift from totally open source innovation to a more palatable form of open collaboration across organizations, with targeted and limited source code exposure. Companies encourage this limited collaboration across corporate lines, extending to external as well as internal developers. The net effect is the creation of previously unthought of solutions, as well as newer innovation and faster time to market with new products. Open innovation by its nature is more transactional and driven by a specific company to increase innovation and, in the long run, profits. OpenPOWER (mentioned in the preceding section) is an example of this model in action.

As with most things, there are trade-offs with open innovation. There are no centralized controls (except perhaps the licensing use cases) and no ability for the company to direct the nature of the development. The loss of control is offset by the new insights and approaches from fresh eyes and the greater security for the company opening its source code to external consumers.

IN THIS CHAPTER

» **Extracting, transforming, and loading data**

» **Handling market data and databases**

» **Checking out data historization and data analytics**

» **Comparing structured and unstructured data**

» **Distinguishing SQL and NoSQL**

Chapter **11**

Grasping Data Management Fundamentals

Data management is the way that companies consume and protect their data. As organizations become smarter and more data-driven, data management processes must change, too.

FinTech companies and all financial systems tend to process significant volumes of data that often changes continuously and rapidly. Processing data efficiently and distilling actionable insights for decision support is the major objective of many FinTech systems.

REMEMBER

Before they can create an effective and coherent data management strategy, business leaders must thoroughly understand that data, including how it's structured, how people use it, and how to care for it. When approaching a data management system, here are some key questions you want to ask:

>> **Sources and volume of data:** Where does the data originate from? How much and what kind of data is required from each source?

>> **Frequency of update:** How frequently should we update the data or collect new data?

>> **Timeliness of data retrieval:** Must the data be available in real time? How old is the data when it becomes available?

>> **Data protection:** What are the policies around data sharing?

>> **Data processing:** Does the data need to go through several transformations before it's usable?

>> **Data ownership:** What is the original source of the data, and who owns it?

>> **Data security policies:** Who can view the data, and who can modify it or delete it?

>> **Data retention policies:** How long does the data and any changes to the data need to be retained?

Based on the answers to these questions, an organization can begin building policies and procedures that support its needs and goals. This chapter helps by explaining the key considerations and decisions involved in data sourcing, collection, cleansing, filtering, augmentation, preservation, and retrieval.

Looking at FinTech's Role in Helping Companies Manage Their Data

As we discuss in Chapter 14, the move to modernization and the refactoring of legacy systems is critical to the future of traditional banking institutions. One major issue that these institutions face is the migration of their data to the new, more open infrastructures and the incorporation of unstructured data into their business intelligence (BI; see Chapter 9).

Would it surprise you to know that the majority of older financial institutions still operate on mainframe technology? The migration off legacy systems is fraught with danger. FinTech helps mitigate that risk because of its specialized knowledge.

If you were the CEO of a bank, wouldn't you want to employ a data management scientist to oversee the transformation to new technologies and avoid that risk internally? That same scientist, working in a third-party FinTech company, can also provide insight into how to access unstructured data and enable greater time-to-market efficiencies, risk management, new product development, and better user experience for customers.

REMEMBER

The use of FinTech companies is key to the success of migration off legacy systems and better business intelligence through real-time assessment and data mining.

Understanding ETL: Extract, Transform, and Load

An important first step in data management is to *source* the data — in other words, to collect it from wherever it resides and integrate it into the destination. You must extract it from its current location, transform it to be compatible with the destination, and then load it into the destination. This process is commonly known as *extract, transform, load (ETL)*. All three of those functions may not be necessary in every system integration, but at least one is always required.

The following sections cover the three main steps of ETL and the software requirements.

Going over the steps

To *extract* data means to take it from a system or a storage medium (for example, a database). This process can be as simple as executing an SQL query (SQL stands for *structured query language*) and writing the output to a flat file, or calling an application programming interface (API) from a system that generates an output file.

However, extractions can also be more complicated. Sometimes more complex SQL statements may be required, or data may need to come from some communication protocol (for example, the data payload in a message queue) or combinations of multiple API calls to a system. Figure 11-1 shows an example high-level ETL workflow for trade data and market data.

REMEMBER

Data *transformation* is usually the most complex and effort-intensive area of a system integration. Transformation involves taking some input data and changing it into a format that a downstream system or user can consume.

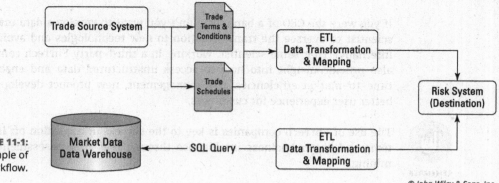

FIGURE 11-1:
An example of
ETL workflow.

Structurally, a data transform may convert Extensible Markup Language (XML) formatted input data to JavaScript Object Notation (JSON), a lightweight data format that general users can read and write. Such a conversion often involves mapping the input data's fields to the fields required at the destination, which may contain the same type of data but have different names. Sometimes this requires mapping multiple input fields to one output field or splitting one input field to multiple output fields.

Another critical data transformation is contextual in nature and requires manipulating the input data itself. For example, not all banking databases store counterparty information in the same way. System A may have a counterparty named JPMorgan Chase, and System B may represent the same counterparty as JPMC. When administrators map the data from System A to System B, they may need to rename the data in each record where that value appears.

The *load* step deposits the extracted and transformed data in its new home. Much like extracting data, loading data can be done in different ways as required by the destination system. Many systems have specified data formats and documented APIs for loading data. Storage media such as databases may require invoking a stored procedure or by calling SQL.

Reviewing ETL software requirements

REMEMBER

Here are some common ETL framework requirements to ensure the process goes smoothly and without problems:

>> The software must be able to handle input data from various formats. At minimum, these should include flat files (.csv), XML, MS SQL (Microsoft SQL Server), Oracle, and NoSQL (non-structured query language databases such as MongoDB or Hadoop). Ideally, the software should also be able to consume data using APIs.

>> The software must be able to perform complex data transformations. At a minimum, it should be able to combine data from multiple sources, use sources as lookup resources, and modify data according to an outside formula (for example, appending a date column to a table row of data).

>> The software must be able to log the transformation process and indicate any errors with data consumption.

>> The transformation process should be capable of running programmatically. In other words, you should be able to call the process as part of a separate application or a script.

>> The software must allow for connection to multiple systems in an enterprise scenario. Ideally, you should be able to configure it to access new systems without having to change the code or recompile.

>> The software must be able to push transformed client data to multiple destination formats. At a minimum, this should include flat file (.csv), XML, MS SQL, Oracle, and NoSQL. In an ideal world, the framework should also allow simple programmatic data upload to systems via APIs.

>> While some of the processes may require technical expertise to handle the most intricate transformations, as large a portion of the process as possible should require little to no prior technical expertise.

Some common ETL tools include Talend, Informatica, and Microsoft SSIS.

Managing Market Data

In finance, *market data* refers to data that changes with the financial markets. Market data can include trade and price-related data for a financial instrument, such as an equity, bond, swap, or option, that is reported by an exchange, clearinghouse, broker platform, over-the-counter (OTC) market desk, or other such quoting medium. Because market data changes with time and is applicable only for the time period in which it's quoted, it can also be considered time-series data. Market data is meaningful only if it's collected in tandem with the underlying static and reference data on which it depends.

Static data, in contrast, doesn't change often. Examples include conventions, calendars, and time zones. Static data may need versioning based on the frequency at which it may change. Having accurate static data is essential because the same market data may imply or mean very different statistics about an instrument if the underlying static and/or reference data conventions change.

The following sections discuss cleansing, normalizing, segmenting, and storing market data.

Cleansing and normalizing market data

In finance, the same data may have multiple data vendors, which may use different conventions in quoting the same data. The market data quoted for many similar instruments may also use a different underlying set of assumptions. Consequently, you can't compare and integrate the data collected from various sources and for different instruments without first transforming the raw data into a common data format. Also, some data points may have stale or missing data due to inefficiencies in data collection, so you may need to filter and cleanse the data.

The process of filtering, adjusting, and bridging market data based on certain criteria to enhance its quality is called *market data cleansing.* The process of converting the raw data into a common data format while cleansing, filtering, scaling, and adjusting the data is called *data normalization.* Figure 11-2 shows the different facets of data normalization and data cleansing.

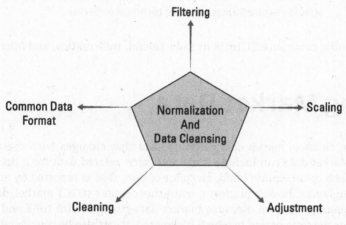

FIGURE 11-2: Methods of data normalization and cleansing.

TECHNICAL STUFF

The raw data may also be augmented with other data that's thought to be useful. Data is needed to provide some basic information required in determining value and risk in financial operations. Smoothing curves and volatility surfaces for rates and foreign exchange data is an example of this type of enhancement. In addition, certain derived data fields obtained during the process of normalization, such as calculation of mean and standard deviation, can be saved along with the normalized data.

Segmenting and storing market data

Poorly managed data poses problems in every stage of the data management process, especially data retrieval and storage efficiency. A simple approach to circumvent this problem is to categorize or separate data based on different parameters, such as time, instrument type, vendors, asset class, snapshots, and regions. *Data segmentation* is the strategy of dividing the data into logical data sets that are easier to work with. Segmentation is particularly useful when working with market data because new data points are constantly being added, and over time the data set can become enormous.

The type of retrieval process also dictates the way the data may be segmented. Here are some examples of different segmentation types:

>> **Time:** Because market data is time-series data, it makes sense to divide it according to time periods. Creating a new archive/collection per day is one of the industry-standard ways to segment the market data based on time.

>> **Asset class and instrument type:** Segmenting the market data based on asset class and/or instrument type optimizes the user's ability to manipulate and store the data in a meaningful way. For example, you may separate equity, bond, and commodity prices.

>> **Vendors:** A best practice is to keep market data from different vendors separate. Vendors may handle and process data differently, and their data can reflect different ways of expressing conventions and reflect different underlying assumptions. The normalized market data may contain a subset or a complete set of market data that differs from that offered by each vendor.

>> **Regions:** The same market data may be recorded in different regions from different sources. For example, the same equity may be listed in different exchanges of the world in different currencies, or in the case of market data vendors, the price of the same equity may be received from different feeds segmented by regions.

>> **Snapshots:** It may be useful to retrieve data by specific snapshots, such as "nyc close" (a snapshot at close of New York markets) and "nyc open" (a snapshot at opening of New York markets), and thus decide to segment the market data accordingly.

Dealing with Databases

Traditionally, organizations have stored their data in relational databases like Oracle, Db2, Microsoft SQL Server, Sybase, and PostgreSQL. However, with the advent of new database models, NoSQL databases are now becoming increasingly popular. No matter what database type you're using, architecting a good database model is still one of the key design areas in a good data management solution.

The database design may influence many facets of data management, such as ease of data retrieval, data retrieval time, and cost and volume of data that the data management platform can handle. As we explain in this section, to overcome these limitations, newer types of integrated data management systems, such as data warehouses and data lakes, are used.

Data warehouses

As enterprises continue to grow, they collect more and more data from different sources, such as new vendors, enterprise resource planning (ERP) systems, legacy systems, internal systems, and so on. Over time, they may end up with several independent systems that don't talk to each other.

Here are some ways to remedy that situation:

>> **Data porting:** An organization ports over all the data collected to date to the latest vendor or in-house data management platform. The old systems are then decommissioned.

>> **Data priming:** An organization may choose to extract, transform, and load the data from the original source (provided it has maintained the original source) over to the new data management solution, thus bypassing the data management systems in place as of the day.

>> **Data warehousing:** A data warehousing system stores data in a cleansed and systematic way, with rules that make access and interoperability possible. Warehousing can coexist with the other data management systems, acting as a central bridge that different data management systems can use to interact with each other. In addition, the storage systems data warehousing systems use are optimized for bulk upload and bulk analysis and may come with integrated tools to manage and analyze it. One example is Amazon Redshift.

WARNING

Using multiple data warehouses may result in data duplication between warehouse storage systems and the other data management system the organization employs. This problem often needs to be addressed in banks and insurance institutions, where a great number of legacy systems and databases are being delivered over many unique interfaces and reports.

Data lakes

A *data lake* is a centralized data storage solution that can store different kinds of data and that has integrated analytical tools for working with the data. A data lake can enable users and administrators to easily query and analyze data, regardless of its type or source.

REMEMBER

Data lakes and data warehouses aren't interchangeable terms. A data lake is raw data that hasn't been processed or defined, and a data warehouse is a defined database that houses structured, cleansed data used for specific operations and functions. Unlike a data warehouse, a data lake takes the approach of collecting all the data without normalizing or establishing all the relationships between the different data sets.

WARNING

Organizations can analyze data from a data warehousing or database solution, using a separate compatible data analysis system. However, unless those creating and administering the system understand the data's use cases very well, such a system is likely to be of limited usefulness. Coherent integration may never be achieved between the data storage/retrieval systems and the data analysis system. For the more advanced and complicated use cases, such as real-time data processing (stream processing) and bulk analysis (big data), the seamless integration of these needs isn't yet achievable.

Thus, one of the use cases of a data lake is to provide a data management solution integrated with data analytics modules. Such an integrated system can perform various kinds of simple, advanced, and customized data analysis in bulk. The storage systems in a data lake are optimized for many different use cases for the same data. Additionally, most data lake solutions (such as Metabase and Tableau) come bundled with various kinds of reporting, visualization, machine learning, pattern matching tools, and advanced analytical software for easy use and adoption.

In Figure 11-3, the diagram shows a data lake system interacting with different data stores, including real-time data, and providing integrated analytics for all data sources.

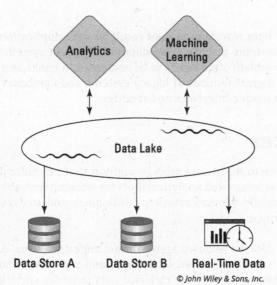

FIGURE 11-3: The input of raw data into a data lake and the distribution of that data into varied data stores for specific uses, including real-time delivery.

Maintaining Data Lineage

Data lineage means establishing the linkage between source data and derived data through every data transformation step so that it's possible to trace back several steps to identify the original source of data elements.

Many kinds of historical analyses require the exact snapshots of data to be present in the database as of a particular day in the past. To ensure data accuracy, a historical snapshot must be maintained for each insert/delete/update operation. This process is called *data historization*.

You can take several approaches to handle data historization. The best choice depends on the kind of database used and the kind of data model chosen. Here are some ways to retain historical information for a relational database:

>> **Having validity fields with an audit log:** Every row in the table must have a "valid from" and a "valid to" field. In every insert operation, the "valid from" field of the new row is set to be the current time stamp at the time of insertion, while "valid to" field is left blank. Every delete operation marks the "valid to" field to be the current time stamp while leaving the row in the database intact. Every update implemented is a combination of a delete plus insert operation.

>> **Creating temporal/system data versioned tables:** If the database tables' schema (structure) changes over time, it's difficult to use validity fields without creating new tables for a historical data model. To accommodate the need for historical records, scheduled snapshot tables can be created at certain intervals (for example, at the start of each day). The old tables are then preserved (snapshotted), and the new tables becomes the active tables. This process is also done for every operation that alters the table's current schema. Therefore, every snapshotted table version could have its own schema. Many database systems like MS SQL Server and PostgreSQL have this feature built into the software.

>> **Creating views and/or stored procedures:** The application can remain agnostic to the data model used for historical versioning of data. It does this by creating views and/or stored procedures for calling the application.

For a NoSQL database, the techniques are different. Increasingly, NoSQL database types are being mined and used in the financial industry. The type of data found in NoSQL comes in mainly four different varieties, as follows:

>> Column based (like an Excel spreadsheet)

>> Document based (like a rich text format or a standard Microsoft doc)

>> Key value pair (hash tables with key types and values)

>> Graph or visual-based stores (like Neo4j)

TIP

Utilization of this form of data presents unique issues. As most NoSQL databases don't have a fixed schema, the need to create temporal tables whenever a change occurs in the schema of the data doesn't arise. By just following the methodology of having "valid from" and "valid to" fields as previously described, a historization of data sets is achieved. In addition, an auxiliary field called the "version id" should be created and used by the data extraction code to model the database entity to the application level object entity.

Breaking Down Big Data

Data analytics begins by identifying the data analysis parameters to be used. This process is like the way a machine learning algorithm identifies what features and how many features its program uses. Defining these criteria may seem apparent to a subject matter expert (SME), but some of the criteria may be quite experimental or arcane.

For example, some of the statistics/parameters that an analysis requires may be derived, and to determine their usefulness, you must understand the correlations between the basic and derived parameters and the ultimate parameter being analyzed. For example, you'd need different derived parameters to determine a cost function than you would for a simple data visualization.

Here are the steps for creating a road map for the data analytics process:

1. **Define the analysis objective.**

   The objective that the business team has stated may be too vague to determine the end goal. Concepts like "optimize productivity" and "reduce cost" are too general and need to be broken into smaller, better-defined objectives, such as "which trading desk has the highest return on capital in the last quarter." The purpose of this step is to quantify the objective of optimization/analysis mathematically.

2. **Disassemble the data.**

   The data may be stored in formats in which the correlation between different entities isn't apparent or transparent. For time-series data, one of the additional factors to analyze the data is over time (as one of the dimensions). Good knowledge of the subject matter is a necessity for this step.

3. **Analyze.**

   When the data has been disassembled into a data format and data sets more suitable for analysis, you can apply a multitude of analytical algorithms and peruse the results for both quantitative and qualitative insights. You can use the insights thus gathered to fine-tune and enhance the first two steps to come out with better analysis.

Differentiating between Structured and Unstructured Data

Myriad data sources may exist within an organization, some of which are untapped. (For example, click logs on an e-commerce site may not have been mined for useful information.) Based on how the data is sourced/tapped, you can divide the data broadly into three different categories:

>> **Structured data:** This is the data received from well-structured sources like ERP systems and databases. Working with this data is fairly easy because it's usually already cleansed and filtered and available in a readily consumable format.

>> **Unstructured data:** This data isn't in structured database format and is often abstract and in a raw format. In fact, it may not be readily gatherable, storable, or analyzable. It may never have been gathered/tapped and stored because it was thought to be of no great use. This data may need to go through multiple cycles of cleansing, filtering, and other adjustments to transform it into a storable and analyzable format.

>> **Semi-structured data:** This kind of data is somewhere between structured and unstructured. It may be readily available in a loosely defined structure or self-describing structure, but not in a ready-to-use storage or analysis format. An example may be data in JSON or XML format obtained from some legacy system. You may need to disassemble/remodel this data into a standard format.

Comparing SQL and NoSQL

Databases can be categorized as either SQL (which stands for *structured query language*) or NoSQL (as you may guess, this stands for *non-structured query language or non-relational query*). Here's a quick look at each of those and the differences between them.

SQL databases

SQL is a well-established and very popular set of protocols for constructing database queries. SQL is the main language for any kind of operation on SQL databases and provides a very powerful interface for different kinds of database operations. SQL can easily handle complex queries across multiple data sources.

SQL databases, also known as *relational databases* (or relational database management systems [RDBMS]), are a category of databases that use SQL or SQL-like language for different kinds of database operations, such as insertion and deletion. Examples include MS SQL Server, Oracle, and PostgreSQL. SQL databases historically have been at the forefront of data management solutions. SQL databases store the data into fixed-schema storage objects called *relations* (or *tables*). All data stored in a table needs to conform to the same schema of the table. Every data entry into the table is called a *tuple* (or *row*, or *record*).

SQL databases are optimized for storing data in normalized format where relations (tables) can be linked with foreign keys. For example, an "Orders" table and an "Order Details" table could have a relationship between them that links each ordered item with a particular order.

Schema (structure) changes are possible in SQL databases but an expensive operation, and all data needs to conform to the new schema after schema change. For example, if you change the maximum length of a field, the data must be checked to make sure no entries violate the new limit.

You have probably heard the term *refactored* used in the context of legacy systems. To refactor data means to modify its schema to improve and modernize the way the data is deployed. As the applications are refactored and more new data is stored over time, SQL databases can become fragmented in terms of normalization and can require significant effort to maintain data normalization. *Normalization* is the restructuring of databases to a predetermined set of norms to optimize performance.

TIP

SQL databases aren't good candidates for in-memory data caching (storing data that is required very often in the main memory for speed); data caching is to be handled at the application level.

NoSQL Databases

NoSQL databases are primarily document, object, graph, or wide-column store databases. Most popular NoSQL databases are document databases, such as Mongo and Cassandra. As the name specifies, unlike the SQL databases, they don't have SQL-like language for different kinds of database operations. Instead, most NoSQL databases have their own nonstandardized language for database (DB) operations, which differs from one database to another.

NoSQL databases store data in a nonfixed schema storage objects called *collections*. A collection is roughly equivalent to a relation or table in an SQL database. Each data entry in a collection is called a *document*, which is roughly equivalent to a tuple or record. Queries are document-focused. Each document can be represented in a JSON-like key-value pairs structure.

NoSQL databases are optimized for storing hierarchical data similar to data represented in JSON format. NoSQL data can be easily cached, because each record represents a document in a standard format (JSON) and is uniquely identifiable.

NoSQL databases, unlike SQL databases, are easy to adapt with schema changes, and little effort is required to optimize the data storage and retrieval. Consequently, NoSQL databases are good for situations with no consistent schema (structure) across the various data sources and where the relationships between different data entities isn't known beforehand and is expected to change over time.

WARNING

The query facilities available in NoSQL databases aren't very advanced and the database isn't very efficient at executing complex queries. Therefore, NoSQL isn't a good choice for situations where complicated data analysis is required.

Chapter **12**

Adapting for Future Technologies

FinTech has already dramatically changed the financial industry, and even more changes are still to come. In this chapter, we tell you about some of the exciting new technologies that have recently started finding their way into the industry and started shaking things up, including artificial intelligence, machine learning, chat bots, and alternative data sources.

Harnessing the Power of Artificial Intelligence

Artificial intelligence (AI) has in recent years captured the public imagination with compelling demonstrations of both novel and practical applications. Voice recognition in virtual assistant devices and apps, facial recognition on social media, self-driving cars — these are but a few of the more prominent examples. For FinTech firms, the use cases include AI-enabled investment management, credit analytics, anomaly detection, data de-noising, data generation, and autonomous decision-making, among others.

The following sections define AI, describe artificial neural networks used in AI, and explain how AI works in FinTech.

A BRIEF HISTORY OF ARTIFICIAL INTELLIGENCE

In many ways, artificial intelligence (AI) isn't new today's breathtaking headlines notwithstanding. Craftsmen have been building realistic humanoid automatons since at least 1000 BCE in China. Ancient Egyptians and Greeks built automatons in the form of sacred statues, which worshippers believed were imbued with minds, wisdom, and emotion. The Muslim scholar, inventor, and mechanical engineer Ismail al-Jazari was making programmable automata in the 13th century CE.

The modern era of AI began in the 1950s with individuals like John McCarthy, a Stanford mathematician who first coined the term. The objective was to start with computers that could play games like checkers and chess using some of the earliest IBM mainframes. The heart of this endeavor wasn't merely entertainment. It was to study and ultimately build intelligent machines as part of our everyday lives, starting with use cases that were familiar to most people in order to demonstrate automated decision-making.

In fact, for decades, practical, commercial demonstrations of AI flourished mainly in games as a means to give players credible challenges and plausible help. For instance, the ghosts in *Pac-Man* (1980), Inky, Pinky, Blinky, and Clyde, were AI-driven. In 2010, DeepMind, using a technique called reinforcement learning (which we discuss later) demonstrated how an artificial neural network (ANN) could learn how to play Atari 2600-style *Breakout* (1976). Games like these and many more have played an outsize role in AI because they're fun and familiar and because they don't risk lives or livelihoods. In other words, whether the AI fails or succeeds, nobody gets hurt.

Apart from games, academia, simulations, manufacturing, and (we can reasonably assume) some classified, national security applications, AI has struggled through repeated cycles of excitement and anticipation followed by disappointment and concern. The reasons for these AI "summers" and "winters" aren't simple. Yet the underlying technology evolves rapidly, and we know from decades of study and experience that some AI problems are far more challenging and nuanced than previously thought. For instance, in the early 1950s, AI researchers predicted that computers would play chess at grandmaster level within a decade. However, IBM's chess machine *Deep Blue* (1997) wouldn't defeat the reigning human champion, Gary Kasparov, until nearly the end of the century — 50 years later than expected.

In 2017, *Time* magazine published a special issue, *Artificial Intelligence: The Future of Humankind*. It covered the major modern themes of AI like ANNs, natural language processing, big data, quantum computing, and Kurzweil's singularity, which posits the emergence of self-aware machines. Such possibilities have stirred anticipation as well as anxiety among the public at large and some of the world's leading scientists and technology experts. In 2015, Elon Musk, Stephen Hawking, and prominent AI experts published an open letter warning of unintended consequences posed by AI that include loss of jobs, violation of privacy rights, and discrimination among AI's "existential risks." According to "Transforming Paradigms: A Global AI in Financial Services Survey," University of Cambridge scholars in 2020 found that 47 percent of 151 firms surveyed believe that AI will exacerbate rather than reduce biases, for instance, in pricing and lending practices.

Defining AI

REMEMBER

The definition of AI is fairly straightforward: automation of a task believed to require "natural intelligence" to complete. AI research and development has traditionally focused on these five areas:

>> **Robots:** Robots used in manufacturing were some of the earliest commercially successful applications of AI that represent an interdisciplinary approach incorporating information processing, mechanical engineering, power engineering, and material science. Today, robots are routinely employed in healthcare, law enforcement, extraction (for example, oil and gas discovery and drilling), surveillance drones, interplanetary exploration, toys, and education (for example, LEGO Mindstorms), to name just a few applications.

>> **Computer vision:** This complements robotics but has its own specialized applications in surveillance, facial recognition, video motion tracking, and autonomous vehicles.

>> **Natural language processing (NLP):** Most people have probably experienced NLP through telephone customer service help, in which it's possible to use usually simple speech commands and requests to navigate the menu system. This same technology also powers virtual assistant devices (such as Alexa, Google Assistant, and Siri), email reading, and contract/content analysis.

>> **Expert systems:** These typically provide some level of decision support that emulates human decision-making in interpreting data sets that may incorporate, for instance, digital imagery. An obvious application is in computer aided diagnosis (CAD) for healthcare, but CAD systems also exist for automotive servicing, equipment troubleshooting, workflow processing, and command and control operations.

> » **Artificial life:** Artificial life is a broad range of techniques that look to nature for inspiration and clues on how to tackle difficult problems. There are many use cases that include transportation scheduling, circuit design, training robots, code breaking, forensic construction of facial composites, and so on. Of particular interest for FinTech firms are valuation of real options, portfolio optimization, design of automated trading systems, and representing rational agents in economic models like the cobweb model, which seeks to explain price fluctuations in a given market.

Breaking down artificial neural networks

Figure 12-1 is a simplified depiction of a biological neural network (BNN) that you may find in the central nervous system. Neurotransmitters bind to specific sites of the dendrite, causing voltage changes in the cell. Those voltage changes travel through the cell body, down the axon, to the synaptic terminal. The synaptic terminal releases neurotransmitters that bind to the dendrites of nearby interneurons. These networks learn by potentiating connections between neurons.

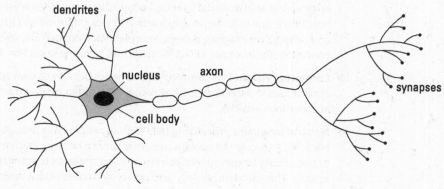

FIGURE 12-1:
An interneuron in the central nervous system.

© John Wiley & Sons, Inc.

Artificial neural networks (ANNs) are mathematical models of BNNs and are core to many machine learning applications (we discuss machine learning later in this chapter). The way that ANNs replicate the behaviors seen in BNNs has long been a source of enthusiasm and speculation about AI's potential.

Figure 12-2 shows a type of ANN known as a feedforward multilayer perceptron. The ANN receives data from the world via the input layer (the X1, X2 . . . Xn nodes), integrates the inputs at the hidden layer (H1, H2 . . . Hk nodes), and forwards the final results to the output layer (Y1, Y2 . . . Ym nodes). The ANN learns by changing numerical values of weights represented by the lines between nodes of the layers.

This class of feedforward multilayer perceptron is among the simplest ANN and forms the basis of many other ANNs such as deep-learning architectures that have complex ("deep") hidden layers.

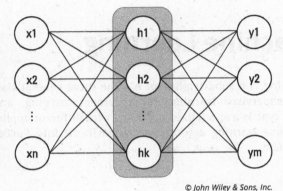

© John Wiley & Sons, Inc.

REMEMBER ANNs represent a connectionist approach to AI — in other words, it's all about the connections between nodes. There are also population approaches. For example, ant colony algorithms attempt to mimic how ants learn through decentralized control to find food and other resources. Genetic algorithms use natural selection techniques to learn through survival of the fittest. There are also Monte Carlo approaches, Bayesian approaches, decision trees, and so on, each of which learns through its own unique method. AI has many machine learning techniques, and the challenge is knowing what kinds of problems are best suited to which approaches.

Exploring how AI fits into FinTech

AI excels at problems in which it's otherwise infeasible to enumerate all possible inputs and outputs. A lot of what goes on in banking is fixed and quantifiable, so it doesn't benefit from AI. For instance, you wouldn't use AI for credit card validation because it's just a simple database lookup. The bank knows all the credit cards and numbers it has on file. The application could just look up a given credit card in the database to determine its status and credit availability.

REMEMBER However, AI is very helpful when the task is more subtle. For example, consider credit analytics. Suppose that the task is to monitor credit card usage for each account, looking for unusual patterns of purchases that may indicate the card has been stolen. This is a great job for AI. To make such determinations, AI considers the patterns — that is, transactions, establishments, times of year, locations, amounts, and so on. If it notices something anomalous, it queries the customer and then learns based on the customer's approval or rejection of the transaction. Over time, the ANN (see the preceding section) becomes very good at monitoring the usage of each account and alerting customer service representatives of anything out of the ordinary for a particular customer.

Leveraging Machine Learning

Machine learning is a subdiscipline of AI. The three general classes of machine learning are supervised learning, reinforcement learning, and unsupervised learning. Each type is a specialized approach with different applications. Any one of these machine learning algorithms can easily fit into FinTech. Figure 12-3 summarizes them.

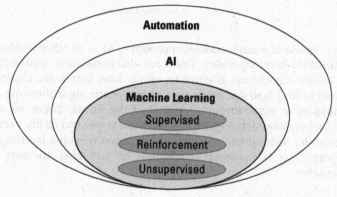

FIGURE 12-3: Three classes of machine learning.

© John Wiley & Sons, Inc.

Supervised learning

In supervised learning, developers train the AI to make an association between a label and a corresponding correct answer. The training in general can be slow, and the goal is for the AI to learn with an acceptable error tolerance. That tolerance isn't usually 0 percent because that's not usually mathematically feasible. A 0 percent error tolerance may even be undesirable because developers want the AI to make generalizations for labels it hasn't been trained on instead of overfitting the data.

Any of the machine learning algorithms we mention earlier can easily fit into FinTech. Here's an example of how supervised learning may fit. The idea for the capital markets may be to use a data-driven, model-free approach to pricing derivatives rather than a model-based approach. A model may be very specific mathematically but inaccurately measured against quoted prices. Often the model makes simplifying assumptions that leave out some unobserved or unobservable variables. An ANN could be trained using supervised learning to price derivatives based on observed quotes of how markets behave in fact rather than how they are supposed to behave in theory.

Reinforcement learning

In reinforcement learning, developers don't have labels and answers but rather an objective — that is, they train the AI to maximize some reward. In an ideal situation, the AI learns increasingly more correct responses on the basis of optimizing the signal. The training reinforces learning by more or less positive feedback. For instance, we could train an AI to optimize data processing while pricing a set of portfolios to minimize the standard deviation of runtime. The input provided would be the number of instruments in the portfolio and tenors of the instruments in the portfolio.

Unsupervised learning

Unsupervised learning has no labels, correct answers, or even objectives per se. Instead, the AI discovers extant patterns and acquires this new knowledge on its own. For instance, streaming music services initially don't know how to serve songs to new listeners. However, through their choices, listeners provide hints or clues about their preferences, and over time the AI builds up a database of what the listener *may* like to hear. It may recognize that in the morning, a listener often chooses upbeat music from the '80s and in the evening, contemporary downtempo. The AI could also play musically related songs (for example, cool jazz) based on patterns from listeners in the same age group and zip code or with similar buying habits it learns through third-party data sources.

Making the Most of Chat Bots

FinTech firms mostly employ long-established, simple machine learning algorithms rather than complex solutions. These could be as basic as regression analysis, cluster analysis, and time-series forecasting. However, in 1950, Alan Turing, a British mathematician, proposed the idea of sophisticated software that engages users through interactive conversation. The "Turing test" asks users whether they're conversing with a real person or a machine. If the user can't distinguish the difference, the bot passes the test for being "intelligent."

Some software embodiments of the Turing test are websites that "chat" with users for customer support. Some client sites provide Level 1 support via a free chat bot service, reserving premium service through a human agent for customers with a paid subscription. Whether the chat bot support option is convincing and worthwhile, free or otherwise, is beyond the scope of this chapter. Suffice it to say that virtual assistants represent the state of the art in chat bot natural language processing (NLP).

Chat bots hold promise to readily dovetail with FinTech. For instance, Payjo provides AI-powered "conversational banking" through messaging (for example, text messaging and Facebook Messenger) to enhance the digital banking experience. Chat bots offer reduced operational and support costs for the enterprise by answering basic questions, hassle-free operations, cross-selling, and real-time, natural communication with customers. These bots also hold potential to widen the customer base by providing differently-abled consumers with speech transcription and synthesis services. A well-designed chat bot is channel agnostic, can seamlessly interpret in different languages, is available 24/7, is instantaneously cognizant of customer preferences, and learns continuously from customer feedback.

TIP

For the latest information about chat bots, check out *Chat Bots Magazine* (https://chatbotsmagazine.com).

Checking Out Alternative Data Sources

For much of the modern history of AI, data sets were varied but mostly small in volume and complexity. For instance, the iris flower data set, which is a benchmark for machine learning often taught to students, has only 150 records each with just five features: the sepal length and width, the petal length and width, and the flower species classification. Data of this nature could be handled on single-code machines.

With the advent of big data, however, new approaches have become necessary that often require parallel and distributed systems (such as Hadoop) to process the data. Here are just a few examples of big data sets:

>> The Landsat-8 satellite photographs the Earth's complete land surface every five days, generating high-resolution optical data that is freely available online.

>> There are IRS 990 records that include 3 million files and hundreds of features on nonprofit organizations' finances.

>> In 2019, there were more than 200 million active websites in the world, and an estimated 200 billion tweets were active and all freely available online.

TECHNICAL STUFF

Data Science Central maintains a list of the top 20 free resources for big data that include data.gov, the United States Census Bureau, the European Union Open Data Portal, data.gov.uk, Amazon Web Services public data, Facebook Graph, Google Trends, and so forth. For FinTech, there is Google Finance, Financial Times Market Data, the UN Comtrade Database containing international trade statistics, World Bank Open Data, IMF Data — the list is long.

According to researchers, one of the major obstacles to AI for FinTech companies is access to data. However, the central issue goes beyond mere quantity. For instance, some data sets contain missing, invalid, and/or hacked values. What good is AI if it learns from the wrong data? There's also provenance, trust, rights, privacy, and so on — all that may need to be assured prior to analysis for AI purposes.

Given that all these issues have been addressed, AI algorithms still can't accept prices, zip codes, pixels, audio samples, and so on directly from the real world. Data must first be normalized or encoded on input and denormalized or decoded on output for human interpretation. Finally, if the AI is to be productionized, resources are needed to process the data on a regular basis. Whether through dedicated infrastructure or cloud services, this kind of operationalization isn't a trivial undertaking and often requires systems and process engineers.

In the following sections, we talk about alternative data sources: companies and devices used, its role in the financial industry, and its sourcing, compliance, and regulation.

Companies and devices involved in alternative data

Many big data resources are free, but the quality and/or formats aren't always assured or structured for ready processing. As such, hundreds of companies are lining up to provide fee-based data and/or data services, including Google, Amazon, IBM, Microsoft, Oracle, Teradata, and SAS Institute. These companies all employ AI to parse and organize the raw data into useful information.

AI techniques excel at identifying patterns and distilling insights from large, complex, interlinked data sets. The ubiquity of devices, including smartphones, cameras, GPS devices, and other Internet of Things (IOT) devices, has led to a huge increase in the amount and range of alternative data sets. Some examples include browsing activity logs, credit card transaction data, social media posts, photos, videos, point-of-sale system data, weather data, satellite images, reviews, online comments, and local news.

Using AI for image and video recognition, natural language processing, machine learning algorithms, and the power of cloud computing, many of these data sets can now be "mined" efficiently. The insights from these algorithms feed expert systems that aid decision-making.

Marketing promotions in retail and credit cards have been using such data sets for many years. Famously, a story circulated that Target was able to predict pregnancy before anyone else by examining customer transaction data sets. Although the story itself is probably apocryphal, alternative data sets and AI have been indispensable for the retail marketing business processes.

Alternative data in the financial industry

In the financial industry, alternative data sets have helped companies prepare precise, targeted promotions or prequalify individuals based on their credit history as well as alternative data sets. For example, bringing together detailed transaction history with demographic information as well as social media activity may help predict someone's need for an investment product or a higher credit line. In the wealth management industry, robo-advisors that rely on a broad array of available data sets are helping bring personalized, data-driven investment advice at a lower cost than traditional wealth management models.

While trading models have historically relied on traditional financial data, such as stock prices and volatilities, we are now seeing increasing use of alternative data sets such as social media or news for sentiment analysis that helps generate investment alpha (return on investment in comparison to a market index). In high-frequency trading, or any trading activity involving high volumes, quants are now purchasing and sourcing alternative data sets that may aid decision-making. In an era where markets are driven heavily by policy, it can be a huge advantage to predict policy based on unofficial farm-roll statistics from transactions data or real-estate data from web platforms like Zillow before the official statistics are published.

Sourcing, compliance, and regulation

Historically, alternative data has been collected directly from the original source, such as by accessing website logs or digitally scraping news from news websites. However, alternative data sets are now available from specialist data vendors as well as many well-known data vendors such as Quandl or Lexis Nexis.

REMEMBER

In the financial industry, it's especially important to keep all relevant compliance standards in mind when using alternative data sets. While compliance and regulatory standards around alternative data sets are still evolving, some regulations such as the General Data Protection Regulation (GDPR) in Europe set clear restrictions around the capture, retention, and transfer of personal data. In fact, most jurisdictions have rules in place or privacy laws that cover the capture, transmission, and use of personally identifiable information (PII). We introduce the role of regulation in FinTech in Chapter 3.

Also, care must be taken to avoid the use of certain types of data that can lead to biases in the model and create the potential for ethical and legal challenges. An example of this type of issue is the use of ethnicity or religion for credit scoring during card or loan approval, which would be a clear violation of laws.

3 Working with FinTech Companies

Chapter **13**

Deciding Whether to Build, Buy, or Partner

A company decides it needs a new piece of software. So begins the traditional build versus buy versus partner discussion.

For what is potentially a major budgetary spend, the decision-making process can be subjective and inconsistent. Within most organizations, big or small, vested interests will argue vehemently for one approach or the other, and everyone believes he is right!

When faced with an important business decision — such as how to acquire new software capabilities — it's helpful to start by asking, "What problem are we trying to solve?" A small start-up business will understand its problems very clearly. However, as businesses grow and require more technology development, it's surprising how many forget that basic, core question. In many cases, decision-making becomes more about internal politics than problem-solving.

A major financial decision should always be based on how best to meet the company's requirements. Moreover, firms need to decide how critical the development is to their business and what revenue or profitability it might generate. Based on this evaluation, they can decide how critical it is to prioritize the development now and whether the company has the domain expertise to build and maintain the solution itself.

WARNING

What *shouldn't* happen is that the internal IT department decides that it can roll out a major new IT initiative without any special expertise in that area. The project then invariably takes longer, costs more, and is of inferior quality compared to a solution from a third-party vendor.

Many IT projects end up being a combination of build and buy. The decision can become more of an art than a science, figuring out which pieces to build and which pieces to buy. In this chapter, we walk you through the points to consider when deciding the best way to acquire new software capabilities. While some of the points may seem like common sense, many companies overlook quite a few important considerations.

Transforming Your Company Digitally

The "build, buy, or partner" decisions are all part of the overarching digital transformation strategies that financial institutions across the world are currently pursuing.

Digital transformation is a recurring point of debate for board members. Analysts are valuing digital companies more favorably than traditional financial institutions. At the same time, the majority of large-scale digital innovation programs fail, and therefore businesses see digital transformation as a significant risk factor. Research has shown that 70 percent of complex, large-scale change programs don't reach their stated goals.

REMEMBER

Here are some of the top reasons digital transformation programs fail:

>> **Lack of ownership and digital transformation skills at the top:** A company's CEO and all senior management personnel must drive its digital transformation. Success is determined not only by keeping up with business challengers but also by adopting the applicable strategies to compete with tech giants and cooperate with FinTech start-ups. Companies that don't have appropriate FinTech and digital governance at the helm are likely to face ongoing complicated and costly issues.

>> **Not changing the business model when change is needed:** While developing and launching new services and products profitably is difficult, reinventing a bank's or asset manager's business model is even harder. Business model changes are often necessary, however, because of the way technological changes affect systemic processes. Senior management must be integrally involved in business model changes, as such changes often involve reallocating capital across various business units. The new model must be integrated across the entire institution.

NUMERIX: THE THIRD PIVOT

Numerix CEO Steve O'Hanlon faced several challenges as a chief executive during times of swiftly changing market environments. These were times when we witnessed the convictions of a man and entrepreneur on the front lines who, in the end, turned bold situations into positive opportunities, even if it required reinventing Numerix. As any good entrepreneur, Steve possesses a strong sense of confidence, built on years of leading, experimenting, taking risks, and always pushing hard for a company's growth — whether it's turning around a Numerix that was deeply struggling prior to 2004 or being the first in the industry to introduce new risk analytic offerings in 2009 in response to the global financial crisis.

Steve's goal was and is currently to position Numerix as a dynamic financial technology company providing a next-generation risk platform. In 2015, the company pivoted again, which started the process of establishing Numerix as a FinTech brand in the market. During this time, Steve positioned Numerix in a direction that broadened its visibility as a pricing and risk-calculation company into a provider of trading and risk management systems that are unique and disruptive to the status quo. As an example, he realized that legacy trading systems were too costly and time-consuming to upgrade from one major release to another. Banking consumers' needs and expectations had changed to real-time, on-demand responses. As a result, Steve has had Numerix leverage all the technological breakthroughs in the area of open source to ensure that the company doesn't reinvent the wheel with certain aspects of the technology stack but instead evolves in the areas that offer a competitive advantage. As such, a goal for Numerix development is to evolve its platform and core applications in the same manner as any SaaS offering, which is to ensure that upgrades happen on the fly and actually occur while people are using their products. At the time of this writing, Numerix is living the vision and offering early aspects of this.

This move to a transformative and disruptive identity can be accomplished only by someone who embraces and leads change in an organization. When dissatisfaction occurs with the present, Steve acquires a vision for how things should be and develops a clear plan for the steps that need to be taken. But he also understands that change is uncomfortable, which is why he cultivates an open, transparent culture that supports Numerix employees during transitions to accept the changes. Employees know why the changes are inevitable and important and why the company as a unit needs to get over the mental hurdle that change represents.

>> **A lack of customer focus:** Many firms focus on the internal benefits that the latest technologies can offer and forget the main reason for digitally transforming the business: their customers. They should be asking "Why are we doing this?" and understanding that the ultimate priority is to improve the customer experience and provide customers greater value.

>> **Inability to build a FinTech ecosystem:** McKinsey, one of the largest strategy and management consulting firms, has suggested that companies facing challenges need to consider the power of ecosystems, claiming that "by 2025, almost a third of total global sales will come from ecosystems." Your FinTech ecosystem is your network of relationships with start-ups, scale-ups, key industry partners, financial regulators, and the investment community. Financial institutions developing strategies focused on a digital platform need to offer the technology and operational infrastructure to attract the top FinTech firms, to collaborate via open APIs, and to present their services (either as a white-labeled offer incorporating the institution's brand or under the FinTech firm's brand) to the institution's clients.

>> **Skills deficits:** Employees must receive appropriate training to enable them to understand and apply the benefits of FinTech, lean start-up methodologies, and Agile development frameworks. Investing in a diverse and knowledgeable group that has adopted such skills can provide a crucial competitive benefit.

>> **Compensation models that don't reward intrapreneurship:** It's important that successful "intrapreneurs" — that is, people who take creative initiative for the benefit of the company — are appropriately compensated. However, many institutions maintain traditional rewards programs and bonus systems, in which taking risks and participating in effective change programs isn't highly valued. Such organizations will find that the best and brightest employees won't find in-house corporate transformation positions appealing. That means that employees who would excel in those positions may leave the firm to go work for a FinTech company.

Exploring Reasons to Build or Buy

Put yourself in the role of a chief technology officer (CTO) at a large bank. Your technology architecture is very old, and neither you nor your IT team wants to change too much too quickly. To rip out the old system and replace it immediately would be too costly and too risky. (If this were to go wrong, you'd have to look for another job!) You need a new technology solution that solves a given technology problem or meets a given opportunity, within a given budget, and that works on top of the old legacy system.

Table 13-1 summarizes the build versus buy decision-making process. Check out the details in the following sections.

TABLE 13-1   **Building versus Buying**

When to Build	When to Buy
You require control over development and functionalities, including regulatory requirements.	Third-party software is critical to maintain your business operations.
You need ad hoc applications specific to your business.	Available software addresses your problem, so there's no need to reinvent the wheel.
Your problem is unique to your firm, and there are no third-party vendor solutions.	The application can be used throughout the organization and interacts with core systems.
You need to solve a specific problem in a given silo of your business.	You want the greater flexibility and adaptability that comes with ready-made solutions.
The company has the resources to build, maintain, and support an application that is built by a team with relevant expertise and loyalty.	Your IT department doesn't have the relevant expertise to build, maintain, and support a custom application. Your IT department doesn't have the time and resources to continually collect user feedback and enhance the software.
A customized application gives your company a competitive advantage over competitors.	
You want to own the source code.	

Looking at reasons to build

Developing new software can be expensive, particularly if the build is large and complex, and can require a large team to build it. Nevertheless, many banks have traditionally opted for the build option, arguing that in-house development ensures better delivery. Internal IT teams tend to agree with that reasoning, having both a vested interest in job security and a delight at the prospect of building something new and interesting.

WARNING

But is that really the best approach? Often it isn't. Why?

» Research from the independent Forrester Group has shown that more than 50 percent of all banking consumer experience projects took longer than expected to complete, resulting in overspending. They also found that projects using (or reusing) internally built modules are more likely to suffer from overspend issues.

» A financial domino effect occurs later in the process, as internal projects are more likely to need further fixes and suffer from high maintenance costs. This ongoing burden takes time and resources from a team that should be focused on keeping the product up-to-date with the latest technological changes. This inevitably leads to architectural inflexibility in the software, with too many elements being hard coded, resulting in frustration both internally and externally. Moreover, because a project has cost so much initially, there's a natural tendency for management to continue to support it, even when the maintenance costs are quite high.

REMEMBER

So if building is such a quagmire, why would any company want to do it? Two compelling reasons to build are (1) that the built software will differentiate you from your competitors in a meaningful way, and (2) that what you want isn't available from a third party and can be considered an extension of an existing in-house application.

TIP

Consider what problem you're trying to solve by developing the technology. Is the particular issue you're attempting to answer connected in specific ways to your primary value proposition? If yes, or if you need a solution that's unique to your business, then you should build it as an ad hoc application that's specific to your business needs.

Of course, this assumes that you have a strong IT team capable of building and maintaining it, so you'll have total control over any development and features. Having control is particularly important if your team will need to install, integrate, support, and update the new software themselves. Because your team will have access to the source code, they can identify and fix any bugs internally to reduce downtime and promptly release updates that resolve any problems. Moreover, in today's environment, many firms are paranoid about data leakage, so maintaining both product and data within their own environment and having control of their own cybersecurity are priorities.

Some financial institutions will also want to maintain control of proprietary development that provides them with an edge over their competitors. For example, a company may have algorithms built by its internal quant teams that provide enhanced trade execution or insight into the market. In such cases, additional costs are justifiable to protect the associated intellectual property. Furthermore, integrating an external solution with such legacy technology can be a potential obstacle to buying external FinTech technology.

Checking out reasons to buy

Is buying the better option? In many cases, it is, but the right answer depends on the factors we explain earlier in this chapter. We review those now from a "buy" perspective.

The pros of buying

REMEMBER

First of all, is the particular issue you're attempting to answer connected in specific ways to your primary value proposition? If no, or if the answer isn't obvious, then buying an existing technology is frequently the better decision in today's technology environment. Your internal resources should be devoted to projects that directly support your core business practices.

Buying can also relieve your internal IT team of the burden of getting and staying up to speed on the latest technologies. Internal development teams are typically less familiar with the required code for a new initiative than third-party specialists are, and they are likely to underestimate the resource or time commitments required.

Buying can save money, which is important in today's financial industry. Capital adequacy requirements have increased to meet regulatory obligations post-2008/2009, and interest rates are low. These factors have led to a contraction in bank balance sheets. Financial institutions don't have the budgets to constantly finance new technology builds, so there's no appetite to build custom software that reinvents the wheel when it's readily available from third-party vendors.

The cons of buying

WARNING

Buying isn't a perfect solution, of course. The license costs to deploy the software can be significant, including annual maintenance costs and version upgrades or new modules further down the line. In addition, choosing a FinTech company can involve risks. If you go with an external provider that ultimately can't deliver on the project, or can't meet performance or security requirements, you're out considerable time and money. To avoid such problems, a tortuous onboarding process may be required, in which FinTech firms are subject to rigorous due diligence from the institution's procurement department and a full-scale information security audit to ensure that they meet the technology, cybersecurity, and/or encryption prerequisites. All of that vetting further extends an already long sales cycle and can seriously challenge a FinTech's company's ability to stay in business while it's waiting for the associated revenues from the contract.

As a result, a potential buy decision requires both the buyer and the FinTech provider to carefully evaluate the benefits of the proposed relationship. The buyer needs to reconcile the licensing costs for the product relative to an internal build. The FinTech provider needs to feel sufficiently rewarded by the licensing and other revenues to go through the onboarding pain imposed by the institution. The real benefit for both, though, is the shared cost of development among all the FinTech firm's clients. This sharing ultimately enables the FinTech firm to continue developing and enhancing the product.

NUMERIX: MEETING EVOLVING DEMANDS

Breaking through the mental hurdles brought about by the financial crisis and its subsequent regulatory remedies enabled Numerix by 2017 to absorb and overcome changing markets and quickly develop industry-leading products and services to meet evolving industry demands.

Steve O'Hanlon took this as an opportunity to figure out the 21st-century incarnation of what would make the company more successful as Numerix advanced toward the next decade. The major goals of Steve's turnaround plan were a new product strategy, a stronger focus on strategic partnerships with complementary technology firms, the development of the industry's strongest pool of quants, employing financial/software engineers and technology platform architects, and building out a more significant global presence.

There's no question each of these goals has been achieved. Today, Numerix is a global force in FinTech, with more than 20 offices, 700 clients, and 90 partners across more than 26 countries. Numerix is now recognized across the industry for its many breakthroughs in quantitative research and its dynamic stack of analytic capabilities, technology, and business services. The company is proud of its reputation for being able to price and risk-manage any derivative instrument — from vanillas to the most sophisticated exotic products. Numerix products and services are utilized in many forms on both the sell side and buy side, including banks, broker dealers, insurance firms, hedge funds, pension funds, and asset managers.

REMEMBER

Generally speaking, a FinTech firm will deliver better technology than an internal team, largely because it has a more developed knowledge of the new technology requirements and can deliver in a more agile way (certain top-tier banks with 10,000-plus developers may be exceptions to this rule). That's not to say that you couldn't hire a few IT specialists with the needed skills in data science, machine learning, blockchain, and other modern technologies, but they wouldn't be cheap, and you'd have to keep them on payroll full time, even when you weren't using their special skills. You'd also have to train your existing staff on the needed technologies, at even more expense. Buying IT expertise is very often a much better value than building internal expertise.

Finding the balance between new and legacy software

Legacy systems are a big problem for financial institutions. They spend a lot of money maintaining legacy systems that probably won't be able to handle future customers' needs. To survive and thrive in the FinTech era, traditional financial services firms have put digital-transformation projects at the top of their agendas. However, while most companies recognize the need to transform their businesses with technology, they struggle to understand how to implement that change and securely move away from their legacy systems.

Here's a very public example of failing to migrate from a legacy platform successfully. The U.K.-based TSB Bank attempted to migrate from its outdated, core banking system to a new digital platform. However, the new system failed, resulting in a period of operational chaos and consumer complaints that continued for more than a month. The magnitude of the problem was so great that the CEO lost his job and the Bank of England (BoE) and the Financial Conduct Authority (FCA) published a paper outlining the significance of operational requirements, warning banks that they would levy fines if service disorders lasted for a prolonged period. Fearing such a scenario in their own companies, many IT leaders have delayed implementing new digital transformation projects, even though they know they need those new technologies to survive.

REMEMBER

Thorough strategic planning is required to replace legacy systems with modern technology. You can't just abandon your current systems. While transitioning from the old system to the new, the new technology stack must peacefully coexist with the legacy systems, at least on a temporary basis. Many established players use FinTech firms as their development sandboxes, reviewing proofs of concept (or proofs of value, as has been more recently coined) using lab-style environments within hybrid cloud solutions. Being able to lab-test a new solution can help organizations plan system upgrades and apply new technologies in a "safe" environment.

Many financial institutions have also invested in application program interfaces (APIs). APIs can specify how software components should interact using a set of routines, protocols, and tools for building software applications. They enable banks to support new technologies more efficiently, work with FinTech firms, and potentially build out their own disruptive offerings. Established firms can add more agile solutions around their core legacy systems, as if they were "satellites" around the core. Banks can adopt alternative digital solutions to replace siloed technology, one at a time. Core technology can also be combined with FinTech firms' solutions through APIs to design market-ready digital products.

As part of this API economy, some financial institutions and larger vendors have developed a digital layer on top of their legacy platforms. This digital layer facilitates API integration with many FinTech firms, allowing them to introduce or withdraw digital offerings based on market response. However, at this point, the number of established players that consistently embrace such approaches is still quite limited.

Finding a FinTech Partner

Picking the right FinTech firms to team up with — the topic of this section — remains challenging for banks, because they're still developing their innovation culture for the new digital environment. For their part, FinTech firms need to better articulate the clear benefits of their technologies and better explain how they can work with banks to deliver change. More banks are lately building FinTech partnerships, motivated by shortages of in-house expertise and the desire to save time and money. In addition, the perception barriers that have previously prevented banks from partnering with FinTech firms seem to be diminishing as the partnerships increase.

The results of such partnerships have been mixed. Banks are still developing the innovation partnership model, and there are still major impediments, such as the time taken for procurement and information security onboarding and the difficulty in contractually defining a longer-term technology retention. This engagement process is also influenced by the contrasting sizes and cultures of the respective organizations, although many of the staff at the FinTech firms have come from banking backgrounds, so finding aligned expectations should be possible.

As part of this process, banks are steering or participating in many accelerators, incubators, and training programs. These initiatives ensure the banks early access to technology and talent without having to take an equity stake in the FinTech companies. Such arrangements offer FinTech companies access to resources, data, space, and networking opportunities to test and showcase their minimum viable product (MVP) while sometimes leading to funding as well.

REMEMBER

There's no single best approach on how to engage with FinTech firms. However, while banks are increasingly looking to such firms to drive innovation, whichever way they choose to partner, banks are still struggling to implement new technology successfully. Many banks are paying lip service to a partner approach in which a head of innovation is employed without having any specific remit or budget. This situation results in a gap with other areas of the organization that have the issues and the budget. Consequently, banks should evaluate whether their partnership models are aligned with their goals and should ensure that any innovation labs are addressing problems that business areas are actually experiencing. It's also critical that the banks commit to providing the necessary budget to implement the solutions if the proof of value proves successful.

TIP

All financial institutions that are looking to partner with FinTech firms need to review the onboarding processes that would be used when deploying the new technology. Procurement and information security processes could be better standardized for most onboarding across all financial institutions. In particular, the onboarding for a proof of concept should be immediate so that both partners can quickly (within a month or so) discover whether there's a fit.

CORPORATE VENTURE CAPITAL AND FinTech

Assuming there's a fit, corporate venture capital (CVC) entities should consider buying minority stakes in the most relevant FinTech firms. Doing so would fully acknowledge the importance of the technology and drive internal engagement with the FinTech firm. However, the CVC should be sufficiently removed from the FinTech firm so that the firm can continue to run its external business and potentially sell to the CVC's competitors. The main benefit that the CVC and its parent bank receive is the shorter time to market of deployment. This gives them a competitive advantage in delivering a product or service. However, that shouldn't preclude the FinTech firm from continuing to build its business.

Longer term, the ideal scenario should be that a consortium of banks owns a stake in the business. They would all enjoy an overall reduction in cost, due to the long-term efficiencies and returns that the FinTech solution provides. The FinTech company can then distribute the improvements to its other clients, who can equally benefit from the technology.

Weighing the pros and cons of partnership

Of course, any transformation project involves risks, and regulatory requirements ensure that senior managers focus on minimizing those risks. However, *not* participating in the digitalization of the industry also involves risks. For example, think about what happened to Kodak, which doggedly kept focusing on film long after digital cameras made film cameras obsolete, even though the digital camera was invented by Kodak!

REMEMBER

An organization needs to have a clear idea of what it wants to achieve from a digital transformation instead of thinking that more engagement will magically improve its competitiveness somehow.

In principle, a financial institution should be in a stronger position the more it digitizes the processes that enhance the customer experience and provide cost and workflow efficiencies. As we explain earlier in this chapter, it's often logical for a financial institution to partner with FinTech firms instead of reinventing a product that's been commercially proven in other organizations. This is particularly true if the product isn't vital for its competitive advantage and it's a new technology domain for which the firm's existing staff doesn't have the necessary domain expertise.

In the new API economy, if banks ensure their integration processes with their core technology work well, they can determine best-of-breed solutions to solve their problems. However, FinTech solutions aren't the nirvana for all issues. If the company's processes are inefficient, automating or digitizing them won't fix them. Companies should review their day-to-day operations to determine whether current processes are inefficient and in need of modification. Smaller financial services firms may not experience this issue, as their processes may be less complex.

FinTech firms' solutions tend to be specific to a given problem that multiple organizations experience. If a large firm requires a customized solution to meet multiple needs, they're probably not going to benefit from a FinTech partnership. FinTech solutions generally aren't easy to modify, so they may cover fewer functions than an in-house or broader vendor solution may provide. Furthermore, newer FinTech technology may have more difficulty interoperating with older or legacy software than a customized solution would.

For larger financial institutions, building custom software rather than partnering is still the way forward for specific solutions where they need greater customization and where it can provide them with a competitive advantage. In building your own software, it's also possible to integrate with a wider set of APIs from different partners, because it's designed to specifically accommodate those requirements. However, such firms need to get sufficient coverage from the solution so that they spread the cost of such proprietary systems over many functions and clients and justify the time, resources, and money spent to build it.

Researching and scouting potential FinTech partners

The following sections provide points on how to research what you need in a partner and where to find suitable candidates.

TECHNICAL STUFF

If a partnership between a large financial institution and a FinTech firm goes well, the institution may consider investing in the company as well as having a commercial agreement for the use of its services. Many examples show where investment banks, or consortia of investment banks, have taken minority stakes in FinTech firms to fully support their engagement, if not buying the FinTech outright, in the same way that the BigTech firms (such as Google and Facebook) have effectively made "acqui-hires" (purchasing companies to recruit and acquire its employees).

NUMERIX: INNOVATIVE APPROACHES

From 2013 to 2017, Numerix was stuck in the $60 million annual revenue range. In fact, in 2016, the company had its first year of down revenue since 2004. The revenue growth trend all but halted, and all employees could see was the reversal trend. In the beginning of 2017, Steve O'Hanlon changed all aspects of the company, and through a series of open meetings, told Numerix employees that stumbling wasn't a liability but a test and that only the great find a way to get quickly to their feet.

Numerix had stumbled for the first time, but in 2017 it would rise again. The struggle to break the $70 million barrier became just as much a mental hurdle as a business one, especially coming off a down year. Every day of 2017, Steve pushed harder, intensely determined to break through that ceiling. As result of three initiatives he introduced and commanded, Numerix achieved the major revenue milestone of exceeding $70 million in revenue by year end and went on to secure its most significant growth of $80 million.

Steve's three initiatives that brought about this success were

- Directing the development team in enhancing the company's solution stack, with the mantra of bringing intelligence to every level, and identifying new and innovative ways clients and partners can apply them. Central to this initiative has been the enhancement of the overall business services focus of the platform, with a greater emphasis on business user workflows and standardizing browser-oriented user interfaces. To put it more simply, the company builds software that customers love.

- Advancing a hands-on and direct approach at integrating the technologies and people into the Numerix culture. This led to the assimilation of TFG Financial Systems into the company (molding different people and skill sets into the Numerix culture), harmoniously bringing together new technologies and new approaches. The success of this effort not only provided Numerix with a unique and market-leading real-time offering but also enabled the company to expand more affirmatively into the hedge fund market, further tapping into a source of company growth and additional revenue.

- Building and introducing a highly competitive managed service offering. Market participants today are continuing to face multiple challenges, such as controlling IT costs, reducing risk, improving operational efficiency, and enabling greater scalability. They are finding that managed services, in contrast to an on-premises system, provide them with the cost efficiency, support, and room they need to achieve their objectives. Agility enabled Numerix to quickly capitalize on this growing trend in 2017 by building and deploying multiple technology solutions through a new managed services platform. This platform offers a range of diverse applications in a microservices format to support valuation, risk, and infrastructure requirements. This was a groundbreaking effort, as was attempting to become a risk company at the fall of Lehman. Today, 30 clients rely on Numerix for managed services, making it the company's fastest growth area.

Performing initial research

REMEMBER

The initial primary research when looking for a FinTech partner should focus on FinTech firms that provide the services that the company needs. They can then investigate potential partners in areas where they believe they don't have internal expertise or where it makes more sense to share the development cost of the solution with others.

The secondary research should then focus on a deeper analysis, including evaluating the technology stack strength. They must determine whether the solution fully meets the requirements and evaluate how easily it can be integrated into some of the internal core systems. They should also undertake a deeper analysis of the company itself, including the credibility of the founders and their offerings and the business's financial health. It's important to feel confident that the company will be around next year — and the next.

This inevitably leads to reviewing the size and success of the firm. Some institutions may be happy to partner with seed stage companies that have developed a specific new-technology solution, such as machine learning. Other institutions will require a minimum level of annual recurring revenue and/or number of employees, both of which can indicate that the company is relatively well established. This is a consideration because well-established companies should be able to scale up to meet procurement requirements.

REMEMBER

Potential customers will also want to undertake a detailed information security review on the FinTech. This includes asking them to respond to an in-depth survey on their technology, explaining its capabilities and assessing how secure the application is. Security is an important consideration, given that the customer will be deploying and distributing the application throughout its organization.

Knowing where to look

TIP

Many FinTech firms claim to provide a solution to given problems, and not all of them are capable and reputable. Therefore, a general Internet search isn't the most efficient way of identifying the right companies. Institutions should search the following types of sites and forums to scout for the most relevant and respected firms to partner with:

>> **Databases:** For later stage firms that have raised funds already, look in databases provided by firms such as CrunchBase (www.crunchbase.com) or PitchBook (https://pitchbook.com). These databases tell how much a firm has raised to date and which investors were part of those rounds. A certain bank investing in the firm suggests that the bank will also be using its product.

- >> **Accelerator programs:** For earlier stage start-ups, sourcing accelerator programs such as Accenture's FinTech Innovation Lab (`www.fintech innovationlab.com`) or TechStars (`www.techstars.com`) can be useful. These programs can help you find firms that have already been prevetted as part of the process to get into the program.

- >> **Incubators:** Incubator programs can help you find companies that have structured programs to help firms grow within the given vertical/technology being considered.

- >> **Associations:** Look at trade associations such as the Investment Association (`https://www.theiaengine.com/`) or quasi-government-led initiatives such as Innovate Finance (`www.innovatefinance.com`). These have several FinTech members and run sandboxes or hackathons around given problems. Platforms such as FINTECH Circle (`https://fintechcircle.com`) also offer custom scouting services for financial players to scout for the most relevant FinTech companies.

- >> **Awards lists:** The top FinTech companies in given sectors or regions are highlighted in various awards lists as some of the rising stars in the FinTech world. If a firm appears among the award winners for several years, and across different awards providers, they'll have shown their worth on multiple occasions. Generally, awards also have an element of vetting, because an industry panel will have nominated and/or voted for the most relevant firms.

TIP

These forums can help verify your initial research findings. To be more confident in what you learn about a company, cross-reference between multiple sources to get additional validations.

Companies have several sources to help identify the right partners to provide a given solution. More institutions are running their own challenges or in-residence-type programs that help them identify relevant firms before they have a specific requirement to keep FinTech firms that provide interesting technology on their radar.

Working with partners on evolving solutions

In 2017, mobile applications overtook desktops as the most popular channel for applying for new services within banks. This triggered a ramp-up in technology investments to adapt and compete in the new digital environment. Banks felt the pressure to make financial products as accessible and convenient as products offered by the BigTech customer service giants.

NUMERIX: COMPANY INITIATIVE AND CULTURE

One could easily argue that only an entrepreneurial CEO could enable a company to spin on a dime to react quickly to new market opportunities. Such rapid response requires new business strategies and new ways of thinking around technology innovation and its early adoption. The key for Steve O'Hanlon's success was to continually and proactively broaden his views on the trends and activities in the capital markets beyond just software applicability. His intention was to focus on broader ways that Numerix could help the entire capital markets space increase trading business, optimize productivity and efficiency, enhance profitability, and meet growing regulatory requirements.

Doing all of this required an in-house enabler. What is that enabler? Adopting a FinTech culture that nurtures and pushes innovation and thinking out of the box. Fostering and maintaining a climate where entrepreneurial thinking, idea generation, risk taking, and the ceaseless quest for innovation are highly encouraged has helped Numerix attract and retain some of the best talent — across several functions — in the industry.

Steve's goal is to continue disrupting the industry. One way he does this is to continue cementing Numerix's position as a dynamic financial technology company that provides a next-generation technology platform built on top of the award-winning and industry-leading CrossAsset software. This also helps Numerix in its continued efforts to pivot to a position as a formative leader in the FinTech industry.

One particularly notable development in 2017 was Oracle entering into a collaboration with Numerix to develop and bring to market solutions that enable financial institutions to meet the computational and business requirements needed to comply with FRTB rules (FRTB stands for Fundamental Rules of the Trading Book). As one of the largest and most powerful tech companies in the world, for Oracle to have selected Numerix as its partner of choice to leverage its analytics in its new market risk solution was an absolute honor.

Steve's entrepreneurial strengths drive Numerix to innovate, enter new markets, and transform old technologies. He has positioned Numerix for sustained success and has proved once again that Numerix isn't a company that shies away from reinvention but embraces it.

The push to digital in today's more complex development landscape, where change needs to be made quickly, leads many institutions to a buy *and* build approach — in other words, a hybrid of both. Where services and offerings are generic and not unique to the bank, they can be sourced from specialist vendors with a proven product. This results in a shorter development cycle and quicker time to market. It also frees up internal resources to concentrate on building functionality unique to the bank's overall offering. The new API economy and platform environments also allow greater comingling of the two approaches.

REMEMBER

Digital transformation can't be a series of one-off projects. As customer needs and expectations are constantly evolving, solutions need to continuously evolve as well. Sourcing and extending components reduces internal customization and spreads the cost of research and development across external players. APIs and a platform approach make it easier for banks to adapt external modules to their own brands and circumstances and make amendments to future needs less difficult. This removes the tendency to revert to big and costly projects on a regular basis.

Describing the Licensing Models

A *software licensing model* defines how the product will be used. What rights will the customer have to use the product? How many people or devices may use it simultaneously? How will updates and new versions be received and paid for? What support is included? It's all in the license.

Enterprise software providers within the financial services industry have traditionally employed a license and maintenance model in which customers bought per-seat or per-user licenses for a particular product release. However, Software as a Service (SaaS; see Chapter 6), a software delivery model where software is centrally hosted and delivered via the cloud, has lately become popular, and much of the industry has moved to a subscription-based model. In fact, Gartner, one of the largest research and advisory companies, foresees that all new vendors, and the vast majority of existing vendors, will provide subscription-based business models, no matter where the software is deployed.

While the subscription model is most popular today, it's far from the only model available. The following sections explain the various licensing models you may encounter when shopping for FinTech products.

Subscription

A subscription is just what it sounds like: You buy the right to use the product for a fixed time period. Subscription licenses are renewable, usually on an annual basis, and include software support and updates during the coverage period. The license is automatically terminated unless it's renewed.

REMEMBER

The subscription model makes license management simple, as it provides the flexibility to pay only for what you use, adding and scaling back respective licenses in line with demand. In addition, upgrades and new features are released in real time and rolled into the monthly price, ensuring that no compatibility or obsolescence issues occur. A subscription model is affordable and offers a predictable payment schedule, which becomes part of operational expenditure.

Ideally, the subscription model allows for a lower initial cost for the user and a faster approval cycle for the provider. This also allows for short-term licenses, with policies subject to amendment at renewal time, and limits problems with duplicate license counts when machines are decommissioned or upgraded. Both parties benefit from an ongoing client-vendor relationship that includes regular dialogue around usage requirements.

WARNING

However, in comparison to other license types, the subscription model can increase the administrative burden of license management, because it requires accurate record keeping, auditing, and management during the license life cycle. Moreover, some vendors complicate the pricing process by adding usage requirements on top of the normal per-user (or per-server) license. Such policies may in some cases be appropriate to prevent excessive data usage, particularly where usage racks up greater costs from the software firm's cloud provider or where the service is specifically data related. However, such policies may create administrative headaches for the client, who must then do extensive auditing and monitoring to avoid racking up excessive extra charges.

Perpetual

Perpetual licenses are nonexpiring licenses to use a given application, where the customer has no obligation to pay for support or update services. Users pay one large upfront fee, which ensures that they "own" the application/software. (They don't really own it, but they own the right to use it in perpetuity.)

However, in today's changing environment, although perpetual licenses can in principle be used forever, they tend have a short life cycle as the software becomes obsolete. Consequently, customers must upgrade periodically to ensure compatibility with other applications or supported hardware.

WARNING

If you continue to use a product that has reached its end of life, you won't be able to get updates, patches, and hotfixes. Not receiving security-related updates can expose a firm to risks such as viruses, spyware, and other malicious software that can steal or damage data. This is particularly true when customers end up using very old software versions to save money and elect to forego maintenance. They then blame the software provider, whose reputation may suffer from it.

Another issue with perpetual licenses is that customers must pay for the software upfront, which requires a larger initial outlay. As a result, the upfront cost for larger software deployments can be significant and need to be attributed to capital expenditure. Then, if they want support, they must pay more annually. In some agreements, the required annual maintenance fee is as much as 20 percent per year of the upfront purchase price.

Term

A *term agreement* isn't bought outright. However, the user does pay a large upfront fee, which is generally based on an annual license rate multiplied by the maturity of the term (generally a five-year term). In almost all instances, the customer is required to take a maintenance agreement, which for a five-year term is generally 20 percent of the one-time initial fee. At the end of the term, the user can either upgrade and pay for another term or stop using the software.

Source code transactions

One of the important questions to ask about a start-up FinTech firm is whether it will still be around in the future. Given that smaller firms are more likely to suffer from short-term cash flow issues, large financial institutions have to consider the risks associated with deploying a start-up's product in the long term if they have a smaller balance sheet.

TIP

To help mitigate such risks, some larger firms require access to the source code of the software product as part of the license agreement. The traditional way of securing access is to put the source code into escrow. In other words, they place the software into custody or trust until a specified condition has been fulfilled, such as the original owner going bankrupt or being bought out by another company. An escrow agreement ensures that if the vendor is unable to manage the product or provide a support service, the purchaser will have access to the code to support its day-to-day operations and ensure it won't be put at risk.

Having access to source code can also be helpful when purchasing from a larger software provider that requires a long-term maintenance and support license to service, update, or reinstall the software. Because the source code required for most software applications is unique, customers may ask for the required information to be put into escrow. If the software provider is unable to carry out a suitable level of support for the software product, customers can gain access to the code via escrow. Offering software escrow as an option assures that customers will always have access to some level of service on their software purchase.

Code escrow is also quite common where a smaller FinTech firm receives an equity investment from a traditional or corporate venture capital investor. If the firm goes into liquidation, the investor wants to have access to the software information, including the documentation and source code necessary to maintain a level of service on the software. To recoup part of its investment, the investor may consider an asset sale to another provider or the clients themselves to maintain access to the product.

An open source approach

As you discover in Chapter 10, open source software has a source code that anyone can inspect, modify, or enhance because its design and code is publicly accessible. Open source products are built on open exchange, collaboration, rapid prototyping, transparency, and meritocracy, all of which lead to a community-oriented development process.

WARNING

Many FinTech firms develop proprietary applications on top of open source components. However, the suggestion that open source is free is a misrepresentation, because using open source software obliges firms to recognize the legal context of open source. If a firm fails to comply with the licensing provisions for open source, it can lead to legal proceedings. To mitigate this risk, companies need to understand open source license conditions and initiate an actionable list of best practices. Open source users need to follow the licensing conditions for each package they use, including subcomponents. Moreover, buyers of open source–driven FinTech applications need to be aware of all uses so that they can assume responsibilities for such use, subject to license conditions.

The bulk of open source licenses are protected by a few agreements, of which there are only two main license groups: copyleft, which obliges developers to ensure that any source code or documentation is obtainable, and permissive, which requires minimal provisions, such as author acknowledgment.

Companies must have a license and compliance policy that covers both categories. At a minimum, firms are required to

>> Maintain documentation for the licensing conditions relating to the open source software being used, incorporating subcomponents and dependencies.

>> Have a strategy for compliance that differentiates between licenses that have simple or complex requirements, such as source code delivery.

REMEMBER

Every open source software license has notice obligations. When distributing a product that incorporates open source, those obligations may require developers to include a simple copyright notice or the complete text of the license that regulates the software.

Copyleft licenses regulate how developers can combine the open source software with privately operated software. The term *copyleft* is intended to both reference the well-known term *copyright* and to differ from it. Copyright is a law that restricts the right to use, modify, and share creative works without the permission of the copyright holder. In contrast, under a copyleft license, the author makes a claim on the copyright of the work and issues a statement that other people have the right to use, modify, and share the work as long as the obligation's reciprocity is maintained. In short, if authors are using a component with this kind of open source license, then they too must make their code open for use by others.

NUMERIX: STANDING ALONE

Numerix's first acquisition took place in 2017. We detail this event and its implications in Chapter 15. For now, suffice it to say that after a tremendous amount of research and due diligence, Numerix entered into a hugely strategic acquisition of TFG Financial Systems, whose unparalleled real-time technology leapfrogged Numerix over its competitors. This acquisition not only advanced Numerix into the micro hedge fund sales channel but also advanced it into a SaaS offering and into new disruptive real-time technologies.

Because this space is crowded, Numerix focused on its key differentiator, which continues to be its unrivaled analytics. In 2019, it was recognized as change advocates by creating and driving thought leadership activities that focused on innovation and disruption technology that point out legacy inefficiencies.

Numerix strategy continues by

- Expanding the applicability and diversity of its Oneview solution stack and deployment strategies
- Leveraging its unique cross-asset real-time risk and portfolio management solution to capture significant market share in the buy-side market, with a focus on global macro hedge funds
- Growing its strategic network of trusted partners as part of an increasing effort to sell more of its capabilities to more markets

Numerix's culture, technological advancement, and unending desire to be the best software company in the world has paved a path where few can compete.

TIP

Component Lifecycle Management (CLM) is a process that allows developers to use cooperative kits, information, and control at each phase of the application development, thereby addressing licensing risk control for a module-based approach. These tools enable companies to choose applicable licensed modules during design and elaboration by

» Recognizing and controlling component licensing through the build stage to identify problems quickly and prevent expensive reworks

» Scanning current applications to recognize licenses and requirements to review dependencies with respect to corporate compliance policies

Chapter **14**

Managing Integration with Legacy Systems

The decision to modernize legacy technology to new, more functional components isn't an insignificant one. A seamless transition from a legacy system to a more flexible component environment may require a complete rewrite of the code and may take years.

It's critical that any company undertaking such a transition has a solid plan in place from the start and communicates that plan to the stakeholders and decision-makers. Employing a FinTech company to help develop that plan can save both time and money. A FinTech company can help identify which legacy pieces should be converted and select the best method for doing so.

This chapter helps you figure out how to evaluate your legacy systems and come up with a strategic plan for updating them, either on your own or by partnering with a FinTech company.

Understanding and Tackling the Challenges of Legacy Infrastructures

One of the most significant challenges the financial industry faces is how to keep pace with technology changes. The systems within banks and other financial and insurance institutions have often grown willy-nilly with little oversight and little eye toward holistic integration.

REMEMBER

The term *legacy* generally refers to any system that is old in age and functionality but still important to the corporation or individual. This definition applies to any technology, computer system, or application.

It can be difficult for an organization to know when it's time to modernize systems and how much effort they should put into the maintenance and/or enhancement of legacy systems. As technology becomes outdated, the capacity to support such systems becomes increasingly more difficult. The following sections lay out the challenges of legacy systems and how to handle them.

WARNING

All the following complexities make the porting of a legacy system and its data into a new environment problematic:

>> Legacy systems may be the base on which the standards for all subsequent functionality has been architected, so unraveling the effects on the entire user base may be hard to plan and predict.

>> Furthermore, it's often impossible to change these aging systems to support updates to real-world business requirements.

>> An organization may have multiple legacy systems, and one or all of them may be at least peripherally integrated into the workflows of other departments.

>> Some systems may share their data in a unique and nonsynchronous fashion.

Comparing old and modern systems

Legacy systems are often monolithic architectural structures that don't adhere to current business practices and aren't flexible, scalable, resilient, or fault-tolerant. In contrast, modern development processes employ advanced architectural modes, such as a service-oriented or microservices architecture at their base. These modalities provide many advantages over the older architectures. (See Chapter 4 for an introduction to microservices.)

Figure 14-1 compares a typical legacy system with a microservices architecture system. With the monolithic structure, all calls draw from a single shared database. This is a single point of failure. It means that any change to any of the upper-level pieces necessitates shutting down the whole structure. On the other hand, each service in a microservice structure is self-contained.

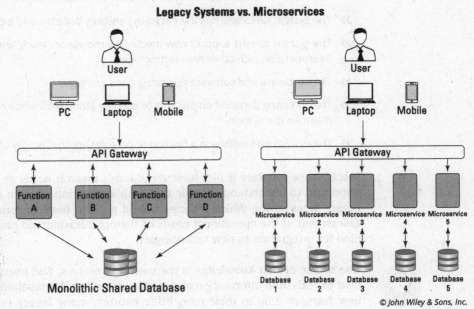

© John Wiley & Sons, Inc.

FIGURE 14-1:
The configuration and workflow differences between legacy systems and microservices.

REMEMBER

Any upgrade to new technologies must include an understanding of the goals of the company and its strategic plan for the use of components such as microservices, application programming interface (API) strategies, real-time delivery, distributed ledger technologies, cloud- or web-based delivery systems, and artificial intelligence/machine learning (AI/ML). Part 2 of this book discusses these components.

Determining whether a legacy system is too old

REMEMBER

A legacy system is typically too old when it becomes cost-prohibitive to maintain (or in some cases, to find hardware replacements or repairs) or when the legacy system can't be extended to meet regulatory or business requirements. Some of the signs that a system has reached its end of life are

>> The system no longer supports the organization's business needs, and the users no longer trust the results it produces.

>> The vendor no longer supports the system, and/or not enough readily available personnel can administer it.

>> The system is inflexible and can't support the functional needs of the end user. It can't handle new workflows or business requirements.

>> The system no longer has the necessary security controls and it crashes often.

>> The system doesn't support new media (like mobile or cloud), and it isn't interoperable with other new technologies.

>> The hardware and software operating costs are high.

>> The company depends on just one or two key employees who know how to maintain the system.

>> The system was written in a fashion or on software that is now obsolete.

Just because software is old, however, doesn't mean it needs to be replaced. It's important to understand the role that each application plays in an organization. Before determining which legacies should go, you need to conduct a complete assessment of the operational needs of the organization and create a prioritized plan for integration to new technologies.

TIP

One source of that knowledge is the users themselves. End users now require as near to real-time information as possible, as well as the capability to quickly add new features. Due to their monolithic natures, many legacy environments are incapable of delivering the level of performance users demand — anytime, anywhere, and in any medium. Listen to your users, and use their suggestions and complaints as an indicator.

When you have an inventory of all the systems, you need to map the use cases for each system or application to the growth needs of the company. A mapping diagram can be effective in minimizing the downtime of any migration of old technologies to new ones.

Your strategy for evaluating and replacing a legacy system must include an understanding of your overall API plan as well as your cloud and data consolidation strategies. All approaches are interoperative within a holistic development plan. You can't develop a successful migration approach without understanding the tools that will permit the successful expansion of these technologies into the future.

Estimating the cost of doing nothing

The costs of maintaining legacy systems are going up appreciably. The cost to an organization that fails to migrate or upgrade away from legacy systems is apparent. Consider the following:

>> One cost comes in the increased time spent on support, maintenance, and updates of legacy systems, resulting in increased costs. Monolithic structures, unlike microservices, can't just be swapped out without taking down the whole system. Downtime costs money and exposes the company to reputational risk. Another cost can come from the potential conflicts with each update across whole departments within the company, not just within the legacy system.

>> By trying to save money sticking with legacy systems, many companies find (ironically) that they actually end up spending considerable funds trying to patch up old systems to speed up compute times and to handle an increase in data storage needs.

>> Legacy systems can also cost a company in labor hours because of their lack of automation. Most legacy systems simply don't have the tools to automate processes the way new systems do.

>> A legacy system can cost more in personnel costs because it can be difficult to find staff to administer and support these legacy systems.

Discovering how FinTech can help

REMEMBER

A company can take several possible approaches when migrating from legacy to new platforms, applications, or systems:

>> Roll it all out at once, a total replacement (a Greenfield approach).

>> Take a phased, gradual approach (a Brownfield approach).

>> Apply band-aid fixes as needed.

>> Improve existing technology only when it's no longer viable.

>> Don't do anything, and just keep adding new technology onto the old.

To determine the best approach, the organization needs to consider the time to implement versus the loss of business, as well as the general cost to the business if it doesn't upgrade. If that sounds like a complex equation to solve — it is.

Many banks are finding that it makes good business sense to partner with a FinTech company for each step in the process, from completing the initial analysis to rolling out the new solutions. FinTech companies can assist organizations in assessing the benefits of a change over the disruption to the organizations. They can also provide manpower and oversight to the actual deployments. (See Chapter 13 for details on partnering with a FinTech company.)

Many organizations are understandably reluctant to replace major systems that have long been integral to the company's stability. Third-party FinTech expertise removes some of the fear around the scope of the projects by

» Supplying personnel to handle the heavy lifting

» Providing expert project management

» Unraveling system interdependencies and avoiding system conflicts that negatively impact the organization

» Reviewing legacy code as well as the proposed system to make sure there's no loss of functionality

» Testing and documenting all replacement components across the entire network

Planning for success

Whether you work with a FinTech partner or not, it's essential to have a detailed plan in place before you roll out any new technology. Make sure your plan includes the following topics:

» A problem statement (a general statement of the issue — for example, the need to automate an online payment process)

» A project goals and benefits analysis

» A detailed review of project constraints (such as time and budget)

» A complete list of stakeholders and their requirements

» An understanding of the organizational culture, structure, and governance and an understanding of the political climate in which the change will occur

» A review of marketplace conditions, which may drive the priorities and the timeline

» An understanding of the best environment in which to house the system (for example, managed services versus on-premises)

» A determination of whether the legacy should be rearchitected, replaced, encapsulated, rehosted, replatformed, or refactored (this choice will affect the time commitment and the cost)

Walking through the Technical Steps of Updating a Legacy System

Working with legacy systems can be challenging. The age of the system, the lack of documentation, and sometimes the lack of personnel are all of primary concern, but a transformative change also has many technical hurdles. These technical issues need to be isolated and addressed point for point. The following sections look at the integration picture from a technical point of view.

Noting areas of concern

Data management (see Chapter 11) provides a good example of a common but major problem. Many legacy systems don't have easy ways to exchange or extract data. Often the data extracted from the legacy systems will require external transformations and/or enrichment for other systems to use it. These operations can be extremely challenging and time-consuming. Data extraction is one area where a FinTech company with data management expertise can be a great time-saver.

Another area of concern is that legacy systems were often written in archaic language and weren't written to handle the digital age in general. Many bank systems were written in languages like COBOL, which are no longer representative of the skill set of the new employee pool. Fewer and fewer coders are available who can provide the coding skills necessary to support legacy systems.

TIP

Using APIs can be helpful when adding workflow or business functionality into a legacy system. APIs can provide business processes without disrupting the rest of the output produced by the system to other users. When upgrading a system, you must run tests to ensure that the legacy system and the proposed new functionality can talk to each other. Using microservices and APIs can enable you to integrate small services into the monolithic legacy structure.

Making your plan

After you're aware of potential updating issues, the first step in the preparation of an integration/migration starts with a plan. We're talking about a technical plan here, not the business considerations we mention earlier in this chapter. In other words, this is about the "how" rather than the "why." You want to make the best technology choices to support the integration.

REMEMBER

The technical plan should include these components:

>> A technology inventory that includes the legacy system's complete technology stack, the programming language, and any known issues with support or obsolescence.

>> An architectural audit, which helps determine the level of replacement or refactoring needed on the legacy product.

>> A code review for quality.

>> A review of past quality assurance (QA) processes and test logs.

>> Recommendations about the appropriate approach to take. Should it be an all-encompassing replacement, a phased, gradual approach, a band-aid fix, a replacement of only the obsolete components, or a do-nothing strategy?

Assembling the team

Implementation services typically involve many activities and deliverables. Here are some examples of these activities in companies operating in the financial arena:

>> Legacy system assessment

>> Business requirements documentation

>> Financial engineering

>> Template and content customization

>> Product hardware sizing and installation

>> Systems integration

>> Customized pre- and post-processing

>> Custom reporting

>> User testing support

>> Project management

Of course, all these deliverables aren't going to deliver themselves, so you'll need the appropriate personnel on board to take care of them. Table 14-1 describes the typical types of personnel for a financial company's migration project. FinTech consultants can fill some of these roles; others will need to come from within the organization.

TABLE 14-1   ## Personnel in an Integration Project

Role	Title	Primary Responsibility
Executive stakeholder	Senior vice president, head of professional services	Provides strategic direction for the project and assists in resolving escalated items
Regional stakeholder	Vice president, professional services	Provides ground-level steering Reviews progress with client project sponsors Manages overall risks/issues Ensures client satisfaction
Implementation manager	Project manager	Provides project direction and oversight of the team and its progress Coordinates various resources and their tasks Schedules resources based on the project plan and project needs Serves as the day-to-day point of contact for all project activities Manages the project plan Monitors the progress made on project milestones and deliverables Provides weekly status reports and other project artifacts and maintains project updates on a shared repository
Project team	Financial engineer	Designs and configures models (calibration and pricing) across all asset classes Performs financial engineering (FE) tests on models Assists in evaluating client modeling options when needed
Project team	Business analyst	Designs functional specifications and workflows and translates business requirements into appropriate system solutions Works with financial engineers to build and benchmark templates Leads System Integration Testing/User Acceptance Testing (SIT/UAT), including the creation of test and use cases
Project team	Developer	Performs tasks related to extract, transform, and load (ETL) Manages system integration and interfacing Manages customization development Provides support during SIT/UAT

Implementing the plan

REMEMBER

After your plan is in place, you can start taking the first steps toward a hassle-free integration/migration by using these best practices:

>> Get buy-in from all stakeholders and senior management.

>> Assess the upgrade needs from an architectural level, and write good use cases that will be used to determine the success of the benefits.

>> Confirm that the technical plan's recommended strategy is the most appropriate choice.

>> Use the best development process from the beginning and create a structure around its continued use. Include testing, documentation, and continuous integration as a standard part of the methodology.

>> Develop new functionality from the new approaches such as microservices and APIs.

>> Create training around the new technology and create a retirement plan for the legacy system.

Figure 14-2 shows a graphical road map for a migration project. Each phase, from discovery to going live, has multiple steps and owners who are required to ensure the expected outcomes.

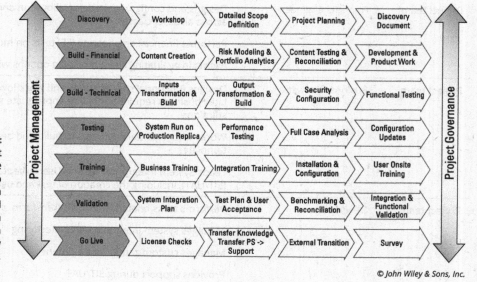

FIGURE 14-2: The variables that must be addressed to assure a successful migration off a legacy system and to new technology.

© John Wiley & Sons, Inc.

Avoiding the pitfalls

For every major mistake a company makes with an integration/migration, hundreds of other companies have already made the same mistake and could have told them what to avoid. But because you probably don't have contacts at all those places, allow us to summarize what we've learned in our years in the FinTech industry.

WARNING

Data integration/migration projects fail most often for these reasons:

» **Not understanding the stakeholders' needs and not building a consensus among them about the project priorities:** It's critical to have meetings early and often, and to do frequent sanity checks as the scope of the project is determined and defined.

» **No commitment to an architecturally driven modernization approach:** There needs to be a respected technical head who owns the success of the project.

» **Lack of senior management buy-in:** It goes without saying if you can't have an advocate among senior management, the project will fail. Getting a commitment to a budget is the first indicator of the seriousness to the engagement.

» **Too little input from and oversight by technical advisors or third-party FinTech teams:** This is tied to the need for buy-in from C-level management and a strong respected technical advocate who has veto power.

» **Lack of project management and project planning:** A project manager is a must for any large modernization project.

» **Not doing a complete audit/review at the project outset of the systems, environments, and user interfaces affected:** This should be step one. There needs to be a checklist and a priority road map at the onset.

» **Poorly defined project goals and vague or unrealistic use cases:** This goes back to the steps outlined in the earlier section "Planning for success." If you follow those steps, you should have a plan that is transparent to all stakeholders and vetted by those who are engaged to deliver it.

Simplifying Integration with Microservices Architecture

As we say earlier in this chapter, many monolithic legacy systems should be replaced for the health of the company. The increased speed to the marketplace, greater flexibility, and greater interoperability are compelling benefits that drive this transformation.

REMEMBER

To be technologically up-to-date, any upgrade must include modern services and technologies, including cloud technologies, microservices, API releases, open source incorporations, real-time delivery mechanisms, distributed ledger applications, automation, and artificial intelligence approaches. Part 2 of this book covers these technologies.

The demand for future development has lately been focused on integrating computational needs with business logic, and most monolithic legacy systems can't deliver that. Microservices, APIs, and cloud technologies are needed to connect the users with their data and satisfy their compute needs. Such new business-driven applications are connected on the service level.

The following sections discuss the benefits of microservice architecture and your options for microservice migration.

The benefits of microservices

Microservices offer many benefits when replacing monolithic legacy systems, including these:

» The separability of function into discrete modules. This separation is found not only in the functionality but also in the nature of microservice maintenance. The development teams are separate, as are the release schedules, and no module interferes with the ability of another module to function or to be separately delivered.

» Continuous integration, continuous testing, and continuous development are key tenets of microservices. Developers submit their code multiple times per day. This code is validated through automated builds and automated test environments.

» Improved bug fix control. Frequent code releases and continuous testing result in better code review and faster identification and remedy of issues.

>> Development language flexibility. Microservices utilize new flexible languages like Python, which are accessible to developers and users alike.

>> Ease of scalability, standardized microservice frameworks, and containerization for rapid deployment.

>> Highly cohesive services (like function with like function) with loose coupling (sharing of well-defined data in a simple database structure).

>> Optimally designed code and architecture that enables any number of users to receive the same data without error.

>> Infinite composability. Microservices are built to optimize composability through the use of design principles that match function sets with loose coupling.

>> Cloud-native construction. Microservices adhere to the concept of the user defining the method of delivery. Therefore, all new development must have mobile and cloud delivery as a requirement.

Migration strategy options

A migration plan can be structured in one of two ways: either revolutionary (big bang) or evolutionary (band-aid).

>> The *revolutionary* method builds a new system from scratch with a hard stop and transfer. This method is fast to implement but can be quite disruptive.

>> The *evolutionary* method is a phased modernization process, as shown in Figure 14-3. This approach takes longer, but the net effect is less disruptive.

Figure 14-3 illustrates the different steps that can be utilized in a legacy review. As you go up the chain, the effort increases as do the benefits. APIs, cloud extensibility, and microservices drive the benefits.

TIP

Both methods have their pros and cons. You can make the right choice by doing a needs-based analysis that considers whether implementation, speed, or minimum disruption is more important and then creating an appropriate migration plan to match.

That plan will also determine which type of transformation strategy is necessary for the legacy technology in question. The options available are

>> **Rearchitect:** Working with the code and altering it to take advantage of better capabilities within the platform.

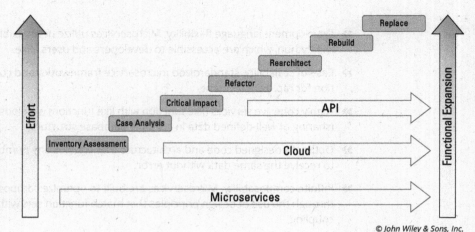

FIGURE 14-3:
The steps that can be taken in a migration and the increase in effort required as the functional demands increase.

© John Wiley & Sons, Inc.

>> **Replacing:** Finding an ultimately better option and writing new code to reflect all use cases required.

>> **Revising:** Extensively reusing the legacy code. This method uses APIs to increase functionality and user interfaces. It's the fastest and most inexpensive approach, but it carries over inherited issues with the old code.

>> **Rehosting:** Moving the same code and functionality to a new infrastructure. Nothing changes with the functionality in this approach — the only change is in how it's accessed.

>> **Replatforming:** Making minimal changes to increase some functionality based on new platform capabilities.

>> **Refactoring or restructuring:** Optimizing existing code without necessarily affecting the external functions.

REMEMBER

Whichever option you choose, it's important to frequently reanalyze the use cases and the technologies available. To be effective in the future, an organization must stay abreast of the current new technologies and weigh the costs against the benefits of upgrading.

Chapter 15

Preparing Your Team for a Successful Project

Any FinTech project's success or failure depends on the same basic issues — whether the project is completely managed and controlled in-house or is fully or partially outsourced. Of course, the complexity increases when there are more cooks in the kitchen. It is therefore especially important when multiple companies are involved to clearly define the areas of collaboration and control so the project managers can work together effectively across the various companies and disciplines.

REMEMBER

As we mention in earlier chapters (particularly Chapter 13), successfully engaging FinTech partners in a project begins by figuring out why you need their help. You need to know the scope of activities required and the level of in-house experience you have to work with. FinTech personnel are best used in areas where no specialists are available, where time to market is critical, or where there is no in-house appetite for change.

This chapter helps you prepare to work with a FinTech company by getting your own house in order first. In it, you find out about assembling your internal transformation team, managing scheduling, supporting change agents, and retaining the best and brightest employees through the stress involved in change.

Assembling a Transformation Team

The first step in identifying the right third party is to determine your company's needs and capabilities. What are you trying to do, and what kind of help do you need? This is important because different FinTech firms have different strengths and weaknesses. Some may be much better at modernizing systems, whereas others may excel at completely replacing them. Some FinTech firms may supply manpower for an integration, while others may supply software as well as integration. The reality is that it's rarely possible to have out-of-the-box solutions that "fix" all the issues of legacy and multiple data sources seamlessly without extensive review and integration. FinTech firms supply specialists as well as best-of-breed technology.

Creating a Request for Proposal (RFP) is a necessary first step in finding a FinTech partner. This document should outline the areas that you want to outsource, the software you may require, and the qualities you want the potential third-party partner to have. To gather the information needed to write an effective RFP, you should complete a full review of the different skill sets required for the project and assess which of those skills are available among the current staff. The project will likely have many areas, especially those that involve new technologies, where the benefits of outsourcing will outweigh those of internal development. Regardless of whether the entire project is outsourced to FinTech partners or split between internal and external resources, the engaging company has to have a committed number of personnel responsible for the interactions and success of the overall project.

REMEMBER

You can establish a good foundation for a successful transformation project, whether internally allocated or with FinTech resources, by doing the following:

>> Get the complete buy-in of senior management, making sure that they understand the costs and personnel requirements.

>> Identify and engage key stakeholders.

>> Identify the project owner/leader.

>> Identify and install a tool set to aid development and track goals.

>> Identify the dedicated team to be focused on the project.

>> Identify areas in which there is insufficient internal assets to handle the development requirements.

>> Identify areas that are best served when outsourced.

>> Develop a complete roll-out team.

Find out more about how to accomplish the tasks in this list with the help of the following sections.

Recruiting the right team members

To assign the right people to the FinTech team's key positions, you must understand the natures of the various roles. This section explains some of the key factors to look for in potential team members.

REMEMBER

If external FinTech resources are engaged, an internal team lead needs to be involved in the selection of the third-party resources as well as the internal team. The internal team lead or the internal project manager should have the right to refuse resources that don't seem to have the right skills or culture appetite.

The team leader is perhaps the most critical role to fill, because his/her vision and skill will drive the entire process, including recruiting other team members. Good team leaders

>> **Know the end goal:** They have a vision about what is needed and how it should be positioned and driven.

>> **Are risk-takers:** They understand that in some instances, they will be operating in uncharted territory and can determine when a risk is worth the uncertainty.

>> **Are inspirational:** They convey the excitement around the goals and recruit for the change.

>> **Have a good eye for talent:** They have a good working knowledge of the skills needed for the project and the people within the organization who can fill the positions.

>> **Manage well:** They set high but reasonable expectations and follow through to attain the goals.

All the other internal team members are important, too, and must be carefully chosen. People with an entrepreneurial bent function well in these more transformational work groups. Good team members will have these qualities:

>> Dedication to the highest quality they can deliver

>> The ability to work well with others and pull out the best work from their coworkers

>> Confidence that their thoughts and ideas are respected within the organization

>> The belief that being dedicated to the outcomes of this project is an individual career differentiator for themselves

>> The willingness to evangelize to the rest of the company about the benefits of the work they're doing

Counting on communication

It's important to have teams that communicate well to those outside of their FinTech project. By doing so, they share information whose reception can be tested. They can clarify the company's strategy, identify the challenges and solutions, and explain the road map and the coming actions. All stakeholders as well as participants in the project are "agents of change" for the project. They must have a clear and consistent message that is shared repeatedly with those outside the group. This helps those external to the project prepare for the change.

The alignment of objectives between different departments that are involved in the project, as well as any FinTech company providing technology, software, or services, is essential. The use of "scrums" and frequent meetings should be part of a daily exercise. External observers of the process, who aren't directly involved but are peripherally affected, should be invited into the discussion on a scheduled basis. The use of company-wide meetings and electronic bulletin boards can help keep all who are curious or nervous informed, and should help to keep the rumor mill at bay. The way change is managed is discussed in the following sections.

Shifting the leadership paradigm

Historically, most corporations have developed hierarchically, with siloed areas of data control and linear reporting. However, many companies have lately been shifting into a more agile structure that mirrors the change in development processes and methods. Both the marketplace and a company's changing development needs drive the growing imperative for faster response times and more flexible process ownership.

Changes in organizational concepts have also created leadership model changes. A transformative team is a flexible team. The organization must reward innovation and proactivity rather than reactive solution-finding. Collaboration and ease of communication within autonomous, focused teams is critical to the success of any project. The leadership within a group must also be fluid, dependent on the task and the skill sets of the individuals. Consensus and testing of the status quo is the new norm.

REMEMBER

The new paradigm for building transformative teams includes these objectives:

>> Build small, cross-departmental, self-contained teams.

>> Empower the teams to act autonomously.

>> Expect frequent revisions and reviews to approaches taken.

>> Expect innovation and customer design-driven input.

>> Enlist the customer as part of the decision-making team.

>> Empower the development of a strong partner ecosystem.

>> Encourage change consistently and repetitively throughout the organization.

>> Embrace knowledge sharing.

>> Make sure you have a complete set of shared tools.

>> Make sure there's a clear understanding of the rules around engagement.

>> Make sure the wins are celebrated and right action is rewarded.

REMEMBER

When FinTech companies are engaged in transformative projects, they must operate as if they are an internal rather than external arm of the organization that hired them. Situating the FinTech company on-premise and having committed resources who interact directly with the internal team is key. The tasks outlined in the preceding list should be established as the guidelines for not only internal but external resources. The FinTech company should have a duly appointed project manager who interfaces with the internal leads and is held accountable to the same goals. The project manager should also have all tasks, objectives, and time frames delineated and defined and a requirements document that rewards or penalizes the third party for non-performance. A carrot with a stick is the best combination for success.

Assigning roles

You may recruit team members for specific positions already in mind for them, but you also may bring people on board first and decide their exact roles and responsibilities afterward. The most successful teams are those that don't have a rigid idea about "job description."

Ownership comes with clear communication and objectives. If you set clear goals and empower team members to own the outcome, it often becomes apparent which team member should take on specific responsibilities and tasks. The internal lead as well as the external FinTech project leader must understand the individual members of their teams and what motivates each one toward their personal excellence.

REMEMBER

At the start of each project, all members of the team, both internal and third-party, should discuss the requirements and outcomes and identify each member's skills and abilities. The project leader must understand the strengths of each team member and draw out their commitment to the project. Team members should be encouraged to reach outside their comfort zones and should be given tools that enable them to be successful. Frequent assessment meetings are highly recommended. The team lead should be able to speak directly with supervisors if any skill set is lacking and draw upon a larger talent pool, internal or external to the organization, as needed.

During the requirements gathering and the creation of the statement of work, a complete understanding of the personnel required will be developed. More expertise may be found to be necessary as the project continues, but the basic needs from a FinTech firm generally lie within certain areas of technical expertise that may reside outside of the institution engaging the FinTech firm. Those positions often are in the areas of data management, application programming interface (API) and microservices development, and cloud security and facilitation, among others. The institution should be prepared to make team members who have specifically unique knowledge of legacy systems, IT, security, analytics, and database architecture available to the project and to the FinTech team.

NUMERIX: LESSONS LEARNED

There's always an inflection point when a company must make the decision of whether it's time to acquire new companies rather than continue to grow organically. All companies start out growing by maximizing the talents of their employees' skill sets and adhering to a strategic development plan. At some point, though, the company needs to accelerate financial growth, take on new areas of development not available through the current work force, or more rapidly bring new products to the marketplace. Those goals drive senior management into the next step of planning: acquisition or merger, or buy versus build.

One area of emphasis for coauthor Steve O'Hanlon, Numerix CEO, was to actively engage with large banks globally to position Numerix's platform technology and analytics as a cornerstone of the banks' innovation and scalability. The potential end state by partnering with key clients is a disruptive move counter to the existing legacy architectures powering many banks today and forging new areas of growth for the firm.

Another cornerstone in his ambitious plan for Numerix was to pursue acquisitions. In this regard, 2016 was a standout year. As an entrepreneur and business leader, Steve always keeps his eye out for additional opportunities. As Numerix crossed into the summer months of 2016, he recognized a breakthrough and differentiating opportunity. He engaged in negotiations, and in February 2017, Numerix acquired TFG Financial Systems, a real-time valuation, risk-management, and integration services company. Its technology, when integrated with Numerix's capabilities, would leapfrog the company over its competitors with a next-generation strategic tech play that no one else would have. The acquisition also offered immediate penetration into a new market for Numerix: the hedge fund industry.

Consistent with his management style, Steve shared his plan with the company at large. He solicited the support not only of his senior team but also all employees, and brought them along on his journey toward enhanced functionality and greater revenue generation. For the integration of a new company into Numerix, Steve felt it was essential that the employees understood the motivation behind an acquisition versus continued organic growth. It was also critical that the selected company filled a void in not only the technology but the skill set of the company.

Steve said, "We conducted considerable due diligence on many firms who have staked the claim to delivering real-time capabilities in the market. It's been well documented how many financial institutions have tried to develop real-time systems on their own and failed. Meanwhile, closed systems like SecDB have operated around proprietary languages and a legacy data model, and select vendor solutions are content to build out similar shell systems without the maturity of data model and analytics. As a state-of-the-art trading and risk system utilizing a dynamic dependency graph, Numerix Oneview is the next generation SecDB. Built utilizing standardized components like Python and a modern market standard data model, Numerix is providing technology akin to what firms like Goldman Sachs and JP Morgan are providing, while remaining independent and unbiased."

Numerix Oneview Asset Management, formerly TFG Complete, provided Numerix with a turnkey SaaS-based real-time front-to-back office solution. They immediately began working with a range of new buy-side institutions, including hedge funds that operated global macro-style strategies, endowments, pension funds, and sovereign wealth funds.

The acquisition also played into Numerix's future plans to continue driving digital transformation.

Setting Realistic Expectations and Timelines

Keeping transformation projects on track is an art form, and it's even harder to do when many different departments and third-party FinTech resources are involved. It's essential that everyone is clear about roles and responsibilities, and frequent meetings are an absolute requirement. The number of failed or delayed ventures in 2005, according to global research and advisory firm Gartner, was in the 30-plus percentage range; today it's at 68 percent. Managing change, and sustaining interest and commitment, are critical to the success of all transformative projects. Any third party utilized in a transformative project must be viewed as an extension of the organization for which it's working. It must be held accountable to the same list of deliverables and to the same standards.

WARNING

Some typical reasons for a project's failure are the following:

>> Misalignment of strategic goals, technical requirements, and business objectives.

>> Poor definition of success. The FinTech resources must be involved in and commit to the goals of the project.

>> Lack of accountability. Setting positive payouts for reaching specific goals and negative offsets for not doing so may be a way of further incentivizing third parties.

>> Poor establishment of timelines and goal monitoring. Project management across all resources, internal or outsourced, is critical.

>> Insufficient investment in tools that would make a project more trackable. All resources must use the same tools.

>> Poor project management and lack of consistent assignment of stakeholder responsibilities.

>> Lack of commitment and focus by the critical team responsible.

>> Loss of key advocates in senior management.

REMEMBER

Aligning a corporation with the best FinTech partner to handle some of the tasks and the administration of the transformative projects assure better outcomes for success. Defining expectations at the outset is critical.

The project leader is responsible for having clear needs and objectives in place. Those objectives come from gathering comprehensive requirements and formulating a statement of work (SOW) that is shared both internally and externally. All stakeholders must be involved in the planning stages of any project, and the sign-off process should include all those who have any level of ownership.

TIP

When you've created a requirements document that includes use cases, test criteria, and approval process, as well as a high-level SOW, the next step is to create a realistic timeline and to assign responsible owners to each component of the plan. It's best to break any large project down into smaller units or phases. Each of these units should have a list of milestones associated with it. Estimates on the manpower requirements and time commitments are integral to the success of a project and should have built-in flexibility. Several tools are available for tracking and overseeing these objectives. Many project leaders use Microsoft Project. (A great guide to help you is *Microsoft Project 2019 For Dummies* by Cynthia Snyder Dionisio, published by Wiley.)

Each plan should include user acceptance criteria, in-date and out-date, and design documents. You must also determine the interdependencies between the different use cases and the required functionality and incorporate them into the project plan. Post the plan on a shared site and update it with all stakeholders regularly.

Developing realistic project plans and delivery timelines is critical to a project's success. Missed deliverables and unrealistic work product commitments are demoralizing to the team, as well as to the internal and external stakeholders. To ensure a successful outcome, you should spend time upfront developing a solid plan that can be later augmented through constant review and task monitoring.

TIP

The schedule and commitments expected from a FinTech partner should be captured completely in the SOW, and there should be negative consequences for failure to meet objectives. This can include return of fees.

Supporting Change Agents

A *change agent* is an individual or team that creates change in an organization. Change agents can come from either inside or outside an organization. Sometimes a change agent can be a single employee who champions a specific process modification. Other times a company may hire a third-party firm to act as a change agent in large-scale organizational changes. At whatever level change is instituted, however, it must have buy-in from senior management.

Change agents provide guidance that comes from a position of strength. Most change agents represent the best and most forward thinkers of a company or division and are already respected in the company for other leadership roles. They have technical knowledge that translates into proactive solution finding, and they are recognized as charismatic leaders. The more change agents know the individual jobs required for a project, the easier it is for them to get team buy-in. FinTech firms often command the necessary respect because they are brought in as agents of change. Generally, the change agent may be the internal team leader of a project, though that isn't always the case.

Change agents are empowered by senior management but are also held accountable for specific deliverables. If they're focused full time on a project, the traditional departments for which they once worked are likely to be strained. Senior management must anticipate manpower disruption and make replacement staff available.

TIP

Because a company's change agents are such valuable assets, their career paths need to be part of the company's overall plan. You don't want other companies to be poaching them! Successful change agents should be rewarded when the project is complete with enrichment opportunities, such as formalized training and increased responsibility.

A change agent should have the following qualities and should encourage them in other team members:

>> The ability to think outside the box

>> The willingness to make mistakes but to identify them quickly and modify approaches

>> The ability to understand the personal limitations of the group and to seek specialized knowledge outside of the normal industry paradigm

>> The ability to listen to criticism with an open mind and empower others to bring their concerns forward

>> The discipline to make sure the project's focus and priorities are aligned with the company's needs

>> The willingness to take responsibility for unpopular decisions that promote the company's objectives

NUMERIX: LEADING DISRUPTION IN THE CAPITAL MARKETS

Founded in 1996, Numerix builds capital markets technology, specifically in the derivatives trading space. It helps firms improve revenues and profit and reduce risk by providing advanced software solutions for accurate pricing, modeling, valuation, and risk management of multiple types of derivatives. Its 2018 billings were $80.1 million, exceeded in 2019 by an additional $12 million.

Derivatives market participants face several challenges, and they need tools to help them navigate through complex market conditions and satisfy changing regulatory requirements. They need to upgrade systems to meet the required transformation of doing business today and in the future. Steve O'Hanlon has responded by building Numerix into a catalyst for innovation, and he approaches the challenges that market participants face as problems that Numerix has to fix better and faster than any of its competitors.

Steve's mission for Numerix is to disrupt existing technologies and business processes in the capital markets via next-generation, leading-edge technology to give clients a strategic advantage in their markets and enable them to make profitable shifts in business strategy. With his entrepreneurial mindset founded on creativity, fortitude, and insatiable drive, Steve has made Numerix essential to the capital markets. Its stickiness in the face of market changes and competitive pressures is unparalleled. Steve focuses the company on the key areas that drive value and make Numerix's clients successful — which leads clients to renew, upgrade, and rarely leave.

Numerix's competitors depend on it as well. Many of them find the need to embed Numerix analytics into their own technology frameworks in an effort to broaden the scope and quality of their own market offerings.

Numerix is very well entrenched in the sell-side community (investment banks), which represents 70 percent of its total billings annually. So in terms of current activity, the company is now developing new product lines that can help it become a more dominant player in the buy-side community (for example, asset managers and hedge funds) as well, since those now represent only 30 percent of their total license billings.

The steps Numerix is taking to assure its success in shaping and partnering with financial institutions are

- **Being a leader in FinTech transformative technologies:** Regulation and the internal driven need by banks and other organizations demand fully integrated platforms that deliver the same consistent data and outputs to all users.

(continued)

(continued)

- **Utilizing and curating new technologies:** Numerix "eats its own dog food." As a company that started out as an intellectual think tank, it has a talent for developing cutting-edge technologies. Numerix has adopted open source, microservices, new development languages, and more flexible development processes that increase its speed to market. It provides prepackaged, easily integrated cloud offerings and has taken a bet on the rapid development of artificial intelligence and machine learning. The position of blockchain in the marketplace and its right position in the future of the financial industry is currently an area of interest and research.

- **Making data homogenous and transparent:** The need for near real-time transparent digitalization is driven by clean and trusted data. Numerix has partnered with the best of breed in the area of data normalization and can deliver results anywhere, any way, and any time.

Retaining Good Employees during Change

All employees at some time in their career wonder whether a future with their current employer is still their best path forward. *Can I grow to my fullest potential here? Is my job secure, with all these changes going on lately? Can I do better somewhere else?*

In this age and this economy, competitors and headhunters are constantly trying to poach good employees. Employees can be especially vulnerable to these attempts when the organization is going through substantial change, because they fear the unknowns that the changes will bring. Employers must understand those fears and do what they can to mitigate them. The following sections can help.

TIP

After a lengthy transformation project, it may be beneficial to hire some of the employees from the third-party FinTech company who worked on the transformation. The contract you sign with the third-party company will likely contain a clause dictating how and under what circumstances you can do so.

Why employees leave

Employees leave companies because they may have some of the following concerns:

» No clear path to advancement

» Lack of respect or no confidence in the management team or the direction of the company

- >> No ability to learn new skills
- >> Compensation isn't sufficient for effort
- >> Lopsided work-life balance
- >> Wrong culture fit
- >> Lack of recognition for work well done
- >> Fear to take creative risk
- >> Fear of reputational risk

When you understand the concerns, you can construct clear policies and practices that help employees develop achievable career goals. All employees should be encouraged to develop a five-year goal plan that they share with human resources (HR) and their immediate supervisors. They should also be encouraged to reach out to more senior members of the organization for mentorship.

TIP

Instituting exit interviews that ask questions about the outgoing employees' perceptions and experiences can also assist in creating policies that decrease the probability of similar exits in the future.

Retention strategies that work

Corporations with successful retention numbers do so by actively supporting each employee's career development. Some ways that companies can help employees grow and succeed in their positions include the following:

- >> Creating programs that encourage and reward creativity.
- >> Developing clear career paths with milestones toward achievement.
- >> Creating incentive programs to reward continuing education.
- >> Making sure the pay structure makes sense. Employees always talk, and everyone wants to be appropriately recognized for the work they perform.
- >> Providing key employees with additional incentives for exceeding expectations.
- >> Offering first-time employees mentorship to help them become acclimated to the organization.
- >> Recognizing that younger employees may not function well within older hierarchical constructs. For millennials, making work fun and offering flexible work hours have been proven to increase productivity.

>> Creating a mission statement that resonates with the employee base and that resonates outside of the company as well. Everyone wants to work for a company that stands for something, is the best at something, or is striving to be the best.

TIP

The use of periodic internal surveys can be used to identify what rewards, policies, and incentive programs work best in an organization. Different types of companies and even different groups within a company may respond to different motivational carrots. For example, in a high-tech company, flex time and the support to do research on a pet project may incentivize a developer more than cash.

Career paths and organizational change

Humans are generally by their nature risk averse. To help employees be comfortable with change (including FinTech changes), the management team must understand the risk to employees (and define the company's comfort level with it), prioritize and rank the risk, and develop ways to deal with unexpected risk through defined processes. Change can be less frightening if employees know there's a process that covers how it's identified, escalated, and mitigated.

Some of the job changes that can occur during organizational change include the following:

>> **Vertical promotion:** A step up is nearly always a good thing, but employees may fear the greater responsibilities and the possibility of failure. The employer should discuss the possible outcomes with the employee, including the "what-ifs." For example, if the employee could potentially return to her old position if the new one doesn't work out well, knowing this could ease her mind.

>> **Horizontal relocation:** Sometimes employees are just in the wrong job for their skill set and should be moved to a different position. The employee needs to understand why management thinks it's the best move. Of course, such a move works only if the employee agrees with that assessment and knows that the leaders and company at large will support it.

>> **Job redefinition:** Outside forces may sometimes cause a job to be redefined, such as a change in a process due to technology updates. Such changes can be hard for employees, because they're comfortable in the old role and perhaps very good at it. It's important to make the employee understand how the change is critical to the company's success so it doesn't seem like an arbitrary and unwelcome disruption.

>> **Temporary change:** A company may need to ask some employees to change their job roles temporarily as they implement a new system in stages. The position may end up being permanent or not, depending on factors beyond the employees' control. To help employees feel more secure in such shifting, employers need to let them know that they won't be fired or laid off should the position fail to be made permanent.

Understanding Data-Driven Decision-Making

Data ownership, mining, and maintenance are all necessary parts of a corporate strategy. Using data properly — and aligning strategically with that use — enables companies to predict future growth more effectively, discover areas of new growth, and streamline operations to maximize profits. This is a new science and often outsourced to specialized third parties and to FinTech organizations.

The more scrubbed the data is that your company controls and uses, the better use senior management can make of it. Most older companies are sitting with large stores of raw data that could help them make more informed decisions if they only knew how to access it. As you find out in Chapter 9, business intelligence helps management utilize these silos of data more efficiently through the creation of dashboards and reports pulled from an array of data stores.

REMEMBER

The use of data to make business decisions is called *data-driven decision-making (DDDM)* and is based on the collecting and parsing of data into analyzable patterns that are driving the company toward key business objectives. These decisions should be driven by algorithms that create output based on metrics and figures. Companies can use the data for either quantitative or qualitative reporting. *Qualitative data* is contextual and not defined by numbers. *Quantitative data* is statistical.

For DDDM to be successful, the following must be true:

>> The data must be scrubbed and true.

>> The matrix used to interpret the data must be reviewed against the changes in the best practices and market needs.

>> It must be tested against biases and preconceived expectations.

Tools now exist that make focused reports and graphs available across the whole of a corporate organization. These tools make it easy to identify trends and to make decisions that are more business-driven than ever before.

NUMERIX: MANAGING THROUGH ACQUISITIONS

The decision to acquire a company is fraught with potential missteps and shouldn't be entered into without much research and fact checking.

In its acquisition of TFG Financial Systems in 2017, Numerix made its first step away from just organic growth to that of a more robust growth strategy, which included acquisition. It did so to attack a new area of revenue growth as well as to expand its technology.

It's safe to continue with organic growth if you've been successful at it. Numerix had always been nimble and astute in understanding the trends it saw in the marketplace and maximizing on its strengths. Consequently, it had seen double-digit year-over-year growth. What it currently faced, however, was a limitation on its horizon. Numerix saw acquisition as a way to expand into other lucrative arenas.

It's easy to be complacent with your growth when it's been organic. With a small to mid-size company, growth is comfortable and there are few variables. The company is well known. The limitations and the assets of its members are understood, and outcomes can be anticipated and are sustainable. It's easy to control the messaging and to provide a consistent vision that everyone understands, both internally and externally. However, at a certain point, it isn't enough.

Numerix understood that to be disruptive and transformative in the marketplace, and to maintain its competitive advantage, it needed new blood as well as new technologies and new avenues in which to sell its products. It saw acquisition as a fast road to those ends.

Numerix looked for a small company that had some sexy cutting-edge technologies that would launch it into new sales channels. TFG Financial Systems offered Numerix entry into the micro hedge fund world through its real-time risk, P&L, and position management system. TFG had new technology that was cutting edge: the dependency graph capabilities at the heart of its SaaS risk and portfolio management software and technology framework. Numerix felt that this new technology would provide core real-time, distributed, event-driven processing capabilities in Numerix Oneview enterprise trading and risk solution.

TFG's graph technology could also be central to future versions of the Numerix Oneview enterprise platform. Underpinning Numerix's technology architecture, Numerix Oneview became the only independent provider of real-time trading and risk with a single source of data and analytics for front and middle office risk.

In the end, an acquisition must be a win-win negotiation. The cultures must work as well as the technology. Due diligence is critical, and clear open communication is key to success. Someone needs to own the process that integrates not only the technology but also the people into one cohesive vision of the "new" company and the new vision.

Breaking the Silos

Three words that should never be uttered in any corporation: *Not my job*. People who hide behind a job description to determine how much work they do aren't focused on the company's success or on their fellow workers' needs. Such individuals are a liability to a company, but it's not always entirely the employees' fault. The company has a responsibility to deliver a work culture that discourages that attitude.

Successful, fully engaged organizations encourage and empower employees to be agents of change. As a matter of principle, they reward and recognize people for initiative.

A corporation's top management sets the tone of the corporate culture. A leader who is willing to perform what may be considered menial work sets an example that no job is unworthy of attention and that all jobs should be performed to the highest quality possible. CEOs who hold themselves accountable can also hold others to the same level of excellence.

A silo is a departmental representation of the "not my job" syndrome. Large corporations often encourage silo structures because they believe they facilitate better control and speedier responses. However, in the long run, silos impede growth and creativity. They form when insular departments and groups keep information away from other areas, either to ensure their own continued status or because they simply don't realize it may be useful to other departments. Such a lack of transparency generally begins as part of the overall corporate culture. When a silo is created, it impacts all aspects of the organization, infects the general morale of a company, and impedes the efficiencies of the corporation.

Here are some simple steps you can take to destroy the mentality that creates siloing:

>> Create a mission statement and set of goals for the whole company.

>> Make transparency the goal across all departments.

>> Use collaboration tools to increase productivity.

>> Form smaller cross-departmental transactional groups that have shared deliverables and accountability.

>> Offer cross-departmental training and pair workers whenever possible.

>> Communicate as often as possible both in teams and on a corporate level.

REMEMBER

Part of the process needed to break down silos starts with respect. Hear and share worker opinions and view differences of opinion as opportunities for growth. An evolving company embraces diversity of thought through action, and disagreements can lead to creative solutions.

Chapter **16**

Investing in FinTech Companies

Many banks are investing strategically in FinTech companies to hedge themselves from disruption, but many are also collaborating with FinTech firms to gain a win-win situation.

Venture capital (VC) firms are in search of the most distinctive FinTech companies that can become the next disruptors to the current banking norm. Private equity (PE) firms are looking for the company that can roll up many "diamonds in the rough" to create a large and significant multibillion-dollar market cap company. The winners and losers will help define the financial industry for decades to come.

Investing in FinTech firms can be like playing a game of chance, but there are ways to increase your odds of winning. This is essentially what VCs and PEs do every day. They try to run their winners and mitigate against risk to improve their returns. Of course, each FinTech start-up wants to take the smart money, and the smart money wants companies that have viable business plans and the credibility or pedigrees to build sustainable, profitable businesses.

In this chapter, we explain who is investing, how to identify future rising FinTech stars, and how to compete against the most well-known VCs and PEs in the industry. This chapter outlines the steps necessary to find the correct FinTech investment vehicles and to perform due diligence so the odds are in your favor.

TIP

The world of investors and investing is changing as a result of the FinTech revolution; this area of FinTech applied to the global investment management sector is called WealthTech. For more information, check out *The WealthTech Book* by Susanne Chishti and Thomas Puschmann (published by Wiley).

Understanding the Players

REMEMBER

When deciding whether to invest in the FinTech space, you need to consider the differences between consumer-driven investments (for example, the company that makes your favorite mobile finance app) and corporate-driven FinTech investments (for example, the company that makes the internal software a bank uses to manage customer accounts):

>> In the business-to-consumer (B2C) arena, some FinTech companies strive to disrupt the industry by providing new financial apps directly to consumers. These apps are appealing because they're easier, quicker, and cheaper to use than those that traditional financial institutions *(incumbents)* provide.

>> The business-to-business (B2B) space focuses on FinTech firms that are looking to collaborate with — rather than disrupt — existing institutions by providing products that increase their efficiency, flexibility, and profitability. The incumbents in turn provide new products to their clients.

>> There's also a middle ground, known as business-to-business-to-consumer (B2B2C). In B2B2C, FinTech firms sell their offerings to incumbents, who then white label (rebrand) each offering as their own and sell to their clients. If you drive a car, you've experienced that yourself, because your car company hasn't manufactured all the parts. Instead, it purchases them from a supplier and assembles them (and you'd never know the name of the supplier). The same happens in banking today: Banks assemble lots of FinTech solutions from FinTech firms and put their own names and branding all over it.

How these entities may attempt to raise funding, and how they deploy their funding, can be very different. Understanding the differentiation between these types of entities, therefore, will help you as you explore your investment options and decide where to put your money.

Challenging financial institutions

As we mention earlier, some FinTech firms are focused on disrupting the existing financial landscape, whereas others recognize that they need to collaborate with existing players to benefit from their size and distribution.

The FinTech firms that provide technology services to consumers or retail clients (B2C), largely in the form of cellphone-based apps (applications), are more likely to act as challengers to financial institutions, because individuals can make the buying decision for those products themselves.

The types of B2C FinTech apps and their functions are numerous. Initially a number of applications arose around payment facilities (PayTech). From there, foreign exchange was a natural segue for international transactions. This led to lending providers with more sophisticated credit scoring. More recently, fully fledged challenger banks have become popular, some of which are mobile-only enabled. Also robo-advisory firms in the wealth management space and InsurTech firms are competing for insurance underwriting.

These FinTech firms are disrupting established financial institutions' higher-margin retail businesses. How sustainable these business models are in the long run remains to be seen, as well as whether there may be consolidation among some of them or they may be bought by the established players.

Offering collaborative solutions to financial institutions

The FinTech firms that provide technology services to established financial institutions are more likely to act as collaborators with those institutions. They're largely based around workflow processes or making manual processes more efficient. Large financial institutions have historically spent hundreds of millions of dollars, if not billions, on technology that either gives them an edge, improves compliance, or helps them cut costs. However, as margins have reduced, interest rates have remained low, and capital adequacy requirements have increased, large institutions are less inclined to continue to build all of this themselves and are looking for shared services.

FinTech firms enable institutions to focus on their core technology and look for best-of-breed offerings in technology areas where they don't need a competitive advantage. The adoption of this model is still relatively fledgling, but demand appears to be growing.

FinTech adoption challenges the cultural approach of a traditional organization and its ability to change, particularly when considered as part of a collaboration with established financial institutions. FinTech has also embraced cultural aspects from a wider society perspective. The "wall of money" that's expected to drown the investment market in the coming years is focused on environmental, social, and governance (ESG) considerations. Companies are investigating how they can become more socially responsible from an ethical perspective but also to remain competitive in an environment where consumers and investors are looking for reasons to support, or not, a given company.

Therefore, new FinTech entrepreneurs are responding with products that promote cultural change, financial inclusion, and diversity. These resonate with some of the investors already described but have also unearthed new "impact" investors that are focused on corporate responsibility as well as a return on investment (ROI).

Navigating the Investor Landscape

Where you sit in the investment hierarchy generally dictates what access you have to given investments and what your risk appetite may be. This is also true for the different investment vehicles in the FinTech investor landscape. The following sections highlight some of the most common investment vehicles.

REMEMBER

FinTech CEOs need to know their potential investors very well and select the best ones in terms of capital, business growth opportunities, and long-term exit opportunities.

Crowdfunding

Crowdfunding is a way for individuals to collectively invest in a business in return for a potential profit or reward by responding to a pitch posted on a crowdfunding website. Crowdfunding can be very exciting for new investors, because they can back young, exciting start-ups and help them raise the money they need to grow. Often multiple banks will have rejected these early start-ups for loans, so these investments can be quite risky.

Several types of crowdfunding exist:

>> **Loan-based:** Peer-to-peer (P2P) lending is provided in return for a set interest rate (such as Lending Club and Funding Circle).

>> **Reward-based:** Money is invested in return for nonmonetary returns, typically samples of the product developed. This is the type of crowdfunding on sites like Kickstarter and Indiegogo.

>> **Investment-based:** This entails receiving shares in return for your investment, which is what we focus on in this chapter.

TECHNICAL STUFF

Investment-based crowdfunding is more the norm in Europe (particularly in the United Kingdom with companies such as Crowdcube and Seedrs) and more recently Asia. Reward-based investment is more popular in the United States due to regulations around investor requirements, although the JOBS Act (May 2016) extended online equity crowdfunding opportunities in the United States.

The very nature of crowdfunding lends itself to B2C-type investments because individuals can relate more to a consumer-focused application (see the earlier section "Understanding the Players" for more information). The product being developed may be something they'd use themselves. Hence, companies may raise a relatively small amount of money from hundreds or even thousands of investors, which in total gives them a decent funding round.

WARNING

Crowdfunding platforms will give you a choice of many companies that need money to grow. The most popular sites make it fun and enjoyable to browse these exciting companies and their products, therefore making it easy for you to part with your money. However, you should never invest money you can't afford to lose because you may not get it back, and you should invest only in what you completely understand.

The amount of due diligence retail investors do is relatively light, given the funds invested. However, firms on such platforms have increased the amount of information they provide, giving a certain standardization around the type of investor presentations produced. The platforms also have an obligation to undertake a due diligence process before allowing companies to list on their sites. The crowdsourcing model is so new that good data isn't yet available to understand how the majority of the firms on such platforms perform from a return on investment (ROI) perspective.

Fewer B2B companies are available for investment on crowdfunding sites, particularly FinTech companies, because B2B technologies aren't as immediately appealing to casual investors. A revolutionary new electronic gadget is just more "fun" to invest in than technology required for workflow processes within a financial institution. And that's why we need angel investors! Read on.

Angel investors

An *angel investor* is an accredited investor who provides financial backing, networking, business expertise, and other support to a small start-up in return for an equity share. Angel investors are typically sophisticated, experienced investors with high net worth and lots of readily available capital.

Angel investors are more likely to invest in businesses that are pre-revenue and seeking seed capital, because they tend to invest in businesses where they feel that they can add value through their domain expertise and network/contacts in that area. Therefore, angel investors generally take more risks than venture capital firms covered in the next section (including investing their own money) and invest more per company than individual crowdfunding investors.

However, angels aren't just guardians. The majority are seasoned professionals who regularly take positions as nonexecutive directors within the firms that they invest in or provide advice and networking to further the firms' opportunities. In addition, many angels invest collectively as a group or syndicate, either within a given theme, such as FinTech, or within random groups coming together under the guidance of one angel who acts as the lead investor.

Europe's first angel network focused on FinTech was established in 2014 by the FINTECH Circle (`https://fintechcircle.com`), where the best FinTech start-ups apply to pitch to experienced FinTech angel investors. The application process is very competitive and normally starts with an online application form, from which the best companies are selected and invited to Selection Days where they present in front of FinTech expert investors. The top seven companies are selected to present at the final FINTECH Circle Angel Network.

In some European countries, particularly the United Kingdom, both crowd and angel investors receive income tax rebates/reliefs from their investments in start-up firms. This acts as an incentive for some investors to become more active in this space and improves the risk-reward ratio for such investors. In other countries, for example the United States, it's more common for the start-up companies themselves to receive tax rebates for their research and development investments.

TIP

Research which tax benefits you'll get as an investor and/or as an entrepreneur early on. This could make your investments much more attractive/cost effective. Here are a few resources:

>> `www.gov.uk/guidance/venture-capital-schemes-apply-to-use-the-seed-enterprise-investment-scheme`

>> www.gov.uk/guidance/venture-capital-schemes-apply-for-the-enterprise-investment-scheme

>> https://startupsusa.org/issues/taxes/

Venture capital

Venture capital firms do what angel investors do, but they do it on a corporate basis. Instead of investing their own money, venture capitalists (VCs) are paid to invest other people's money.

Managers of the venture funds, known as general partners (GPs), are typically investors who have years of experience investing in and taking minority stakes in early stage firms. That's what they do for a living, unlike investors in crowdfunding sites or angel investors. GPs are either good at investing or lose their jobs.

Venture capitalists receive money from high net worth individuals, family offices, and corporations, all of which become limited partners (LPs) in the fund. Each of the LPs is looking for a diversified but higher return than what it can achieve from less risky investments, ordinarily for a fixed period of up to ten years. The GPs receive management fees (typically 2 percent of funds under management) to scout and invest in the right types of investments, conduct due diligence, and manage the resulting portfolio.

TECHNICAL STUFF

GPs and their firms typically take a carry fee (for example, 20 percent) of the performance of the fund (this management fee and performance fee are commonly referred to as "2 and 20"). The remainder of the profit (for example, 80 percent) is distributed to LPs. However, many funds have to achieve a *hurdle rate* — a return rate that investors must receive before the fund managers can receive their carry fee. For example, a fund's agreement may specify that the LPs must be paid back their invested capital, in addition to an agreed annual percentage yield, prior to the GP receiving their return.

To reduce the number of LPs that a fund services, a substantial minimum investment is typically required, putting such funds outside of the scope of most regular investors. To invest in VCs, you must either be very rich or indirectly invest via a fund that serves as one of the LPs; this is called a "fund of funds" structure.

REMEMBER

Because they're investing with other people's money, VCs tend to invest in businesses that are relatively established, with a given level of annual or monthly recurring revenue, at the Series A level of fundraising or later. Series A is generally the first funding round by VCs; Series B is the second funding round; Series C the third funding round; and so on. Crowdfunding and angel investors are normally investing in seed or post-seed rounds that come before Series A.

Some VC firms are lately shifting their focus to later stage investments (called scale-up funding), because the ROI for many funds have been lower than anticipated. Generally, VC investors should anticipate that about four out of ten firms will fail, and another four out of ten firms may return the monies invested. The remaining two firms would therefore need to have returns of 10 times or more to achieve the type of returns expected. The very successful firms are called unicorns, a term that refers to start-up companies that achieve a $1 billion market valuation.

To protect their interests, VC firms are more likely to demand preference shares for their investment and receive veto or minority investor rights that aren't available to other investors. They also tend to act as the lead investor in a funding round, thereby dictating the valuation, total monies raised, and the terms of the investment. Those terms may include the pre-money valuation of the firm, prior to investment, and the post-money valuation, which includes the funds raised added to the pre-money valuation. For example, a firm raising $1 million at a pre-money valuation of $10 million will have a post-money valuation of $11 million.

Corporate venture capital

As the name suggests, *corporate venture capital (CVC)* firms are like regular VC firms, but they invest on behalf of a given company. Their initial motive is therefore to invest in companies that will give some form of strategic benefit to the company, either immediately or in the future. As such, they tend to be focused on later stage firms that can bring immediate revenue and/or profitability. Some CVCs also take outside money, where LPs invest alongside them. However, such funds may be split in focus between providing a good ROI to all investors and delivering a strategic benefit to the parent company.

For example, suppose that your bank has a corporate venture fund. It could decide to invest in a FinTech company before it rolls out its FinTech app to millions of consumers globally. The bank must decide whether it will immediately separate the funds made available as CVC or whether it will draw down funds from the bank's balance sheet to support the investment. *Draw down* refers to collecting funds when an investment occurs, based on an agreement that such funds will be available when the CVC requests them.

This decision can have a significant impact on the commitment to the investment, or at least the perception of commitment. The employees who manage the CVC aren't necessarily rewarded in the same way that a commercial VC would be, with respect to management and performance fees. Therefore, the incentives, and hence the commitment, can be questioned.

TIP

Good VC investors should make lots of money, because they share the performance fee. However, the manager running a CVC won't get such unlimited payments. Therefore, if someone is driven by money, he'd probably want to run his own VC fund. Having said that, in principle, CVCs should be better venture partners to FinTech firms than regular VCs, because they have a competitive advantage due to their domain expertise, knowledge of markets, client networks, and technologies. In addition, their stronger balance sheet makes them a more patient investor. They aren't looking only for mutual growth but also more strategic benefits, such as direct synergies with their company's business that further drives additional revenue growth and valuation.

However, not all CVCs leverage these benefits. Internal stakeholders can question the start-up's ability to deliver or suggest that they can build the same thing themselves internally. Those that do succeed follow the mantra that "rip and replace" isn't the solution to managing old legacy systems and that "core and satellite" is a better strategy.

Of course, FinTech firms need to consider whether a CVC minority investment gives them the necessary short-term capital injection to meet their scale-up aspirations in conjunction with the corporate "mother ship." They may find that aligning closely with one large corporate infrastructure reduces their ability to scale into other competing corporate infrastructures due to a paranoia around access to confidential data. In addition, the obvious exit may be full integration into the CVC's company, which may not give the same return as selling the product on the open market.

Private equity

Historically, private equity (PE) funds have been viewed as more similar to the traditional asset managers of private investment. They tend to invest in much later stage companies that already have substantial revenue and are therefore less risky investments. (Blackstone buying a majority stake in Refinitiv is a recent example.) Not many FinTech firms are sufficiently large to qualify in that regard, so PE activity is more often found in other commercial sectors.

PEs have a similar structure to VCs, in that they involve GPs and LPs. However, the pools of capital raised for such funds tend to be much larger, as the company valuations of invested firms are much higher, given the firms' maturity, revenue, and profitability. PE funds typically have a fixed investment period, typically ranging from seven to ten years. There are similar management and performance fees (2 percent and 20 percent, respectively), although when institutional and ultra-high net worth individuals invest substantial funds, fees are often negotiable.

PE funds can also support investments such as leveraged buyouts, management buyouts, and company restructuring, whereby they regularly take majority or outright stakes in a company and use debt to finance large transactions, with the resulting burden of servicing that debt left with the company. They may then appoint management to make the company more profitable and valuable, which may include selling off pieces of the business in a "sum of the parts being greater than the whole" strategy. Alternatively, they may exit the investment through a trade sale to a strategic buyer (for example, Blackstone subsequently selling its stake in Refinitiv to the London Stock Exchange) or to another PE firm, or they may list the company on a stock exchange via an initial public offering (IPO).

Conducting Due Diligence

After you know the major types of investors (described earlier in this chapter), you can consider what firms these investors may be looking for and what assessment criteria they may use.

It's important to do your own research to determine whether you're making a viable investment. This is true whether you're a private investor monitoring some crowdfunding opportunities or a portfolio manager at a large private equity fund. The level of research will of course differ, but the principles are the same:

>> Your initial primary research should focus on companies addressing the areas in which you're interested in investing. For example, you should decide whether you're interested in retail or corporate opportunities and whether you want to limit your search to a given business sector that you think has growth potential.

>> Your secondary research should focus more deeply on individual companies. You'll need to determine whether there's a real market for their product, the size of the market opportunity, and the strength of the technology stack. Secondary research enables you to understand the business itself, its founders' credibility, and the potential of its offering.

The following sections look at the various types of research you may want to do in evaluating a potential FinTech investment and how investors can analyze the data they gather.

Performing primary research

Primary research is all about finding investments that meet your criteria. So of course, the first step of this process is to determine what your criteria actually are.

You may want to start by looking at where a company sits in the overall value chain: Is it B2C, B2B2C, or B2B focused? In other words, what is the general market sector the company targets? (See the earlier section "Understanding the Players" for more information.)

After you choose an overall sector, your next step is to determine whether to focus on a given vertical, such as WealthTech or RegTech (which we discuss in Chapter 1), or on specific technology areas. Examples may include artificial intelligence (AI; see Chapter 12) or blockchain (see Chapter 7). You could also go for a combination of two or more technology elements.

Then you must decide on the size and current success of the firm. Crowdfunding or angel investors may be happy to invest in seed stage companies that are pre-revenue but may require the firms to be eligible for certain tax benefits, preferably available to the investor. VC, PE, and CVC normally require a minimum level of annual recurring revenue and/or number of employees, which can indicate the company is relatively established and on a growth trajectory that suggests it can scale up.

TIP

There is a wide universe of FinTech firms out there, so a general Internet search is certainly not the most efficient way of identifying the right companies. Review the list of research sources in Chapter 13 for some ideas of where to do your research.

Doing secondary research

After you've identified some firms of interest, it's time to perform your own due diligence to ensure that the firms meet your requirements. Here's a general checklist to use as your starting point:

>> Are they producing a real solution to a given problem, or are they producing a technology solution that is *looking* for a problem?

>> Is the technology solution sufficiently differentiated from existing solutions, or does it create more efficiency and/or revenue?

>> What is the differentiating business model, and how sustainable is it?

>> What regulatory requirements, if any, does the business need to meet? Are there licenses or approvals to obtain?

>> What is the addressable market for the solution? Is a small percentage of that market still sufficiently interesting to make the solution viable?

>> Where is the current or likely competition for the solution? Does the FinTech firm have a sufficiently superior approach to differentiate it from the competition?

>> Is the product more likely to disrupt or collaborate with existing financial institutions' offerings? Are the founders clear on their direction?

>> What is the sales approach for the solution, and what challenges does that provide? For example, for B2C, how critical is search engine optimization (SEO)? For B2B, what is the sales cycle length required for larger financial institutions?

>> What is the current traction in terms of existing sales and potential pipeline?

>> What are the current projected revenues and related cost structure that create the expected burn rate and associated runway for the business?

TIP

The *burn rate* for a company is the regular monthly spend required to keep the firm in business. The *runway* is the length of time that a company can survive before needing more funding. Runway is determined by dividing the current funding available to the firm by the regular monthly spend. Of course, some firms start reducing their costs as they get closer to the end of their runway, to leave further time for revenue or funding opportunities.

>> Who is on the team? What credibility and/or experience and network do they have? Do they have the right personalities or chemistry? Have they worked together before?

REMEMBER

For some investors, the team is the most important factor, superseding all other analysis. The company may have a great product, but if the team isn't aligned, or if the chemistry is wrong because their respective ambitions or drive don't fit, they may not be able to reach their goals collectively. Founder issues occur surprisingly frequently, perhaps driven by the stress of meeting short-term objectives with limited resources. Looking for those who have worked successfully together in the past can be a key indicator. In addition, understanding the founders' home life challenges and ability to support themselves while bootstrapping the company — that is, building the company from the ground up with nothing but personal savings — can help you assess the overall situation.

>> What is the anticipated valuation of the business, pre-money and post-money? What amount of funding is required for what time frame to fund the business to the next milestones or funding requirement?

>> What is the longer-term exit plan for the business? For example, do the founders hope for a trade sale or an initial public offering (IPO)?

Analyzing data

Some investors can take all or some of the primary and secondary market indicators and use them to scientifically score firms and build up an objective matrix to evaluate the right firms to invest in.

Other firms focus more on diversification. They calculate the optimal number of firms to give certain return levels, and those calculations may drive them to diversify across industry verticals, types of technology, thematics, and even geographic regions to achieve a blended portfolio that will give the greatest ROI with the lowest risk profile.

Some firms have built a business around objectively scoring investments based on the secondary market research factors, and investors will pay for such scorecards to simplify their due diligence process.

In addition, some investment platforms have enabled machine learning algorithms to matchmake certain FinTech firms with established serial investors in that vertical or theme, alerting investors to firms that are looking to raise funds.

Artificial intelligence/machine learning factors are frequently applied at this stage to establish a scientific approach. However, as we mention earlier, personalities and leaders can also be a key element to success with some firms, and those things are more difficult to quantify.

TIP

To further find out how artificial intelligence is used and benefits financial services, refer to *The AI Book* by Susanne Chishti, Ivana Bartoletti, Anne Leslie, and Shân M. Millie (published by Wiley).

Evaluating a Company's Growth Strategies

When considering which FinTech firms to invest in, it's important to understand a company's growth strategy (with the help of the following sections). This information can help discern whether a small company will be able to grow into a larger one. Many start-up firms fail to grow into their potential, either finding and maintaining a plateau or ultimately failing.

Studying the competition

One way of deciding on a FinTech firm's ability to scale is to study its potential competitors. (You can find those competitors by looking through accelerators and FinTech award lists, or the firm may find itself in direct competition for sales on a regular basis.) How did those companies grow, and what can the company in question learn from that?

Understanding the competition can also help you assess the market saturation. What is the size of the market, and how well is it already being served? Does the complexity of the product enable multiple products to compete and win in that space? What is the company's USP (unique selling proposition)?

Listening to customers

Many investors will request a call with some of the FinTech firm's customers to understand how they use the product and whether that usage is consistent with the firm's objectives. Recurring revenue is a major factor in determining a firm's viability and valuation. Therefore, it can be helpful to understand how important and "sticky" the product is to the client.

The ability to penetrate the market and increase sales is a vital factor in growing the business as well. Understanding how the product is distributed and delivered as well as understanding what the client anticipates in customer service and future product development is vital.

Asking about technology

Given all the recent technology advances, it can be difficult for investors to fully understand a company's technology stack. Does it do what the FinTech firm claims it does? How scalable will the architecture and infrastructure be if the business grows quickly?

TIP

Some investors will use technical domain experts to ask the FinTech firm the right questions to determine the technology's uniqueness or viability. Meanwhile, some independent firms have begun to produce objective, standardized scorecards on FinTech firms that they sell to investors (for example, see www.thedisruption house.com/technology-providers).

Inspiring innovation

A founder may start his own FinTech firm out of an ambition to build a more efficient and innovative product than currently exists. This ambition needs to be infectious, not only in selling the founder's vision to an investor but also to attract talented employees who want to join the journey of growing the business.

To scale, firms need to convey a passion that others will follow. This inspiration and passion is important to today's millennial workforce, where companies are likely to find the relevant new-technology skill sets. This is why some investors find the team and their capability and credibility important in determining which firms have growth capability.

Considering a Company's Culture

FinTech, as a whole, is more culturally progressive than the traditional financial industry (or at least its reputation). FinTech companies and projects are leading the way to more inclusion and diversity. *Inclusion* means finding ways to help more people participate fully in an experience. For FinTech firms, that means helping more consumers qualify for and use financial products.

FinTech firms can help promote greater financial inclusion, particularly in the consumer/retail space. Some of the products that FinTechs provide make banking accessible to low-income individuals who may have poor credit or limited access to brick-and-mortar banks. Making banking services available via smartphone — not just desktop and laptop computers — further improves service accessibility, because most people today have smartphones. And objective, data-driven qualifiers for loans and other products can bring more opportunities to customers who have traditionally been discriminated against in human-biased evaluation processes.

Financial inclusion is also a key theme in emerging markets where large parts of the population don't have bank accounts. Instead, they use telephone credits to pay each other, referred as mobile money. For example, M-Pesa is a money transfer service that was launched by the largest mobile network operators (by Vodafone in conjunction with Safaricom and Vodacom) in Kenya and Tanzania. The cellphone-based service is also used for microfinancing, particularly in rural areas.

TIP

The number of products and institutions supporting such activities is likely to increase as more of these products are proven in the market and socially responsible corporate activities increase.

Despite the perception that the vast majority of FinTech founders are white guys in their 30s with beards, FinTech employee diversity is very high. When working for a start-up, you may have to struggle on a low income until the company finds success, and many immigrants and students are used to surviving on low income! Joking aside, a strong correlation exists between computer science skills and international workers and students. Many immigrants end up working for FinTech start-ups, which naturally increases the workforce diversity.

The number of women founders has increased recently, but there's further room for improvement on that front. In 2018, 93 percent of technology investments in technology were received by all-male founding teams in Europe. All-female founding teams received only 2 percent of technology investments made by European Venture Capital, with start-ups made up of both men and women receiving just 5 percent of funding. The UK Business Angel Association states that only about 15 percent of the total angel population are women. Its research highlights that 30 to 50 percent of the portfolio of investments made by women investors are in women founders, although just 7 percent of partners in the world's top investment companies are women. Therefore, the investments in female entrepreneurs are likely to increase as the percentage of female angels continues to increase — for example, 40 percent of the FinTech firms in the 2020 Barclays/Techstars Accelerator cohort have female founders.

Many FinTech start-ups have international scale ambitions, and a diverse workforce is also a clear reflection of that reality. The fact that international employees feel they have less to lose can also lead to a higher risk-taking mentality and more entrepreneurial spirit, which can be useful in a FinTech environment.

Chapter **17**

Figuring Out the FinTech Endgame

A s we discuss throughout this book, technology is driving innovation and disruption across financial services. Banks and financial institutions will have to embrace technology and innovation if they are to succeed in the coming years.

The banking sector has generally recovered from the financial crisis, and the resulting new regulations have required banks to improve their capital adequacy to prevent a recurrence. However, in a low interest rate environment, their profit margins are reduced, and their earnings outlook has shrunk. They've also faced increased costs in meeting the new regulatory criteria required to ensure a secure financial system. Consequently, financial institutions have had to consider new business models, including different pricing structures, cost reductions, and perhaps consolidation.

The new wave of digitalization across the industry has made people feel optimistic and has motivated even the most traditional institutions to develop innovation agendas. The scene is set for disruption, revolution, and transformation.

REMEMBER

FinTech firms have largely been successful in implementing online payment spaces and new lending platforms, but that's just the beginning. Traditional institutions fear that FinTech will offer state-of-the art financial services far more cheaply — and it's a very realistic fear to have. This fear drives banks to voluntarily disrupt their own practices and structures before someone else disrupts them. Challenger consumer retail institutions such as online-only banks are a few years away from challenging the full economic functions of a traditional bank, but that time is coming. The "digital genie" has left the bottle.

FinTech companies do have some challenges on the horizon. The closer FinTech firms get to fully replicating a bank's offerings, the more regulatory oversight they will have to face, which will be both challenging and costly for them. Regulators will review a firm's business model and determine whether it needs a license to undertake banking or payment services. Financial institutions or FinTech firms will need to provide services that are efficient, cost effective, and, most of all, secure to meet their customer base's requirements.

So what is the FinTech endgame? Who is going to win at the end? Will it be the FinTech start-ups that have disrupted the market? Will it be the BigTech giants that have applied all they know about social and e-commerce platforms toward financial services? Or will it be the incumbent players that will learn to fight back? That's a highly charged question in the finance and FinTech sector and often debated in the media. This chapter considers some of the factors involved in answering that question and discusses some possible outcomes.

Bringing the Board Up to Speed on FinTech

We are board members ourselves, so we can appreciate the balancing acts that CEOs and boards of financial institutions must navigate. There is constant pressure to do it all — maximize revenues, reduce costs, reduce headcount, upskill their employees, replace their legacy core banking systems, and partner or acquire tech or FinTech companies. It truly is a balancing act, because you can't do everything at once. When you put resources toward certain performance and financial metrics, others deteriorate.

In the following sections, we explain the challenges that financial boards face and provide some guidance on how they can adapt to the use of FinTech.

Noting the challenges that financial boards face

Boards prefer as much information and data as possible to make good decisions. Greater insight helps "de-risk" them. Often, however, reliable data points don't exist, especially when you move into the uncharted territories of innovation. This can lead boards to be hesitant to act, so they try to wait until more information becomes available. However, by that time, the competition has moved ahead, and it's too late.

Another challenge for a board is to measure the return on investment (ROI) of FinTech transformation programs. This is very hard, because it depends on so many variables and how you defined the baseline to which the end result will be compared. Some board members also see FinTech as a temporary activity, which becomes apparent with questions such as "When is the investment in technology completed? What will the tech team do afterward?" Boards must understand that technology isn't a time-boxed investment and activity on a project plan. To stay competitive, companies must make technology an ongoing focus.

Senior management at most financial institutions are anxiously monitoring the shifting competitive environment within financial services. Digital transformation is a regular agenda item in board meetings, given its potential bottom-line impact, and therefore all financial institutions will go through digital transformation programs. However, McKinsey research has shown that 70 percent of such programs have failed or don't reach their stated goals.

Transformative innovation relies on collaboration, participants sharing ideas, and agreeing on the common pain points. This is increasingly apparent in the FinTech sector, with various reports suggesting that companies will have to think in terms of ecosystems, where a growing percentage of global sales will be transacted.

Some financial institutions and vendors are creating platform-based strategies where they provide the operational platform to allow FinTech firms to integrate via open application programming interfaces (APIs) and provide their offerings (via the bank's brand name as a white-labeled service or operating under their own brand) to the bank's clients. A successful FinTech ecosystem enables banks to coordinate start-up and scale-up development. They need to create their own community or partner with firms such as accelerators or incubators. (See Chapter 13 for more about partnerships.)

Having a strong ecosystem enables institutions to move quickly and gain a first-mover advantage. The focus should be to trial and analyze in iterative cycles, to develop minimum viable products (prototypes) within shorter time periods, and to decrease the build and launch times within both the business-to-consumer

(B2C) and business-to-business (B2B) offerings. However, to create such a flexible environment, financial institutions need to review their procurement and onboarding processes. In many organizations, outdated processes stifle the vast majority of initiatives by not being quick and agile enough. It can take more than six months to arrange a proof of concept, by which point the parties involved have already moved on.

The final reason FinTech is so important for boards of financial institutions is because it drives company valuations. In the past, there was almost a direct link between the earnings power and profitability of a company and its ultimate value and valuation. Naturally, valuation drives shareholder decisions because it helps raise money at higher valuations at the next financing round (for private companies) or is a public sign of approval and confidence in the future strategy for companies listed on the stock market.

However, as we've seen in the recent tech and FinTech boom, the link and positive correlation between earnings before tax and profitability metrics, compared with the valuation of a company, is broken. In today's tech-driven world, loss-making companies with convincing technology platforms are seen as much more valuable than profitable financial institutions with old-fashioned technology architectures. Incumbents need to convince the investor community that their potential for future earnings is made stronger by having a scalable technology infrastructure.

REMEMBER

Regulated financial entities can't focus only on maximizing their shareholder valuation at all costs — which is what most tech giants and nonregulated FinTech companies seem to be focused on. They also must be compliant with all regulatory requirements. So that's why regulation has often been a hindrance to larger financial institutions, because it makes their ability to innovate and experiment that much harder. (Flip to Chapter 3 for more about regulation.)

Embracing digital transformation

Digitization is the process of converting information from a physical format to a digital one, or something nondigital (analog) into a digital representation, to automate processes or workflows. Digitization enables businesses to automate collecting and leveraging their data. Consequently, it's the information you're digitizing that matters, not the processes by which you do it.

Digitalization is the process of leveraging digitization to further improve business processes by applying technology and information to transform business operations. Digitalization helps create a digital culture, using digital information at the core, to enable the business to be more efficient, productive, and profitable.

Whereas digitization and digitalization are essentially about technology, *digital transformation* focuses on using efficiency and productivity gains to better serve the customer through cultural change in the organization. Digital transformation involves reviewing all aspects of business and determining a new growth strategy based on new business models that can lead to a new market environment. Therefore, digital transformation isn't just a series of digitalization projects. It requires an organization to embrace change, making it a core competency of the business so that the new culture drives an end-to-end focus on the customer.

The vast majority of digital transformation programs fail, largely because many financial institutions have entrenched business silos that have created a noncollaborative culture. An inflexible enterprise structure acts as a barrier to an innovation culture. Therefore, any strategy incorporating digital transformation needs to be driven by the CEO and key management personnel.

Unfortunately, most leaders don't know how to lead digital transformation. They have earned their positions by showing great awareness in managing traditional business models but aren't well prepared for the platform economics of digital competition. Few leaders have a strong FinTech or digital transformation background, nor the experience to change a traditional culture by encouraging an entrepreneurial attitude and cooperative behavior from senior management down. It therefore becomes difficult to sustain the impact of transformation due to the general lack of employee engagement.

Many institutions have digitalized their products and solutions, which has maintained retail and corporate customers in the short term. Nevertheless, these solutions are often disjointed attempts or tactical initiatives that don't exploit their full transformation potential. Existing heads of silos see them as disruptive and give them less priority.

It's already challenging to create and promote new products and services profitably but introducing a new business model at the same time makes it even harder. Such decisions are made at the board level, as they often require capital reallocation within multiple business units, such as retail, corporate, investment banking, asset management, and private banking.

Digitally altering an institution requires far-reaching strategic plans, rather than narrow focus on new products or services. Associated platforms and data sets must be integrated across the institution. Some institutions will survive and develop alternative digital business models, but other institutions will react too late and will either collapse or have to move into special markets.

Developing digital skills

It's fair to say that most financial institutions have a skills deficit. Understanding lean start-up methodologies and agile development frameworks is necessary, because these are the skills required when steering and employing large digital transformation programs within financial institutions. Moreover, having a diverse and experienced team with these skills, incorporating many entrepreneurial talents, is a critical competitive advantage for any institution. Talent and skills development via FinTech master classes, for example, can build the innovation muscle of an organization so that the company can correctly analyze and respond to digital disruption. (See the nearby sidebar for more about classes.)

REMEMBER

When staff have been enabled to recognize and implement digital transformation goals, it's required that they're recompensed appropriately. Outdated payment models and bonus systems view taking risks and successfully implementing change initiatives as less valuable than revenues produced in the front office. In such environments, the best and brightest employees won't consider championing corporate transformation attractive from a career perspective. They already have to battle the bureaucracy erected by people who don't want change. Companies must reward digital transformation leaders for the professional and personal career risks they undertake and must make sure they know that they have the full backing of their CEO and senior management team. Otherwise, the more entrepreneurial people may jump ship and start their own FinTech firm or act as advisors or nonexecutive directors to existing FinTech firms.

Organizations need to discard top-down, hierarchal management structures and move toward multidisciplinary teams that are collaborative and team-oriented. Managers must adapt, applying their experience of organizational history and culture and employing their expertise to make decisive business decisions. Creative thinking and experimentation, data analysis and interpretation, and strategy development are some of the main skills that management must develop further in the future.

The digital skills required across an institution will focus on data scientists that can integrate artificial intelligence (AI) and machine learning (ML) practices into an organization. The ideal approach is to build internal teams of expert product people and engineers who understand the application of AI/ML, working closely with the teams delivering customer services. These strategies will also require unstructured data, where the natural language processing of ML can deliver results, alongside the more structured data AI conclusions. (See Chapter 12 for more about AI.)

A FinTech MASTER CLASS FOR THE C-LEVEL

A midsize bank had a very progressive CEO who had published in its annual report that digital transformation was a top priority for the bank over the next three years. However, there was no clarity as to what this actually meant in relation to being a wholesale bank, which combines retail, commercial, investment banking, transaction banking, and wealth management/private banking activities all under one brand.

The board and C-level executives attended a FINTECH Circle MasterClass that explained the strategic options the bank had to consider based on the various FinTech trends and changing, competitive landscape. The leadership teams utilized enterprise innovation methodologies and developed several new business propositions during the class, and they developed a road map to get those new value propositions implemented.

The class challenges attendees to break down the silo thinking that normally exists in large financial institutions and to form cross-functional teams to both fully understand existing customer pain points and develop potential solutions that can be tested in an iterative cycle. (Chapter 15 has more information on breaking down silos.)

In these classes, financial services managers come to understand the urgency for change and are able to develop a concrete vision of their strategic options and acquire a tool kit to lead digital transformation.

Although some commentators have focused on the challenges of using AI and ML for future professional work, these technologies offer huge opportunities for promoting new fields of expertise and delivery. The key challenge for management is to reconsider the ways in which it develops and balances emerging technological tools. Successful managers must understand both data science and human factors such as empathy and emotional intelligence.

Managers must develop systematic approaches to leverage the digital transformation of an institution's strategy, processes, and technologies. They will need to introduce strategies to manage change and assist staff to adapt to change in a proactive environment. This suggests that they will have to make decisions based on real or forward-looking, predictive analytics instead of making decisions based on historical data.

Figuring out how to participate

Many financial services board members learned fundamental business and financial rules and strategic planning skills a long time ago, and those skills have continued to serve them well for most of their careers. Many financial institution executives have been slow to recognize the threat of digitalization and the new competitive situation. They have significant insight into traditional business practices and industries, but the principles that have served them in the past are often at odds with the new-platform economics of BigTech (very large tech companies that provide products and services across multiple industries) and FinTech, their key competitors. Digital transformation is a regular point of discussion for board members as they recognize that their company is falling behind those companies that have already digitalized.

Financial institutions' management boards must learn how to participate in this new environment where just keeping pace with competitors isn't sufficient. They must also understand how to compete or partner with BigTech and collaborate with FinTech start-ups and scale-ups. Of course, that advice also assumes an openness to new ideas and developments. Board members must understand how to develop digitalization as a force for innovation within the current business model and how to proactively adapt to the new digital environment. Without a strong FinTech and digital transformation leadership team in place, companies will struggle to compete and can potentially commit to a range of complex and expensive mistakes that may be impossible to fix in the future. Therefore, many institutions have created the new role of Chief Digital Officer to drive the transformation required.

WARNING

Being technologically current is important, but riding the bleeding edge of new technology is not. When contemplating digital transformation, don't focus heavily on the latest radical technology, because the risk-reward balance isn't optimal there.

There's also a risk that board members may forget the main reason for digitally transforming the business: its customers. They need to understand that staying customer-focused requires the institution to test, evaluate, and modify its approach to match or exceed client expectations, pivoting whenever required. Such customer responsiveness also requires the board to embrace a new open culture that encourages and empowers employees to not be afraid to try and fail when pursuing innovation.

Meanwhile, these boards will need to think in terms of ecosystems. Financial institutions must provide the technology and operational platforms, the underlying ecosystem, to which FinTech companies can connect via open APIs and present their services to customers (either white-labeled under the institution's brand name or under their own brand). A successful FinTech ecosystem enables institutions to engage meaningfully with tech start-ups and scale-ups, suppliers, investors, regulators, service providers, and, of course, customers. They therefore need to create their own ecosystems or partner with firms that have built such an ecosystem. Doing so enables institutions to move faster and develop a learning advantage. The goals should be to decrease the build and launch times within B2C and B2B approaches.

REMEMBER

Transformation isn't about ripping out and replacing legacy systems overnight. Systemically important institutions shouldn't take the risk of failing to meet their obligations, however that may be defined. Developing a hub-and-spoke model should be a key objective. In such a model, internal staff continue to maintain and develop the core systems ("the hub") while they partner with satellite FinTech partners ("the spokes") to deliver the technology required to meet their digital challenges.

Looking into the Future of FinTech

Technology in general is constantly developing, and a number of new technologies are being applied to the financial services arena. This section highlights some of those new technologies and how FinTech firms are putting them to work.

Authentication methods

Biological authentication (*biometrics*) is the future of authentication, with authentication methods such as facial recognition, voice recognition, retina scans, and fingerprint scans becoming ever more accurate and widely deployed:

>> In particular, voice biometrics represents a major step forward in eliminating passwords and making authentication more reliable and expedient for the client. To activate voice recognition, a customer must record a statement that needs to be said aloud when logging in. Consumers like it because they're recognized more quickly, and they don't need to answer additional security questions. Businesses like it because tech support fields fewer calls for help.

WARNING

However, while banks claim that voice authentication is more secure than fingerprint reading, there are some concerns about the rapid increase in such modern technologies. Voice biometrics are accepted on the theory that each person has an inimitable voice, but the current research is still based on a relatively small sample. In addition, it's still unsure how background noise may restrict the attributes of voice biometrics.

>> Other institutions employ facial recognition technology to authenticate customers, when granting access to mobile banking apps. To set up facial recognition, the bank takes a picture of the customer as part of the

onboarding process, and that picture is compared to the picture taken with the mobile device's camera when someone tries to sign in on the device.

>> Iris recognition is also common. With this technology, the device's camera captures an image of the person's eyes and analyzes the unique patterns inside the ring-shaped area that surrounds the pupil. Dual-factor authentication can combine facial and iris recognition by also monitoring blinks and eye movement. This additional layer of security helps counter fraud, because a video of a user wouldn't be able to blink at the right moments.

>> Fingerprint recognition is the other main biometric authentication option available. Fingerprint recognition has been around longer and is the most common means of authentication that's used in the majority of digital devices, partly because it's inexpensive to implement.

Customers can be given the option to log in to an app using their preferred method — voice, face, or fingerprint — or they can opt out of biometrics and enter a PIN or password.

Apart from these biometric options, another approach to multifactor authentication is the use of device identification, where an encrypted token is sent from the device to the institution, which is then matched against the ID of the device registered at the time of enrollment.

Voice technology

Voice technology has become common in the home, with consumers now able to talk to smart fridges, thermostats, vehicles, and many other devices. Voice assistants such as Alexa, Google Home, and Siri have also changed the way people get information using mobile devices and home management systems. People are becoming increasingly comfortable talking to computers rather than humans to get things done.

Voice technology is expected to soon transform the finance sector as well. Gartner Research has suggested that AI bots will control 85 percent of customer service interactions in the near future.

Many banks are looking into using voice authentication technology alongside voice-controlled virtual assistants. In such a system, consumers would be able to make a payment by talking to their smartphone app. The app would not only authenticate users by their voice but would also follow their orders to make the payment.

As machine intelligence becomes better at voice recognition and conversation, businesses are applying it in many different forms, from biometric security to helpful chat bots (see Chapter 12). While past technological limitations perhaps delayed consumer acceptance of these technologies, radical breakthroughs introduced over the past five years have made widespread adoption more achievable.

Voice technology usage is certain to increase in the next several years, further enriching customer experiences with digital devices. Voice recognition will become an integral part of daily transactions by bridging the gap between human and machine conversations.

Artificial intelligence

Artificial intelligence (AI) is an overall term referring to a group of computing technologies and methods to enable computers to make adaptable rational decisions in response to often unpredictable conditions. The elements of AI (discussed in more detail in Chapter 12) include natural language processing (NLP), machine learning (ML), intelligent agents, and rational decision-making. The process involves developing systems that can perform a range of basic tasks better and more efficiently that have traditionally been done by humans. AI is developing at an unprecedented rate due to developments in big data and cloud computing technologies (see Chapter 6), both of which make it easier to store vast amounts of data, and through the benefit of accessing elastic computing power.

ML is effectively a subcomponent of AI but is also its natural ally. Whereas AI involves training a machine to learn from a large amount of ingested structured data using algorithms, ML then adapts its program pattern based on what it learns. For example, ML plays a major role in tools that companies use to analyze data or identify intelligent activities and their applications for organizations and management. ML is therefore one of the most common and effective approaches to achieving AI.

WARNING

However, many challenges remain to complete and maintain a successful implementation. Some of these include data management (such as accessing data from unrelated sources into a common data lake), IT infrastructure, and employing the essential human talent to deploy the technology as the complexity of these techniques has noticeably increased.

In addition, the scale of applications across different client segments has seen considerable progress. Initially, machine learning was primarily used to make credit decisions in retail portfolios based on the structured data that financial institutions already had on their retail clients. Nowadays this analysis is being extended to larger corporate and wholesale sectors, where the structured data is being combined with multiple sources of unstructured data where natural language processing can be employed, including news feeds and internal and external supply-chain data. To achieve further advancements, data sets must be unified across institutions to allow more wide-ranging decisions to be made.

Identifying Industry-Driven Networks, Accelerators, and Incubators

Several institutions are sponsoring incubators, accelerators, and hackathons to encourage tech experimentation and provide advice, connections, and mentorship to FinTech start-ups. It can be mutually beneficial for institutions and start-ups to participate. For FinTech companies, particularly in strongly regulated sectors, it's more sensible to leverage large financial institutions' infrastructure and investment spending.

The FinTech Innovation Lab

Run by Accenture, the FinTech Innovation Lab (FIL; www.fintechinnovationlab.com) helps start-ups build connections with relevant decision-makers at partner organizations (many of the largest financial institutions) and gain valuable insights to accelerate their businesses to the next level. Started in 2012, FIL is a global accelerator program with hubs in London, Hong Kong, and New York.

FIL immerses start-ups in a community of their peers, advisers, experts, and partner financial institutions that may become clients and investors in the future. Networking among this ecosystem brings insights, feedback from mentors, and support from influencers from global financial companies. Ambitious start-ups receive three months of mentoring, networking, and advice, which helps them refine and test their value propositions.

Even better for start-ups is that it's also free. Accenture takes no fees or equity stake. Its stated aim is to find ways to support its customers in the financial services industry by providing an opportunity for them to engage with and learn from FinTech firms.

Startupbootcamp FinTech

Startupbootcamp FinTech (www.startupbootcamp.org) is a global program supporting innovative companies in the financial services industry. The program is run from Amsterdam to Mexico to Mumbai, with the flagship program traditionally run out of London. They have a large group of partners that provide direct access to an international network of the most relevant mentors, partners, and investors in the industry. Partners include firms such as Bertelsmann, Lloyds Banking, Mastercard, Rabobank, and Route 66. In addition, they provide expertise, exposure channels, APIs, and access to their FinTech network of industry professionals from around the world.

They also help early-stage tech founders rapidly scale their companies by providing office space and seed funding, for which they receive an equity stake in return. The London program has now taken a new format and is focused on growth stage companies with Scale and CoLab programs. The latter also works specifically with partner organizations to provide specific scouting and dedicated programs to individual institutions with an identified problem looking for an innovative solution.

Techstars

Techstars (www.techstars.com) is a global program supporting innovative companies across a range of industries. It provides access to financial, human, and intellectual capital for portfolio companies within the accelerator to drive their successes. Once accepted to a Techstars accelerator, each company is offered an investment of a $100,000 convertible note. Techstars provides $20,000 of this amount, which is generally used to fund attendee living expenses throughout the program. In return, Techstars receives 6 percent of the token reserve (tokens held back for the founders and the company at network launch) and 6 percent equity of the company (on a fully diluted basis, issued as common stock) until the company raises a priced equity financing of $250,000 or more (a qualified financing). Techstars has developed a specific FinTech program in London, New York, and Tel Aviv in partnership with the Barclays Accelerator.

At the end of the three-month accelerator program, Techstars organizes a demo day, where 100 to 200 angel investors and venture capitalists (VCs) are invited to listen to the start-ups pitch their companies. In addition, Techstars Ventures has $265 million under management and has a third fund ($150 million) that it uses to co-invest alongside the angel and venture capitalist communities.

FINTECH Circle

FINTECH Circle (https://fintechcircle.com) is a global network of more than 130,000 FinTech entrepreneurs, investors, finance professionals, academic, government representatives, and solution providers that produces content and updates on the latest FinTech trends. It provides a range of services for different participants in the FinTech ecosystem.

Its angel network, established in 2015, was the first FinTech-focused investment platform in Europe, and its investors have already enjoyed three exits during this period. FINTECH Circle's ecosystem has enabled it to crowdsource three bestselling books: *The FinTech Book, The WealthTech Book,* and *The InsurTech Book* (all published by Wiley).

More recently, FINTECH Circle has expanded into educational courses, with both face-to-face FINTECH Circle MasterClasses and online FinTech courses, covering topics such as a FinTech foundation, enterprise innovation and digital transformation, WealthTech, InsurTech, RegTech, LegalTech, PayTech, and blockchain/cryptocurrency. It also provides an external acceleration program to help firms develop internal teams and coach their own intrapreneurs.

Finally, FINTECH Circle also produces a China FinTech Bridge conference, which is the only conference dedicated to FinTech investments and business trade deals between Greater China and the UK/Europe.

Level39

Level39 (www.level39.co) is wholly owned by the Canary Wharf Group in London and was launched in March 2013. Level39 supports fast-growth businesses by providing access to world-class customers, talent, and infrastructure. They have established a well-connected tech community, providing access to a well-appointed workspace at Canary Wharf, a crowded events calendar, and some well-established mentors and facilities, all aimed at helping businesses achieve scale.

TECHNICAL STUFF

Level39 has since grown into an 80,000-square-foot accelerator, spread over three floors, based on the 24th, 39th, and 42nd floors in Canary Wharf, London.

Mulling Over Mergers and Acquisitions

The FinTech endgame will naturally include many mergers and acquisitions as the industry matures. Some important questions are

>> **Will financial institutions continue to co-invest in or buy FinTech companies outright to provide them with a competitive advantage in the endgame?** It's interesting to note that all the BigTech giants have made multiple acquisitions over the years to stay ahead of the curve.

>> **Will larger FinTech companies buy smaller FinTech companies?** This approach has been seen already with larger traditional vendor firms buying

midsize vendor competitors. It will be interesting to see whether this extends to them buying smaller firms developing new, innovative technology in the same way that BigTech firms have done in the pure technology space.

>> **Will tech giants buy FinTech companies?** The BigTech firms may consider buying FinTech firms that are pure technology providers that can collaborate with larger financial institutions rather than buying FinTech firms that are disruptive and potentially expose them to regulatory oversight.

The short answer to all these questions is *potentially yes*. There have been huge investments in smaller FinTech firms over the last few years on a global scale, and this trend will likely continue. The following sections discuss two types of mergers and acquisitions: consolidation and corporate venture strategies.

TECHNICAL STUFF

The United States is the leading country for FinTech investment, with $9.37 billion invested across 477 deals according to an Innovate Finance and London & Partners report. The United Kingdom ranks second, with $2.29 billion across 142 deals. Germany, China, and Sweden complete the top five in terms of deal value. However, in terms of cities, it's interesting to note that San Francisco is currently the major city in North America for deal value, rather than New York City, while London remains the largest city in Europe, both in terms of value and number of deals, and has seen more individual deals than San Francisco (114 versus 80).

Consolidation

Consolidation is the merger of two separate corporate entities to form one larger entity. Consolidation can result in cost and revenue synergies that lead to greater economies of scale. Consolidation makes good business sense where companies are complementary in nature and therefore increase their product portfolio and customer reach or when companies want to secure greater market share within a given product area. The payment processing sector is already experiencing the effects of business consolidation.

TECHNICAL STUFF

During the first half of 2019, three transactions accounted for $87 billion in deal value. These top three transactions were Fidelity National Information Services' acquisition of Worldpay for $43.6 billion, Fiserv's $22 billion First Data deal, and Global Payments' $21.2 billion purchase of Total System Services. These consolidations, on their own, accounted for more than half of a record-breaking $120 billion in disclosed transaction value in the first half of 2019. This trend for larger deal sizes was also highlighted in that 65 percent of deals recorded exceeded $100 million in the first half of 2019. Outside of the three big payments deals, enterprise financial software is the largest FinTech subsector, with more than 75 percent of the remaining deal value and close to 50 percent of all deal volume, 98 deals in all.

It seems natural that consolidation will occur among some of the smaller FinTech firms, but there will always be issues around valuations, leadership structure, and strategic visions that will make founders reluctant to give up their babies. Angels, VCs, and other investors can highlight where consolidation may lead to a more successful outcome for the firms. Founders may prefer to "take the money and run" if they receive an attractive bid for their shares.

However, the more likely outcome is that larger firms will determine that acquiring new companies, for the specific product sets or the capabilities of the teams, is more efficient than building a competitive product internally. In addition, as with the payments sector example, creating synergies through cost reduction or economies of scale will always be an option. Many of the early-stage FinTech firms are focused on a specific piece of the workflow or life-cycle management of a broader issue and therefore won't develop into unicorn valuation on their own. Therefore, a trade sale to another entity with a complementary product set can provide a way forward.

The larger firms have to decide whether they're best positioned to integrate such firms from an early stage, perhaps buying a minority stake early on and building on that stake, or whether VCs and private equity firms are better positioned to create a roll-up strategy for firms within their portfolio.

Corporate venturing strategies

Many financial institutions, investment banks in particular, have a dedicated fund to channel corporate venture capital (CVC). As we explain in Chapter 16, CVCs are a subset of venture capital in which funding comes from corporate funds instead of acting as a third party that manages money on behalf of external investors. CVCs tend to be more strategic in nature rather than purely ROI focused and therefore should invest in smaller businesses that are specifically relevant and beneficial to achieving the strategic vision of their parent entity.

To achieve this, either they set up a dedicated fund, which generally has at least $100 million available to draw down for given investments, or they invest directly off their own balance sheet. Having a dedicated fund can suggest that they have a dedicated team that will be focused solely on the portfolio, but it does depend on the structure of the institution. Some institutions have dedicated innovation or digital transformation teams that feed into this process with a broader strategic investments team. However, depending on the institution, they may also be more risk averse and prefer to invest later in the funding life cycle, perhaps Post Series A, to ensure that the FinTech firm has sufficient traction and development to meet their requirements.

WARNING

The benefit for the FinTech firm is that it wins both a commercial agreement and an investment agreement from the CVC and can access the expertise and network (including client distribution) of the financial institution. CVCs can bring knowledge and access to potential clients, but the FinTech firm needs to be careful that it isn't subsumed within the broader entity and fails to receive the external support it requires to grow its business. In addition, firms should be aware that they're exposing their intellectual property to a potential competitor. While such risks should be covered by legal agreements, they represent a factor in determining the right CVC partner and formulating the expectations on both sides.

The vast majority of banks now have a CVC offering, with some proving more proactive than others. In addition, some focus more on accelerator/incubator-type activities to spot interesting technology firms to partner with instead of making direct investments. This trend is likely to develop further into the asset management and insurance domains.

The Part of Tens

Chapter **18**

Ten Symptoms of Ailing Legacy Technology

D ue to perceived costs, fear of potential business disruption, and attachment to their familiar legacy systems, many financial institutions have been reluctant to touch their monolithic dinosaurs. We've even seen some cases where organizations try to apply band-aid fixes to legacy systems from the 1980s!

If financial organizations with aging systems don't rapidly move toward replacement, they may end up obsolescing themselves. But how do you know when that time has arrived when an upgrade is a necessity? Here are some symptoms of an outdated system that needs an overhaul. For more information on legacy systems, see Chapters 13 and 14.

A Band-Aid Overload

Many institutions have chosen to follow the path of least resistance in their technology. In other words, they change nothing until they absolutely have to, and then they make the smallest change possible. In the short term, it may seem like doing only the minimum necessary to maintain the functionality required by the end user is a thrifty and reasonable strategy. However, such a strategy can result in many hidden costs that, when factored in, make it not such a great value after all. It can also result in dissatisfied customers and frustrated employees.

If this describes your company's situation, it's time to act. The problem is only going to get worse the longer you delay. Your first step is to assess the current system and develop a strategy for improving it (either updating/fixing or replacing). The best approach to take depends on the scope of change required. Will you be adding a couple of lines of code, replacing everything all at once, or something in between? Is the nature of the change revolutionary (all at once) or evolutionary (gradual)?

As its name indicates, the revolutionary method is the more radical. It requires a concerted review of how the change will affect the end user, the infrastructure, and the organization. The two types of revolutionary deployment strategies are rebuilding and replacement (see Chapter 13):

>> With the replacement strategy, the legacy system is essentially taken offline in its entirety and a completely new technology is inserted in its place.

>> The rebuild approach utilizes the legacy system only as a point of reference, and a new system sits inside a new technology-based infrastructure.

The evolutionary approach is a well-planned, less drastic, and incremental method of modernizing old legacy systems. It's less intrusive and less risky. However, it can also be a band-aid solution and, just like a band-aid, can be painful when it's pulled off. You can mitigate the issues around supporting and maintaining a legacy system with one of these five evolutionary approaches: revision, rehosting, replatforming, refactoring, or rearchitecting.

REMEMBER

It's important to understand a legacy system thoroughly before you make any changes to it. You'll need to know its functions, its use cases, its user population, and any pending functionality or issues. Stakeholders in the system must help determine how any replacement or modernization will affect meeting the critical business needs. This includes considering any unmet business needs that a new system could potentially help with and understanding how associated systems rely on the legacy system.

A Lack of Backward Compatibility

Backward compatibility is the ability for new code/hardware/software to work with older data formats and applications. Backward compatibility is critical to a legacy system's continuing viability when new technology interfaces with it.

Good programmers today understand that they must consider backward compatibility with legacy systems when they design new systems. Unfortunately, though, backward compatibility wasn't such a programming focus in the past, so many legacy technologies were *not* built with any compatibility, and most old systems don't recognize the languages in which new code is written. Consequently, although new systems may be constructed to be "backward compatible," that doesn't guarantee that legacy systems will work well with them. A legacy system is often a compilation of unique snippets of code interspersed with larger formatted enterprise weight systems. There are millions of lines of code, and most of it is poorly documented and only inconsistently quality-checked. Upgrading in such environments is problematic.

One way to increase a legacy system's compatibility is by employing a "wrapper" layer that provides new functionality and extensibility through application programming interfaces (APIs). Testing can be more complicated when this mode of expansion is used because the new code must not only be compatible with the legacy system but also be backward compatible with the APIs.

WARNING

Old code often isn't extensible, and that limits the ability to build new functionality through a wrapper. If the code isn't backward compatible, the two versions of code will be inoperable and will throw errors and crash when called. The only remedy is to remove and rewrite such code.

Incompatibility with Other Systems

Before you can modernize or replace a legacy system, you must understand how it interfaces with other systems in the infrastructure. You must run tests to confirm the nature of the exchanges between systems. Do they call the same databases? Do they access the databases in the same or different ways? Do they share web services? Does your system call APIs from another system? Does your legacy system call external data sources? Do other systems call your legacy's data sources?

Ascertaining the level and areas of interaction between systems isn't necessarily difficult, but it is time-consuming. If you fail to do this due diligence, you risk disrupting other operations or corrupting databases.

It isn't enough that you isolate the other systems engaged in sharing infrastructure or data; you must also understand the nature of the exchanges. Some questions to be asked are

>> Is the exchange bidirectional?

>> What data within the database is being accessed or exchanged?

>> What functions and operations are being called?

>> When are these calls or exchanges taking place and with what frequency?

>> Are the services that are shared performed in the same or in a compatible fashion?

WARNING

Some tools can help you map these uses, but if you don't determine these relationships either manually or through some form of automation, your replacement or modernization strategy won't work seamlessly.

Disparate Data

Integrating data from legacy systems into new technology is often not simple or easy. Many legacy systems don't incorporate data management software and are written in nonstandard database formats. Whether you're replacing or modernizing the legacy system, you'll still have to understand how data is handled, stored, accessed, and written in that system to ensure the data isn't compromised. Procedural scripts and reengineered database architectures often are required. The database structures you're dealing with between the legacy and new systems can be fundamentally different. For example, one may be a relational database and the other may be an object–oriented system or an XML file. You can manage such differences by defining constraints that help you avoid conflicts within a diverse database.

Before you can determine the level of engagement required, you must perform an audit to determine how data is used and stored. The questions that this audit should answer include

>> What is the volume of data to be handled?

>> Where is the data currently stored?

>> How do you increase data availability without affecting overall system performance?

>> What is the required regulatory security model, and does it comply with new country-regulated personally identifiable information (PII)?

>> How is the data used?

>> How do you extract end-user value from the data that is stored?

REMEMBER

When determining the data structure, you must take into consideration the other systems that may be sharing this data already with the legacy system. Some data areas to be concerned about when planning to modify or retire legacy systems are these:

>> What is the quality of the data?

>> How is the data is formatted?

>> How many different databases are there, and what are their structures?

>> When is the data accessed, and how is it accessed?

Spreadsheet Risk

Spreadsheets are great tools for data transformation. If you put data into a spreadsheet, you can augment it, transform it via alternative data sources, and develop customized analytics bespoke models. In a recent survey conducted by Deloitte, it was found that 80 percent of all enterprises use spreadsheets as drivers for business-critical functions.

WARNING

Although it's a great work-around tool, a spreadsheet isn't a great medium for permanent, large-scale data storage. The ubiquitous, unmonitored, and uncontrolled use of spreadsheets for analysis and risk management can be problematic because individual spreadsheets generally fall outside of the main data lake, making them difficult to monitor. Most banking or financial firms don't know how many reports are generated off unmonitored spreadsheets throughout the organization. Generally, no inventory is made of how and where these sheets are used and maintained. There's always a risk that the spreadsheet's creator may leave the company, in which case the thought and methodology behind the model construction may be lost forever.

Other risks include the following:

>> Spreadsheets are prone to data entry errors and aren't usually peer reviewed. Since the passage of Sarbanes-Oxley, companies have faced pressure to control, review, and monitor end-user computing. To understand and mitigate the risks, organizations conduct assessments and maintain inventory lists. Many banks have run their risk management off models developed on spreadsheets. Because all the inputs in these sheets are manual, and often the output is carried into other spreadsheets or added to the systems of record manually, the chance for error is high. Spreadsheets in constant use

"harden" over time, and any errors can become a basic component of the output. When spreadsheet errors are allowed to persist without peer review, senior management ends up making decisions on potentially flawed data and compounding those flawed decisions over time.

» Spreadsheets are also not always safeguarded properly. They're easily passed around a company, and sometimes to external contacts, without much thought to confidentiality. With the passage of laws internationally protecting PII, this kind of careless sharing can leave a company open to fines and individual suits associated with privacy violations.

WARNING

Spreadsheets are high on auditors' lists of items to review due to regulatory concerns. Companies need to be prepared to assure auditors that they understand the risks of storing data in that form. By facing the issue head-on, doing a review, and creating policy and procedures to limit risk, a company can perhaps sidestep some of the liability associated with spreadsheet use.

REMEMBER

Because spreadsheets will likely continue to be pervasive in the financial workplace, companies are developing new solutions to mitigate the risks. Some of these solutions allow for flexibility within the system and provide controlled and auditable connections to third parties. These benefits greatly increase a solution's value while meeting a broader set of individual user needs. If the primary value of your system is being derived outside of it in spreadsheets, this is a clear sign that your legacy system may have outlived its usefulness.

You can take some simple steps to limit some of the operational risk exposure associated with spreadsheet usage. For example, having read-only servers and a required accompanying process document can protect against inadvertent changes and key man loss. Creating an oversight committee that provides clear policy rules about spreadsheet use, maintenance, version control, and security is essential to good governance. Every spreadsheet that becomes institutionalized should follow well-defined formatting guidelines and should be reviewed in a scheduled periodic fashion. Users should receive spreadsheet-creation training.

TIP

Spreadsheet applications have features that can help mitigate some of the risks on an individual spreadsheet basis. For example, Microsoft Excel includes auditing and versioning controls, and you can centralize and restrict access to shared files with SharePoint.

REMEMBER

Here's a summary of the steps to take to understand, prioritize, and limit liability:

1. Define the risks and scope of end-user computing throughout the organization.

2. Determine the policy and procedures around the use and versioning of the spreadsheets that must be used institutionally by the company.

3. Create controls, and monitor and review them for adherence.

4. Review potential replacement of spreadsheets used in critical operations.

Defining controls starts with understanding the governance responsibilities and needs, educating responsible personnel, creating a process around the restriction of risk, and prioritizing the risks to make sure that the first remediation addresses the areas of greatest vulnerability.

Latency

Latency is the amount of time it takes for a request to go from client to server and back again. Many conditions can increase latency, including network configuration, volume of data calls, caching models, stand-alone applications, system architecture, aging hardware, and Internet speed.

The main causes of latency issues are

>> Number of hops between devices and server

>> Data bottlenecks

>> Data formatting

>> Central processing unit (CPU)/graphics processing unit (GPU) distribution

>> Poor workload prioritization

>> Hardline connections versus Wi-Fi

>> Configuration issues

REMEMBER

If your system experiences latency and it's not a problem — great. Not every system needs lightning-fast response times. But if users or customers complain about latency, that can be a signal that it may be time for an upgrade. Latency issues weren't an important consideration during the development of many legacy systems because real-time performance is a relatively new demand in the marketplace. A decade ago, developers didn't prioritize performance, database optimization, or workflow maximization when coding. Systems weren't structured to maximize productivity. In contrast, new systems are very latency-conscious.

Increasing Demand for Support and Maintenance

Supporting a legacy system isn't always easy. As systems age, they may become more stable because of fewer changes, but they may also become more brittle and less reliable. The knowledge base is often limited to a few old engineers and service specialists. The documentation on the total system is often thin. Upgrades may be difficult and poorly supported.

At some point, the cost of maintaining aging software or hardware begins to outweigh the benefits of keeping it in place. Global research and advisory firm Gartner has estimated that the cost of maintenance and support of a customized system can exceed its development budget in fewer than five years.

Here are some of the most common legacy system support issues:

>> There's no readily available pool of already-trained support staff. Or, if there is staff, retaining them may be difficult because there's no clear career advancement path for them.

>> There's no established user community and no easily maintained knowledge base.

>> When issues arise, developers may no longer be available to diagnose and fix issues.

>> There's no impetus to make the system better because it's near the end of its life.

>> The codebase is probably large and difficult to manage.

>> Fixes may require shutting down the whole system.

>> As the system ages, crashes may increase.

>> There are no tools available except those the in-house developers have created.

>> Upgrades can be extremely painful.

>> If developers have employed API wrappers to augment the system's functionality, it may be hard to determine where a specific problem lies.

Short-Term Gains and Long-Term Pains

As we explain earlier in this chapter, small fixes don't often provide long-term solutions. While revising or rehosting are the fastest and cheapest modernization approaches available for the legacy dilemma, and may offer short-term benefits, those benefits come at great operational cost.

TIP

We advise taking an inventory of the corporate goals and doing a cost-benefit analysis on upgrading before attempting a short-term fix. A comprehensive, phased plan that gets you to an end position free of the legacy system and on new technologies is usually a far more effective strategy.

A Shrinking Talent Pool

As we state in Chapter 14, maintaining and supporting a legacy system can be difficult because of the shrinking talent pool over time, particularly if the legacy system is written in an obsolete coding language. As an example, a number of these systems are in COBOL, a language prevalent in the late 1960s to early 1980s. Many developers who once used this language are now retired. Table 18-1 provides some insight on the aging of the COBOL developer community.

TABLE 18-1

Developers with COBOL Skills

Percent of Available Developers	Age of Available Developers
52%	45–55 years old
34%	35–45 years old
7%	55+ years old
5%	25–35 years old
2%	Unknown Age
100%	

Lost Market Opportunities

The banking industry hasn't committed to any major innovation since the inception of the ATM system in the 1980s and the legacy systems they're dealing with, which were developed then. The industry's failure to keep up with user expectations and new technology has left many institutions vulnerable to customer poaching by disruptive new paradigms, such as cryptocurrencies, start-up online banks, and tech giants with cash and inclination to enter the fray.

Today's customers expect to have information on demand, user interfaces that fit their lifestyles, and self-service capabilities. Most legacy systems aren't compatible with these new demands. Even the ubiquitous cellphone can't be utilized to its fullest potential through the legacy systems. The functionality that APIs and wrappers offer isn't enough to quell users' desires for immediate results.

Robotics and artificial intelligence (see Chapter 12) will likely play a role in the banking experience of the future, and the cost of these technological changes will be offset by a decrease of 10 to 30 percent in back-office staff. According to Pat Patel of *Payment Week*, "Support of legacy systems accounts for 15–25% of the total IT spend for the banking industry." Past estimates have put that number at up to 50 to 70 percent of total IT spend. Any savings will underwrite a portion of the cost of migration or modernization. Upon converting to more user-friendly systems, companies will also achieve savings from the decrease in maintenance and support costs.

REMEMBER

It can be tempting to see a legacy system as being "free" because its initial capital expense is many years in the past. However, to explore the potential hidden costs of maintaining legacy systems, ask yourself the following questions, and if your answer is yes to any of them, your system isn't "free" and it's impacting your bottom line:

>> Are the legacy systems reducing the developers' and IT staff's productivity?

>> Does the team supporting these systems have to create work-arounds?

>> Are you losing business due to failure to respond to customers fast enough?

>> Is your annual support cost greater than the replacement cost of the entire system, including hardware and software?

>> What is the cost of the team that keeps the legacy running?

>> What is the risk to revenue if the legacy system fails to perform?

>> Can the legacy system support the anticipated company growth? For how long?

>> Does your system interface with other internal and external systems easily?

- » Is the system auditable as required by regulations and company policy?

- » What is your growth strategy for the future? Does it require a more flexible and open platform?

- » Is your legacy system easily adapted to web services?

New online banking institutions can provide end users the choices they want in customer support and self-service. These new virtual banking approaches are starting to steal market share from the more traditional structures. Banks are also beginning to feel limitations due to lack of speed to market of new products and services. Siloed data is making it hard for the financial industry to pull value out of their customer exchanges.

The door to getting away with only minimal change may be rapidly closing, as banking regulatory agencies are also starting to look at the security vulnerabilities of the legacy banking systems. These vulnerabilities, coupled with privacy laws, may be the final straw on the legacy's back.

FinTech app

» Understanding the building and
  buying processes

» Speeding up a build through open
  source and vendors

» Asking vendors the right questions

Chapter **19**

Ten Questions for Determining Whether to Build or Buy

To buy or to build new FinTech technology is a thorny issue not without its adamant stakeholders and points of view. However, the mystery behind the problem can be resolved by asking some key questions about your situation, which we address in this chapter. Find out more about the build versus buy decision in Chapter 13.

REMEMBER

Whichever choice you make, success is driven by thorough planning and clear communication.

Is This Functionality Core to Our Business?

Working with a FinTech company enables an organization to focus on mission-critical operations and outsource the rest. Whenever a company contemplates rolling out new technologies or functionalities, the first question to be asked is whether the new initiative is core to the business. If it isn't, then engaging with third-party FinTech sources is nearly always the best way forward.

REMEMBER

Put your development dollars into the creation of code that provides your business market differentiators. If it isn't core to your financial objectives, you're stealing money from other areas of the company that will generate business. Even if you have the greatest development team, if what they're developing is peripheral to their area of expertise, the net effect is that the software will rapidly degrade and become obsolete over time. Identifying what is core to your business is key to your success.

Is the Application Unique?

Don't waste time or money on building what already exists. It makes no sense, either financially or operationally, for a company to build standard applications like customer relationship management (CRM) systems, human resources (HR) and payroll, time management systems, licensing applications, and so on.

On the other hand, if the application you want is unique and original, you won't find it on a third-party vendor's product list. To get the features and capabilities you want, you may have to either build it yourself or start with something generic and modify it to fit your use case. The latter is often your best bet; it's a much less daunting proposition to modify an existing application than to start from scratch. Finding applications that are extensible, that are used for many operations, or that integrate easily with other applications and can share databases is a real positive for a rapidly expanding company. Such an application can grow with the needs of the organization while requiring less specialized support.

TIP

If you choose to go the third-party modification route, you need to make sure that it can be done contractually and that the core third-party application will continue to be supported and updated over time. A thorough review of the application programming interfaces (APIs) available for the product is critical.

Which Approach Is More Cost-Effective?

Building or buying: Which represents the best value? It's not a simple question to answer, because of all the auxiliary costs involved in both building and buying.

On the surface, the question seems like a no-brainer. Buying is cheaper than building, by tenfold. In other words, it costs ten times more to build a system than it does to buy an equivalent system. The maintenance costs are higher for house-built systems, too — 40 to 60 percent more over seven years than the same large, complex, modified vendor model. This is mainly due to economies of scale because a vendor can build a system once and then sell it to many customers, whereas if you build a system yourself, you are its only customer.

On the other hand, buying carries its own cost burden, including costs specific to the deployment, both before and after, and annual fees, both maintenance and support, over the life of the contract. With that said, one of the most compelling arguments for buying is that you don't have to deal with legacy systems, and the technology that's purchased is constantly being rejuvenated over time.

Buying software means paying upfront for the licensing and then (usually) paying again each year for support. License fees can be not only for the software but also any peripherals that are needed to support the software.

TIP

Look at the projected costs of a live contract over seven years to determine the all-in costs of a purchase versus the all-in costs of an in-house development. You also need to reflect on the cost of deploying the software. Vendors will supply estimates. Be sure to tack on 10 percent to their estimates for hidden and internal costs.

Should This Application Be Built?

These are the main decision points in deciding whether to build an application:

>> **The nature of the application:** If it's unique and/or critical to your core business, build it. If neither is true, buy it.

>> **The need to control the nature of the application:** In-house building means you have more control and privacy. Privacy can be an issue if it's important that the code not be shared with other organizations.

>> **The cost to build, maintain, and support it:** Buying is nearly always cheaper, as we explain in the previous section.

>> **The risks involved in the development and maintenance:** If you can't afford for the system to go down, or if you don't have the in-house staff to support it, you should buy. (More on risks is in the next section.)

TIP

The availability of robust Software as a Service (SaaS; see Chapter 6) offerings has lately shifted the balance in favor of buying or subscribing for many organizations. SaaS has substantially altered the need for organizations to own, build, or maintain generic software. SaaS is generally rented on a subscription basis. It's offered in the cloud, which makes it ubiquitous, and it scales based on user and compute requirements. The vendor provides all support, maintenance, and automated upgrades. This model is particularly appealing to small and start-up organizations.

REMEMBER

Everything is a trade-off. Within the build versus buy discussion, the amount of control you have is inversely proportional to the cost. Buying the product is less expensive than building it, but you have less control over the direction, distribution, focus, and support of a third-party licensed product than you do over a unique in-house project.

What Are the Risks of Building versus Buying?

WARNING

It can be difficult to determine the risk level associated with a build versus buy strategy because there are so many potential risks and each one has its own uncertainties:

>> If you build, the time to delivery is your highest risk. Proper project management can help mitigate the risk of failed delivery dates. Schedule slippage is less of an issue when buying because the software is already created and needs only to be integrated with your systems.

>> When buying, the lack of access to source code can be a risk. You must rely on the vendor to address concerns, fix bugs in a timely manner, and develop new functionality in response to your requests. If the vendor doesn't meet your support needs, you may find yourself stuck with them anyway because of your contract, or because it would be too expensive to change to a different vendor.

REMEMBER

Due to personal information retention and privacy laws, and country-specific regulatory controls, data management and visibility are also mounting concerns. If you allow a third-party vendor to store and manage your data, it's important to choose a vendor that will keep you well informed about what's happening with your data and what security risks its network may be facing. If you manage your data in-house, you must be responsible for adhering to all regulations yourself and bearing the administrative costs of that.

When Does Open Source Make Sense?

You can reap the benefits of a vendor system while avoiding some of the liabilities by incorporating open source applications with either vendor-supplied or in-house built software. With open source (covered in Chapter 10), you're getting the reach of a user base that far exceeds your own specific group. The software is tested in ways your team would not. Open source is free to acquire but not completely free to use because of the associated costs, like integration, support, and maintenance. Because support and maintenance costs can be significant, it's imperative that the open source project you select is vetted and mature and has an active user group and contributors.

Open source also mitigates the issue of some elements of control. Your team can develop custom work for critical functionality not currently in the open source package. It can also release updates in an automated fashion, taking advantage of the changes noncompany developers have made. By always contributing new code back to the project, the user company is assured of backward compatibility and shorter update cycles.

Unlike vendor code, open source code isn't a black box. It utilizes the more flexible newer development processes like microservices and is cloud-enabled.

TIP

The open source community is robust and should be utilized when doing due diligence on any project you're entertaining. Here are some sites you can use to assess a project:

>> Bitbucket (https://bitbucket.org/)

>> Tigris (www.tigris.org/)

>> SourceForge (https://sourceforge.net)

>> OSDN (https://osdn.net)

>> Freecode (http://freshmeat.sourceforge.net/)

>> FossHub (www.fosshub.com)

>> GitHub (https://github.com)

>> LaunchPad (https://launchpad.net)

>> Open Source Software Directory (https://opensourcesoftware directory.com)

You must source the discussion boards before selecting any open source project. When you have finally narrowed your selection, the following list should be used to determine which is your most robust option:

>> Does it have a large user base?

>> Does it have a good reputation?

>> Is it interoperable?

>> Does it require specialized skill to use or maintain? If so, this could be costly.

>> Does it have sufficient, well-written documentation?

>> Does it have a good support network? The support network includes a community as well as paid support options.

>> How often has the code been updated since its inception? What is its most recent update?

>> Is the project site well trafficked and well maintained?

>> Is the open source license associated with the product clearly defined?

>> Is there any larger group or company supporting the development of the project?

REMEMBER

Frequency of updates to the code, longevity of the project, good documentation, and a large user and support group are clear indicators of a successful open source project.

When Does Building Make Sense?

If any of the following are critical to the organization's success, building is your best bet:

>> Does the software have specialized functionality that only your company needs?

>> Does the software need to be customizable? On the fly?

>> Are data control, security, and privacy a must?

>> Is the output or the workflow specific to your company's use case?

>> Have you searched and not found software that solves your critical problem?

>> Does your company have the IT and developer resources to create and maintain the software?

REMEMBER

The benefits of building can be summed up in one word: control. With building, you own the code and the functionality being built.

The potential liabilities of building are just as apparent. Your company may not have the inside expertise to accomplish the build, and you won't know until it's completed whether it fulfills all the objectives. In addition, because the software is unique to your company, it will require specialized user training.

How Can We Accelerate a Build?

One way to accelerate a build is to create a hybrid system that combines third-party components with some internal development. Some examples of the type of systems that lend themselves to this collaboration are

>> Customer relationship management (CRM) systems

>> Content management systems (CMS)

>> Business process automation systems

>> E-commerce software solution

>> Business portals

As an example, Salesforce.com is perhaps one of the best SaaS software offerings for customizing out-of-the-box functionality. It enables customers to build their own custom processes or to hire third-party developers to develop applets that provide greater functionality. Salesforce.com retains the responsibility for the infrastructure it provides while making tools available for the company and the end user to customize.

For such collaboration to be successful, the vendor must assemble a very exacting set of requirements, objectives, and deliverables. An expert project manager is key to staying on schedule, along with having a concrete statement of work.

Another way to speed development is to embrace DevOps, which is a new discipline that automates standardized operations and processes used by development and quality assurance teams. It's an outgrowth of the small cross-functional teams used in open source, microservices, and Agile-like development. DevOps is for automating processes in a controlled way, developing continuous integration and deployment environments. Automation and continuous integration make it easier for teams from different organizations and different locations to work together in real time.

Application programming interfaces (APIs) in third-party software make it easier and faster to deploy third-party code. They enable internal developers to collaborate with third-party vendors and open source projects easily. In-house developers can utilize APIs to build layers of functionality on top of a third-party black box or to make their software available to a third party without revealing any of the corporation's secrets.

When Does Buying Make Sense?

Just as there are clear indicators for when building makes sense, there are also indicators for when it makes more sense to buy. Those reasons are the inverse of why you build.

REMEMBER

One of the most critical questions to ask is, "How soon do you need this functionality?" If your answer is "now" or "very soon," then buying is your solution.

You should also buy if one or more of these things are true:

>> The functionality is ubiquitous and used across companies.

>> It isn't core functionality required to drive the company's success.

>> It's outside the company's area of competence.

>> It isn't cost-effective to build or maintain.

>> Development of it deflects labor that could be working on more core functionality and thereby takes money away from the company.

>> Applications already exist in the marketplace that can be deployed out of the box, that are mature and bug-free, and that have a support and user network.

The benefits and drawbacks of buying should be apparent when you review your spec and scope document. Some reasons for buying include economies of scale, focused domain expertise, rapid deployment, ongoing maintenance and support, complete QA and documentation, wide user groups and external support, and known predictable costs.

WARNING

Just like building, buying has its own set of liabilities. With buying, you own nothing and are completely dependent on the supplier. You have no control over data integrity. You can't dictate the levels of security, and you can't drive the areas of new functionality. And if the vendor goes out of business, you may lose your software support and be unable to get updates.

TIP

If the application you're selecting is important to the day-to-day operation or to the company's bottom line, you may want to build an escrow component into the terms of the contract.

There are also some hidden risks involved in buying. Consider these possibilities, for example:

>> The request for proposal (RFP) process could be flawed and the product may not match the company's needs.

>> If the application is being integrated into some other system, there may be compatibility issues.

>> It may take more time to deploy than anticipated.

How Do We Select a Vendor and a Product?

When you're shopping for software to buy, the vendor is just as important as the product itself. Make sure that the vendor you choose

>> Has economies of scale

>> Provides support and training

>> Has a focused skill set that drives development and functionality of the application

>> Has a proven track record for supplying needed functionality

>> Has designed the software to be flexible and interoperable

>> Offers regular reviews and upgrades, making the software future-proof

REMEMBER

Many vendors offer multiple software products to choose from. Before you finalize your buying decision, you should be thoroughly familiar with the software, its capabilities, and any potential drawbacks, including any areas where the vendor doesn't provide strong support. Here's a partial list of questions that you should ask about the software and vendor you're considering:

>> How often is the software updated?

>> What does the update process look like?

>> Is there free software training? If not, what type of training and cost is available?

- **»** What is the level of support during deployment? After deployment?

- **»** What type of reports are available out of the box?

- **»** What other software does this system interface with?

- **»** What are the hardware requirements?

- **»** What is the cloud capability?

- **»** What is the mobile capability?

- **»** How is data integration carried out?

- **»** What is your road map for the product's future functionality? How far out does the road map go?

- **»** What is your security model? Have you ever had a breach?

- **»** What certifications do your system and team hold? Do you have a Service Organization Controls (SOC) report? What is your disaster recovery plan? Has it been tested?

- **»** What is your data management plan, and what is your data disposal process?

Chapter **20**

Ten Considerations When Using Open Source Technology

I f you're going to use open source in your organization, it's critical to have a well-thought-out plan for doing so. There are many moving parts and many factors to consider when developing an open source strategy. This chapter summarizes some of the factors that may make a difference in how you want to proceed. Flip to Chapter 10 for the full scoop on open source technology.

Your Business Model

Before determining the place for open source in your company's plan, take a careful look at the company's business model, current needs, and future goals. A FinTech company can help you identify what technologies are available, what the new trends are in the industry, and what future areas of growth you may want to plan for.

You should also think about what open source can offer and how those offerings fit with the company's goals. Some of the most compelling benefits open source can potentially offer include

>> Speeding up development and time to market

>> Reducing overhead

>> Removing redundancy

>> Increasing efficiency

However, those benefits don't just magically materialize. The company must take a comprehensive approach to open source usage and management within the company's structure. This includes having versioning and provisioning processes and takes into account the company's general tolerance for oversight.

TIP

As a company is developing its strategy, it should invite and encourage employee input. The objectives of all stakeholders must be reflected in the plan. Feedback from naysayers and skeptics is just as important as feedback from open source true believers, because they can help you anticipate and overcome objections.

Open Source Community Health

Keep in mind that one of open source's great potential benefits is the large pool of expert users who share their expertise and updates with one another. Therefore, one important consideration when looking at a particular open source solution is to what extent you'll have access to such a community.

TIP

Here are some easy benchmarks for evaluating the health of an open source community:

>> How well is the project site developed?

>> Have the project site owners thoughtfully curated the resources and tools provided?

>> Is there a ticketing system?

>> Is the documentation well conceived and regularly updated?

>> How many releases have there been and over how many years?

>> How many forks in the code have taken place?

>> How many contributors have there been over time?

>> How many users are there?

>> How well known is the code outside the project home?

>> Have there been any financial contributions/donations over time toward maintaining and further developing the project?

>> Do any large corporate users contribute to the code or its support?

>> How many maintainers are there?

>> How much has the code changed over time?

>> Are any statistics available about the code's return on investment (ROI)?

>> How many organizations contribute to this project?

>> How often are there new releases?

>> How often is there code review?

>> How many regressions have there been over time?

>> How many bugs?

A good project site should be able to supply answers to all these questions.

Tech Support

As we explain in Chapter 10, open source doesn't follow the traditional support model. No single company is responsible for after-development support. Instead, a community of users and developers have freely assumed the responsibility of providing support and bug fixes.

REMEMBER

Technical support for open source code can be problematic if the code doesn't have an active user community, as we say in the previous section. An active user community can offer information and support that enables a company to deploy a stable open source code logically and systematically. The factors we list there can reliably indicate the code's stability and quality because they point to there being people who care about the code and its viability. You must do your due diligence and research to determine the community health and, by association, the prospects for getting good technical support.

Keep in mind that the online user support community isn't your only option for technical support. If you're deploying a whole open source system versus utilizing a small snippet of code, your expectation of support may be different, and you may opt for different approaches:

>> For large deployments, it may be beneficial to have in-house support. That support person may also be the developer who integrated the system into the company's network. If you're working with a mature open source offering, a service and support network may have grown up around the project and may be available at a cost. If that's the case, there may be multiple candidates to fill the support function. The same due diligence is required in determining the best service provider as was required for selecting the open source code initially. There are also service groups that support all manner of open source code for an annual subscription fee.

>> On smaller projects, it may be possible to subcontract support directly from project's owner/creator or maintainer. There are tools you can license that can report on the code's health through a constant heartbeat.

WARNING

If you're embedding open source in your proprietary software, you must weigh the risk of having no control against the level of support and the level of error fixing for the included open source code.

Security

Depending on how you plan to use the open source code, its level of available security may be inconsequential, critical, or somewhere in between. It's important that you know your company's security requirements and then compare them to what the product or code provides.

One important security consideration is how well the code has been tested/proofed against security attacks. Several out-of-the-box "defects and analytics" tools are available that produce static security reports. These tools reveal possible defects in the code and report them back to the project maintainer.

When reviewing a project portal and its documentation, it's important to note whether you can easily report bugs, review the security protocols, and review any reports of vulnerabilities. Vulnerabilities should be included in the release notes.

WARNING

Some vulnerabilities are extremely common and readily identified, and any good development process avoids them. Finding such vulnerabilities in an open source product after its release can indicate sloppy development.

REMEMBER

The open source world has no quality assurance standardization, so all open source code comes "as is." You shouldn't release or use anything that your own company's quality assurance process hasn't validated.

TIP

Also, no centralized database lists open source vulnerabilities. There is, however, a National Vulnerability Database (NVD) that collects vulnerabilities as they are known; see `https://nvd.nist.gov`. Unfortunately, this database often points out vulnerabilities to hackers, who then exploit them. Most deployed open source is checked against this database, either manually or using automated tools, and any vulnerabilities found are fixed quickly. Someone in your organization should be responsible for reviewing this database and managing any needed changes on a weekly basis.

Code Audits

As we point out in Chapter 10, many organizations are hesitant to use open source code because of the potential for operational and security risk. Such risks can be minimized by regular and rigorous code audits.

Open source code audits are important for two reasons: They expose any potential security concerns, and they expose any potential infringement issues. Not only must an organization have policies governing software selection, vetting, and review, but it must also demonstrate an understanding of the potential interdependencies entailed in the actual use and deployment within a larger framework.

Auditors typically look for more than a simple spreadsheet as proof of proper oversight. To survive an open source audit, a company must demonstrate that it has educated its developers on the proper processes to follow before using even one line of open source code. There should also be a centralized repository of all contracts associated with open source that counsel has reviewed.

REMEMBER

Staying on top of releases of open source code is crucial to the success of surviving an open source audit. A company's policies and tools should require regular open source code review. The primary purpose of such a review is to verify that the code has been updated with latest releases and that any known vulnerabilities and errors reported have been fixed. This review should entail

>> Listing all open source components, the version in your product, and the most current version available

>> A list of vulnerabilities associated with those components

>> A scheduled date by which to remediate any critical issues

Reliability

When selecting open source software or code, future sustainability is of major concern. Open source code is sustainable only if there are dedicated user and contributor bases. Open source, like all code, has a life cycle, so it's not unusual if the number of developers decreases over time, as long as the consumption of the product doesn't wane.

TIP

You can easily gauge the value of open source code by simply using standard Internet search tools. Social media also supports open source discussion through blog posts and articles discussing projects.

Narrow down your selection to three possible candidates by using this checklist. If your open source candidate holds up positively to these questions, it will pass most internal and external audits:

>> **Does it have a large user base?** If so, it's likely to have strong support and a good likelihood of longevity.

>> **Does it have a good reputation?** Reputation isn't everything, but it is important.

>> **Is it interoperable?** You want to be able to use this code easily.

>> **Does it require specialized skill to use or maintain?** If so, maintenance could be costly.

>> **Does it have sufficient, well-written documentation?** Because contributors to open source have varying skills, review of documentation is critical. In fact, the use of the documentation to support the code should be part of the quality assurance (QA) done on the open source code before it's incorporated into production.

>> **Has it used open standards?** Code built on open standards and practices is easier to maintain.

>> **Does it have a good support network?** A support network can include not only a user and developer community but also paid support options.

>> **How often has the code been updated since its inception? What is its most recent update?** Frequent is better.

>> **Is the project site well trafficked and well maintained? Does it exhibit good governance and community participation?** A review of release notes and user statistics can help in determining this.

>> **Is the open source license associated with the product clearly defined?** Your legal counsel should review it, and you should make sure no conflicts occur with other open source agreements.

>> **Is there any larger group behind the development of the project?** A large company that relies on the code or regularly contributes to it is a benefit.

After reviewing the general field of projects in open source, you should next apply a narrower set of criteria to determine the best code for your needs. A plethora of Internet tools can assist you in evaluating open source code; they can be found through a simple search for tools to be used for managing open source code. Fossa (`https://fossa.com/`) and GitHub (`https://github.com/`) offer some good starting points, but you'll need to do your due diligence by reading user reviews.

After you've concluded your review and found three likely candidates, you should be able to drill down into this attributes list to determine the best.

Hidden Costs

Open source is appealing because there's an implied understanding that it's "free." But as we say, nothing is ever really free. You must understand the open source offering and the organization's needs before you can understand its potential costs.

On the surface, there appears to be savings from the outset because you pay nothing for the license and use of the code. There are hardware, maintenance, support, and legal costs, but these too may be less expensive compared to enterprise third-party offerings.

Cloud strategies (see Chapter 6) and the use of open source platforms can eliminate some of the network overhead. Though the use of these items isn't free in that development and deployment costs are associated with them, they should be significantly less expensive than in-house company-owned equipment. There are also other intangible benefits in using open source. For example, faster development time is a real and quantifiable benefit.

To understand and manage costs, take a look at the following areas of setup and maintenance, where there can be ownership costs, and determine ways to control and scope them prior to making a commitment.

Setup costs include the following:

>> **Hardware:** Review the project site for hardware recommendations and make sure you have them on hand. If not, the cost of the hardware will need to be built into the budget.

>> **Integration:** The size of the project will determine the size of the staff. If it's an application, outside resources may be required. Create a deployment project plan. Analyze interfaces and interoperability. Specialists may be required.

>> **Replacement:** If this is a replacement strategy (see Chapters 13 and 14), you must understand what components are needed. Data transfer can be time-consuming and may require specialists.

>> **Customization:** Open source doesn't mean "one size fits all" out of the box. You must budget for developer costs to modify code to fit your unique needs.

>> **Training:** New software implies new training and perhaps some slowdown in productivity.

Maintenance includes the following:

>> **Updates:** Someone will need to rigorously monitor the project site for available patches and releases and take charge of applying them.

>> **Customization:** Any customization your organization does to the code will require support throughout the life of the product.

>> **Support:** User and developer support must be available throughout the life of the product.

TIP

When selecting open source software, pay special attention to these areas that may necessitate additional expenses:

>> **Interfaces:** Because of poor user interfaces, less and inconsistent documentation, and lack of training, there could be increased time spent on administrative functions with some open source products.

>> **Support complaints:** Because of the lack of designated support and inconsistent documentation, your internal team may spend more time on troubleshooting.

>> **Bug fixing:** Because not all open source projects have a standardized approach to QA and regression testing, your in-house team may be responsible for finding and fixing bugs themselves.

>> **Additional development:** After you've implemented an open source solution, you may find that you need further code development due to some unanticipated issue, such as poor network performance.

>> **Extensibility:** There are no guaranties that any code will be future-proof. The only insurance you may have is that the code has been built on the latest flexible architecture in any easily utilized language.

Updates and Upgrades

Through new releases, programs get new functionality, bug fixes, and higher levels of security and usability. However, with open source, there's also a more pressing reason that updates and upgrades have to be current — the code is open to all. Anyone can see it when issues arise, including hackers looking for vulnerabilities they can exploit.

WARNING

As we mention earlier in this chapter, once a vulnerability is found, it's published to the project and later to websites that list all open source vulnerabilities. These lists are fodder for hackers. Luckily, you can use tools — such as Zoho (www.zoho.com), Bugzilla (www.bugzilla.org), and MantisBT (www.mantisbt.org) — to make sure that you don't miss updates and that check against the current open source code you're using for vulnerabilities and severity of them. With internal accountability for fixing issues as they occur and resubmitting them back to the project, you can handle maintenance and security with minimal risk.

REMEMBER

Updates and new releases should go through proper quality assurance. Because no standards are established in open source for quality control, it's your company's responsibility to see that the standard of the open source code meets the company's quality standards.

When engaged in updating or upgrading, note that backward compatibility isn't a given. Testing is a requirement to guard against fatal errors caused by version conflicts. The compatibility issue becomes more complicated when there are multiple uses of different open source projects. In such situations, you should test open source components in the actual environment they function in rather than in isolation.

To avoid the risk of vulnerability attacks and of third-party update incompatibility, your company will need to take a regimented approach to updates and releases. The regimen should include a calendared weekly review of all open source updates. You can automate this process using code management tools. All security issues and bug fixes should be prioritized for immediate updates as determined by their level of severity. New functionality should be prioritized according to business needs.

TIP

There should be a centralized repository that developers use for all open source code. By limiting the accessibility to the open source code to one repository, you avoid the possibility of different teams using different versions.

Educational reviews of all open source products in use should be shared with the development teams on a scheduled frequent basis.

Potential Hardware Impact

The ever-increasing demand for real-time computation has driven companies to search for cheap compute environments. As virtual servers and in-the-cloud burst delivery mechanisms are replacing brick-and-mortar server sites, it's important to understand the costs involved in moving away from physical on-site environments.

FinTech companies are well situated to advise members of the financial industry about tactics and strategies to be used to reduce operating costs and still deliver as near to real-time analytics in the areas they are required.

Speed isn't a requirement for probably 80 percent of the data store and manipulation that goes on in most financial firms. With that said, open source has often been a trailblazer in the area of reducing costs by creating and facilitating "free" operating systems.

TECHNICAL STUFF

Before 1974, there were no concepts of, nor mechanisms for, the copyright of software. All software was public domain. Source code was routinely delivered with any software product. In the 1950s and 1960s, software development was a collaborative event among academics, government, and researchers. Of course, this position rapidly changed with the increase of proprietary software and the need for corporations to protect their rights.

TECHNICAL STUFF

The first functional open source operating system with a kernel was released in 1991 as a Linux project. Sun Microservices and Apache soon followed suit. The Apache web server project has been so effective that it has cornered the market with at least 70 percent market share.

There are of course costs associated with the creation of hardware, which has made open source hardware development projects challenging to achieve. Even with its success, Apache's web server and Tophat are funded only through corporate sponsorship and user conferences.

With the cost constraints around creating free open source hardware (FOSH), FOSH projects rely on the community to build hardware based on the intellectual properties developed (such as data layouts, integrated circuit schema, mechanical drawings, and so on). The academic community has driven FOSH's creation and development to date. Its hardware development artifacts are captured via hardware description language (HDL).

However, utilizing open source software code with open source operating systems and the available security and efficiency tools can result in significant savings. Cost reductions have been reported as high as 44 percent for hardware costs based on intelligent strategies around open source, cloud-based deployments and virtual servers.

TIP

Companies hoping to achieve such reductions must make some policy and procedure changes. For example, they need to deploy tools that monitor system health, and they need to implement on-demand compute and workflow provisioning. Open Compute Project (OCP), a newly formed group, has taken on the challenge of creating hardware that will more efficiently deal with the need to handle large amounts of data at high computation speed. NASA, Rackspace, and Goldman Sachs started this group in 2011, and it has corporate buy-in. Visit www.opencompute. org for more information.

As a result of many large companies working together, a quantum shift has lately occurred in the way companies use servers. Instead of a single server with many different functions jammed together, the new approach is to break down the tasks a server performs into smaller units that perform limited tasks efficiently and speedily. This is somewhat like the shift to microservices (see Chapter 4). Of course, this new approach needs to be reviewed and implemented over time to be cost-effective.

One of the remarkable characteristics of an open source project like OCP is the incredible speed at which development takes place. The challenge now can be that of keeping up with all the new technology changes. A good FinTech company can help with that.

Legal Considerations

Open source/free licensing contracts test the complexity of good governance and legal adherence. Unfortunately, there isn't a one-type-fits-all generic contract available for open source.

Another layer of complexity becomes apparent when reviewing all open source contracts a company uses. The contracts often have interoperability issues with each other. And finally, international use of open source may raise other legal restrictions that have to be understood and resolved.

When reviewing the licenses associated with open source, pay particular attention to the following:

>> There should be no audit rights that reach into an organization's network directly.

>> There should be no fines associated with the inadvertent deployment of unlicensed open source code.

>> See whether you can purchase an outside warranty for the open source used. There are no warranties with open source code. If you use it, the liability for it lies with you as the user.

>> Check to see whether conflicts exist with the use of libraries within the open source code.

>> Make sure there are no requirements to provide written notification of initial ownership or code creation within the code.

>> Make sure there are no restrictions on the use of proprietary code with open source.

Be sure to check the open source project for pending legal actions. Your rights aren't protected should a lawsuit be launched against a project; your right of use may be obstructed.

There should be regular training about the policies around the use and maintenance of open source for users and developers.

Copyleft is the most common version of an open source license agreement. It allows anyone to change the code, but code the company develops as part of that open source can't be repackaged as third-party or proprietary software. With copyleft, anyone making changes to the code must make the new iteration available to all.

Non-copyleft licenses permit developers to make any changes to the code, including retaining the modification as proprietary. Purists of open source don't like this version because it violates the spirit of open source and restricts the sharing of all functionality as it's developed. Corporations, of course, would like to retain control over what they pay their developers to create. Non-copyleft code is therefore more acceptable to corporations and for projects needing fast and ubiquitous adoption. One of the issues with non-copyleft code development is that new functionality may not be resubmitted back to the project and may result in the original code's use and growth being stifled due to forking.

Maintaining a directory of all open source components in your organization is no easy task. Along with the components, you must also track the license requirements and understand the potential for licensing conflicts. There are hundreds of different types of open source licenses, and the licensee must adhere to terms of each agreement it has accepted.

TIP

The amount of open source integrated into proprietary code has been growing exponentially. In the most recent review, approximately 60 percent of all companies are using open source in some form or other. If you're using open source across your company's organization, it's no longer feasible to do it manually. Software Composition Analysis (SCA) is a relatively new tool that maintains inventory reports that list the licenses associated with each code and its known vulnerabilities. It automatically reviews the code against known open source vulnerability databases. SCA does this by code-scanning at build time or when the code is committed. It reviews the code each time it's run and tests the code's interoperability within the larger codebase. Such a tool will become more critical as governance rules expand and open source audit reviews become de rigueur. A fairly extensive list of free and licensed SCA applications can be found at `https://owasp.org/www-community/Free_for_Open_Source_Application_Security_Tools`.

REMEMBER

One of the early fears surrounding the use of open source within proprietary software remains a concern today. The broad reach of the open source agreements provides the potential loss of ownership of proprietary software if the proprietary code is inadvertently embedded in open source. This concern can be mitigated only by "best practice" development process, review, and vigilance.

Appendix

Building a FinTech Company from the Ground Up

Interested in creating your own FinTech company? This appendix is here to help you get started with some practical tips.

REMEMBER

We wish you good luck on your quest to develop your FinTech start-up! It will be a test of your patience and perseverance, and you certainly won't have worked harder in your career, but the true entrepreneur will embrace those challenges, and the exhilaration of the highs and the lows, along the way.

Writing a Business Plan

Success in business starts with an idea, but an idea won't suffice. The real metric of success is in the details, and the details are found in a good plan.

Thousands of good ideas are floated out into the ether every day, but few of them ever end up being put into production. Why? Mainly because writing a good business plan is just step one of many psychological hurdles you must get over to succeed in business. When you've finally completed that plan and had your closest allies read and comment on its efficacy, you're ready to start on the biggest piece: executing and adhering to the plan that you've concocted.

REMEMBER

Good business plans are living documents. They should be constructed to be changed when needed and to be shared often. A great hazard of many potential entrepreneurs is that they're mired in their own point of view. As the saying goes, "You may know what you know, but it is what you *don't* know that will get you every time." By involving others in your plan, you're building your base and broadening the emotional and intellectual investment of others in your project.

TIP

For more help with business plans, check out the latest edition of *Business Plans Kit For Dummies* by Steven D. Peterson, PhD, Peter Jaret, and Barbara Findlay Schenck (Wiley).

Doing research

The first step in the creation of a business is research. If you have a good idea, others have probably had it as well. So before putting inordinate amounts of time and energy into a concept that may have already had its day, you need to research the feasibility of what you're trying to accomplish.

Research starts with the marketplace. Is your FinTech product/service already there? Do you have a unique spin or differentiator that makes your idea better than those already out there? Going into business is like going back to school. You must immerse yourself in all aspects of the industry, market, and product before you even determine whether a plan is needed.

REMEMBER

If you find similar products or services, don't get discouraged. Calmly go about learning how others have approached the problem that you have a solution for. Most first entrants fail to survive. Followers learn from what has come before them and execute on a new exciting approach that eventually can result in becoming a leader and first mover.

Determining the audience and structure

A good business plan is a road map that can be used to guide a young company to its future. You should write your business plan for at least four different audiences: financiers, technocrats, marketing specialists, and ultimately the implementors of the plan.

TIP

To reach those audiences, you may have to build four different strategic plans, each targeted to the appetites and interests of the group it's intended to influence. A plan written to raise money will emphasize different aspects of the business than one written for a techno-geek, or to someone you're trying to attract to work with your company. Bankers are interested in profit-and-loss statements, and the technocrat is interested in the new sexy software you have or are using.

The structure of a business plan is straightforward. It contains these basic sections:

>> An executive summary, which is an overview/synopsis of the salient points presented in the rest of the document.

>> A business history and company description, including the overarching achievements and key stakeholders. A statement regarding the uniqueness of the products and the company and its differentiators is well positioned here. List any awards you've received.

>> A mission statement, a description of the business's objectives, and an explanation of how you'll meet them.

>> An organizational chart and management profiles. It should include a plan for growth and an estimate of future personnel needs.

>> The products/services to be offered. This section should include any traction, any sales history, and the products' technical specs.

>> A market analysis that shows the total value of the market and any positioning currently being exhibited, as well as future positioning.

>> A marketing and sales strategy. How will you capture the market? What is your growth projection in that market (based on what metrics)? This is a very important section. What concrete goals do you have, and how will you accomplish them? Your sales approach should include the type of sales structures and any contract prototypes.

>> Your funding needs, both the current needs and the three- and five-year projections.

>> Your financial projections. Tie these to financial needs and market analysis. Make sure you include expected costs, cash flows, and break-even states, and tie everything back to your funding needs.

>> Appendixes containing any reference documents such as contracts, leases, job descriptions, or technical manuals.

One thing that separates market changers from idealists is their ability to understand where their products fit into the marketplace. A concrete marketing plan helps drive home the level-headed approach of the plan creator. Your marketing plan should show your complete strategy, from new products to cross-selling to repositioning. Your plan should also include a content marketing plan. Tell them how you'll capture customers. Your plan must also include appropriate budgets for each initiative.

REMEMBER

As the famous Scottish poet Robert Burns said in his poem "To a Mouse," "The best laid schemes of mice and men often go awry." We want you to avoid that unpleasant possibility. To do so, you need to make sure that

>> Your financial projections are realistic.

>> You don't promise things that can't be delivered.

- » Your research is good.

- » You've accurately identified your audience.

- » You haven't given too much information in an unwieldy fashion.

- » You understand the market and your distribution within it.

- » You know your competitors, and you have a strategy to mitigate them.

- » You have identified your strengths and your weaknesses accurately.

- » You have been consistent in all your projections and numbers.

- » You have created focused plans for different audiences.

Developing a Prototype

We all think we have great ideas, but what happens when we commit to a development and get it all wrong? It does happen, and more often than you may think. Prototyping is one way to avoid the risk of overcommitment and to test your assumptions in the marketplace.

FinTech and software developers at large have embraced the use of prototyping because it speeds up product development, reduces costs, and engages end users earlier.

Partnering with customers

Numerix, LLC, has put an interesting spin on the concept of prototyping. It makes its customers partners in development. The benefit to this approach is that you've committed external users and an initial first customer right out of the box.

For example, at the beginning of 2018, Numerix secured a new client, based in Switzerland, that wanted to leverage the Numerix tech stack from the lowest layer (analytics) to the top layer (graphical user interface, or GUI). The customer wanted a Structured Product Trading System, and Numerix assisted with its design. Numerix used its platform (tech stack), called NXCORE, to accelerate the creation of a trading system.

If built in-house or through an external service company from the ground up, such an endeavor would have taken two to three years and would have cost $10 million or more. Numerix was able to work with this bank in January 2018, spec out its requirements, and launch the product by September 2018, at a fraction of the cost. The resulting offering was so good that in January 2019, Numerix made it one of its official products, and other clients have purchased it as well. "Build once and deploy to many" is Numerix's motto.

Understanding the process and downsides

REMEMBER

Prototyping allows a developer to test assumptions and enables end users to supply insight into the proposed functionality. Microservices and Agile development processes make prototyping faster and more efficient. There isn't a lot of difference between regular development and prototyping except for the limitation of scope of functionality and the speed of iterations.

A basic prototyping process follows these steps:

1. **Create a use case or requirements document.**

   This is a minimum product viability document.

2. **Create a mock-up to ensure the accuracy of the input/output and user interfaces.**

3. **Give customers access to the prototype and collect their feedback.**

4. **Create a second iteration based on feedback.**

   This process continues until the users concur on the viability of the product.

Throwaway prototypes, as their name implies, are constructed rapidly to be reiterative. They're created to test and eliminate functionality. Beadboard prototyping, on the other hand, is a very cohesive approach to prototyping. It refines and reuses the prototype over multiple iterations, all the way through to the end production model.

WARNING

However, prototyping also has quite a number of disadvantages to be understood and mitigated:

» It's easy to fall down the rabbit hole when prototyping. The developer is in direct contact with the end user, and that can become a time sink because user objectives may be ill-defined.

» The developer may confuse the prototype with the end product and become emotionally invested in it.

» There's no project manager to be responsible for managing costs, so prototyping activities can wildly exceed their original budgets unless there's oversight.

Operating Off the Grid

When creating a FinTech start-up to develop a groundbreaking idea that no one else seems to have thought about, you should operate off the grid, in "stealth mode," for as long as possible.

Guarding your secret development efforts is challenging but can also be rewarding:

>> One challenge is that you're basically alone, with perhaps one or two people thinking through the company and the market problem. You may not have all the correct talent around you. Nonetheless, you're about to break new ground, and maintaining anonymity becomes critical to building a disruptive FinTech.

>> The other challenge is that you can't test the waters with your idea, and you may not be able to move rapidly to an offering. Other entrepreneurs are likely trying to figure out how to solve the same problem as you, but you can't work with them because you're trying to be stealthy. Perhaps they're not attempting to operate in stealth mode; they may be putting all their energies into being first to market, rather than shielding themselves from the public eye. Their aggressive pursuit of first-to-market status could stifle companies trying to proceed more methodically in stealth mode, forcing them to play catch-up.

REMEMBER

The benefit to operating in stealth mode is that you can be thinking about the problem long before others have even identified it. If you have the right small core team who can get a product to market in a reasonable time period at an affordable cost, then as a stealth mode operator, you can be a first mover and can secure large sums of capital from a venture community that can accelerate the product and the company's position in the market, thus creating enormous wealth for the founders and investors.

WARNING

Venture capital firms are the last companies to speak to about your general disruptive idea, even if you have a prototype and are looking for your seed funding round. Venture capital companies could easily back people in their own network to replicate a stealth-mode company's idea.

Raising Capital

The process of raising capital (covered in more detail in Chapter 16) works differently depending on the size and nature of the company involved.

Capital can come at a very high cost. New businesses generally start off by tapping family and friends. Crowdfunding is a new "wild west" approach to start-up sourcing. With that said, however, crowdfunding in the EMEA (Europe, the Middle East, and Asia) financial sector is booming with very serious players who are all regulated by their regulatory agencies, like the Financial Conduct Authority in the United Kingdom. Crowdfunding in the EMEA region is a fully established and respected business model. Two examples are Seedrs (www.seedrs.com/) and Crowdcube (www.crowdcube.com/).

Only by proving a young company's viability can start-up firms begin to engage in securing larger seed money. Some start-ups bootstrap their company with a great idea and a client that funds the initiative. The client gets a breakthrough product at a reasonable cost, and the start-up founders give up no equity but gain a partner in defining the perfect product.

The next level of capital infusion can come from "angels," private investors, and then venture capitalists:

>> Angels are just rich individuals who want to get in on the ground floor of start-ups that seem to have potential.

>> Private investors tend to want large returns on their risk. They look for companies that have solid credentials and perhaps some new technologies.

>> Venture capitalists are much more critical in analyzing companies in which they invest. They require stronger financials and take much longer to complete the review process. They often require significant operational changes when they do invest.

Traditional bank loans may be available to some. They follow a similar process as venture capitalists. They may make specific demands on the way money can be used.

Larger public firms have the ability to raise cash by using either debt or equity capital. Equity comes from the increasing value of stock and dividends, and debt capital comes from loans with interest-bearing terms.

'The future of Fintech post the Corona crisis?'

Whether you are an optimist or a pessimist there is widespread acceptance that financial services, if not the world, is unlikely to return to the 'old normal', and that new ways of working and servicing clients seems unavoidable. As we see throughout this book, the concept of "old normal" was already in transition. History reminds us that a crisis, or any shock to the system, inevitably acts as a catalyst for change. The dotcom crash in the early 2000's spawned the creation of BigTech giants such as Facebook and Google, while the global financial crisis of 2008/09 encouraged the development of FinTech itself. The Corona Virus has merely escalated the urgency and prioritization that is motivating innovation. It is providing a test bed for the "new normal." What might the Corona crisis engender and what will that mean for the current FinTech community?

The optimistic view focuses on the principle that the FinTech model is well placed to 'weather the storm,' because the total cost of their operations are relatively low, due to a lean operating model, cheaper and more flexible systems and an infrastructure that is built to scale resiliently. The requirements that flexible working entails has highlighted the need for larger financial institutions to adopt cloud strategies in a meaningful way, embrace agile services and engage with their clients through improved digital experiences. Acceptance of Cloud and Software as a Service (SaaS) functionality, which can be operated with low infrastructure costs, scale with usage and have proven their cybersecurity credentials, allow products to be developed and amended quickly. In fact, what we are seeing even at the start of Phase 1, is what we anticipated and discussed through out this book, while FinTech is well positioned to navigate dispersed environments and rapid deployments, banks and other financial institutions are feeling the weight of monolithic structures and legacy systems that do not lend themselves well to the more flexible needs of this "new normal."

Smart FinTech companies are using the Corona Virus as an opportunity to test the scalability and flexibility of these new technologies, as well as to harden the best practices for maximizing group productivity in decentralized work environments.

REMEMBER

Financial institutions had paid 'lip service' to these benefits previously but questioned their security, however the necessity of flexible working has further facilitated their adoption (although, the main providers of the cloud infrastructure include BigTech firms, such as Amazon, Google, and Microsoft)!

Their reticence was historically due to financial institution's inability to be sufficiently agile to innovate at speed. But it was equally due to a 'blame culture' which layered internal technology development concerns of keeping control on top of procurement bureaucracy and draconian information security requirements. Some of this will still need to be addressed post Covid-19 to allow banks to fully collaborate with FinTech firms. The importance of this is underlined by the confirmed potential for Artificial Intelligence (AI) to be more widely deployed to support new business. The benefits that AI could bring to areas such as investment algorithms to improve portfolio management, predictive analytics to endorse credit facilities and strengthen fraud detection and back office functions in their future business plans are clear. Regulation around new technology will be a potential impediment to the adoption of technologies such as AI and support the historical cultural barriers.

TIP

Therefore, the pandemic should also be a catalyst for regulators to continue with initiatives such as Open Banking which compels banks to embrace the new technology ecosystem.

The pessimistic view is that we will see a 'flight to quality' which entails that customers will revert to familiar, household names that are perceived as a 'safer bet' in troubled times. After the 2008 financial crisis, consumers were obliged to try out new digital alternatives. However, the current crisis may make consumers move back towards traditional financial institutions as they seek trust in more household names and accept a more risk-averse attitude. This could have the greatest impact on some of the more recent unicorns, such as challenger and neo banks, payments companies, specifically around transaction interchange and foreign exchange transfers, peer-to-peer (P2P) lending platforms and B2C FinTech firms in general. This will result in some failures and consolidation amongst FinTech firms as they preserve cash and working capital where possible by cutting costs, rather than further scaling the business, as income drops.

B2B firms will argue that digitalization will develop far faster than forecast, bringing forward years' worth of tech progress to financial institutions as they also look to create cost savings while improving clients' digital journey. This is further supported by the fact that, relatively speaking, the financial industry is still lagging other industry verticals such as telecommunications and media in their digital take-up.

WARNING

However, post Covid-19 we've seen FinTech funding drop back to levels seen 3-years ago. The likely changes in the investment landscape, at least short term, will see venture capital and private equity houses supporting businesses in their existing portfolios but more cautious about supporting new ventures, particularly seed funding or early series raises.

Funding rounds for later stage FinTech will take precedence, with those that raised just before the pandemic better positioned to 'weather the storm' and seek opportunities. For those raising now, valuations for some have reduced significantly as investors become more rigorous and maintain their 'war chest'. Before COVID-19, there was an increasing appetite from the corporate venture arms of financial institutions to actively buy stakes in promising FinTech firms. As we emerge from the crisis, will this accelerate or will BigTech firms leverage FinTech firms' capabilities within their cloud offerings, as part of a broader 'FinTech-as-a- Platform (FaaP)' strategy?

As Winston Churchill was forming the United Nations after WWII, he famously said, "Never let a good crisis go to waste." This can also be applied to the post pandemic crisis we face today. From crisis comes innovation and opportunity and it is inevitable that the 'new normal' in financial services will require new ways of working and engaging with clients and adapting will need digital transformation. The cynical post distributed on social media of late asks:

Who led your digital transformation?   A) CEO, B) CMO, or C) COVID-19.

and Microsoft CEO, Satya Nadella, recently said, "We've seen 2-years' worth of digital transformation in 2 months."

The general conclusion is that, while elements of the FinTech sector will be under stress, there is a huge opportunity for incumbents and FinTech firms to 'collaborate to innovate.'

Index

A

accountants, 2

acquisitions
  discussion, 308–309
  Numerix, 245, 266–267, 276–277

AFM (Authority for the Financial Markets), 47

Agile development process. *See also* microservices
  discussion, 61, 71, 73–74
  open source software and, 176, 183
  programming languages and, 89
  prototyping and, 355
  rapid application development (RAD), 71, 73, 77–78
  waterfall development versus, 71–73, 176

Agile Project Management for Dummies (Layton, Ostermiller), 74

AI. *See* artificial intelligence (AI)

Alibaba, 24, 29

Alipay, 28

Allaire, Jeremy, 101

Amazon, 21, 28–29, 33

Amazon Web Services (AWS), 28, 112

American Institute of Certified Public Accountants Auditing Standards Board, 130

AMF (annual maintenance fee), 12

AMF (Autorité des Marchés Financiers), 47

AML (anti-money laundering), 42, 56

Android OS, 152, 158

angel investors, 284–285, 357

ANN. *See* artificial neural network (ANN)

annual maintenance fee (AMF), 12

Ant Financial, 14, 21, 24, 26

anti-money laundering (AML), 42, 56

Apple, 28–29, 151

Apple Pay, 28

application programming interfaces (APIs)
  benefits of, 62–64
  cloud computing and, 110
  discussion, 18, 30, 61–62
  gateways, 74
  graphical user interfaces (GUIs) and, 160

legacy systems and, 253
management, 76
open source software and, 183
strategy for building, 64–66

apps
  banking, 153
  capital markets trading, 156–157
  developer mentality toward, 151–152
  discussion, 151–152, 154
  graphical user interfaces (GUIs) for, 157–160
  hybrid, 152
  lending, 154–155
  native, 152
  RegTech, 155–156
  requirements in developing, 160–161
  types of, 152–153
  wealth management, 153–154
  web, 152

artificial intelligence (AI). *See also* machine learning
  alternative data for, 218–221
  for analyzing investments, 291
  artificial neural network (ANN) and, 212, 214–215
  banking apps and, 153
  capital markets trading apps and, 156–157
  chat bots and, 217–218
  decentralized applications (DApps) and, 102–103
  developing skills for, 300–301
  discussion, 32–33, 211, 305–306
  disruptions caused by, 34–35
  in Fintech Cube, 11
  history of, 212–213
  Julia programming language and, 91–92
  learning methods within, 215
  open source software and, 183
  opportunities presented by, 37
  practical applications for, 211, 215–216, 219–220
  Python programming language and, 90
  reinforcement learning, 212
  subcategories within, 213–214
  wealth management apps and, 154

cloud encryption service (CES), 123–124

cloud service providers (CSPs)

  discussion, 111–112

  encryption by, 123

  security and, 129–130

  self-service provisioning via, 127–128

CloudMargin, 157

COBOL programming language, 253, 323

Commodity Futures Trading Commission (CFTC), 46

Communications Platform as a Service (CpaaS), 113, 117

complex event processing (CEP), 170

Component Lifecycle Management (CLM), 245

compute nodes, 137

computer aided diagnosis, 213

computer vision, 213

computing technologies. *See also* decentralized applications (DApps)

  capacity planning, 93–95

  discussion, 93

  quantum computing, 104–108

confidential data (CD), 122

consensus protocol

  in blockchain, 96, 104, 138

  in decentralized data structure (DDS), 97–98

  discussion, 137–138, 141

  manipulation of, 145

  in permissioned blockchain, 103, 141

consolidation, 309–310

consortium blockchain, 140, 143

Consumer Financial Protection Bureau (CFPB), 46

containerization, 78

Convercent, 156

copyleft licensing, 177, 245, 348

corporate venture capital (CVC), 235, 286–287, 310–311

CpaaS (Communications Platform as a Service), 113, 117

CPU. *See* central processing unit

crash fault tolerance (CFT), 141

Credible, 155

credit default swaps (CDS), 9

Credit Karma, 155

credit value adjustment (CVA) calculations, 27, 50, 54

CRM (customer relationship management), 115

CrossAsset Software, 9, 19, 47

crowdfunding, 11, 282–283, 357

cryptocurrency

  discussion, 32, 36

  online courses on, 308

  regulation of, 43

  traditional institutions and, 24, 149

CSPs. *See* cloud service providers

currencies, 11

customer relationship management (CRM), 115

CVA (credit value adjustment) calculations, 27, 50, 54

CVC (corporate venture capital), 235, 286–287, 310–311

cybersecurity. *See also* security

  in cloud computing, 111–112

  discussion, 23, 33, 56

  regulation, 42

  third-party software and, 44

D

DAE (distributed autonomous enterprise), 139

DAO (decentralized autonomous organization), 139

DApps. *See* decentralized applications

data

  semi-structured, 209

  structured, 164, 208–209

  unstructured, 164, 209

data at rest, 124

data cubes, 166

data designations, 122

data governance, 56

data in transit, 124

data in use, 124

data lakes, 55, 205–206

data lineage, 206

data localization laws (DLLs), 132

data management. *See also* ETL (extract, transform, load)

  accuracy versus speed in, 82

  database architecture and, 55, 204–206

  differentiating data in, 208–209

  discussion, 18, 81, 197

  efficiency in, 83–84

  ensuring accurate data in, 83

  historization in, 206–207

  key questions, 198

  with legacy systems, 198–199

  lineage in, 206

  market data and, 201–202

United States
  FinTech in, 26
  regulation in, 39, 45–46, 132
unstructured data, 164, 209
unsupervised learning, 217
Upgrade, 155
user experience (UX), 157–158

V

value-at-risk calculations, 8
Varo Money, 153
vendor risk issues, 39, 44
Venmo, 154
venture capital (VC)
  discussion, 2, 13–14, 356–357
  investments, 279–280, 285–287
virtual machine monitor (VMM), 126
virtual private network (VPN), 124
virtual reality, 11
virtualization
  cloud computing and, 126–127
  discussion, 95, 114–115
  Function as a Service (FaaS) and, 117
Visual Basic programming language, 70
VMM (virtual machine monitor), 126
VMware Fusion, 127
VMware Server, 127
VMware Workstation, 127

voice technology, 211, 303–305
VPN (virtual private network), 124

W

waterfall development, 71–73
wealth management industry, 21, 45–46, 153
WealthTech
  challenges by, 281
  discussion, 9, 13, 32, 280
  online courses on, 308
  portfolio self-management in, 34
web apps, 152
WeChat, 14
Whitten, Greg, 9
Windows, 158
Woerner, Stefan, 107–108
workflow engine, 160
WorldRemit, 51

X

XML (Extensible Markup Language), 200
XVA, 27, 54

Z

Zopa, 155

About the Authors

Susanne Chishti is the CEO and founder of FINTECH Circle, the leading global Fin-Tech community focused on FinTech investments and corporate innovation strategies, and founder of the FINTECH Circle Institute, a FinTech learning platform offering innovation workshops to C-level executives and FinTech courses. She is also the coeditor of the bestseller *The FinTech Book*, which has been translated into ten languages and is sold across 107 countries, *The WealthTech Book*, *The InsurTech Book*, *The PayTech Book*, *The AI Book*, and *The LegalTech Book* (published by Wiley in 2020).

After completing her MBA, she started her career working for a FinTech company (before the term "FinTech" had been invented) in Silicon Valley 25 years ago. She then worked for more than 15 years across Deutsche Bank, Lloyds Banking Group, Morgan Stanley, and Accenture in London and Hong Kong.

Susanne is an award-winning entrepreneur and investor with strong FinTech expertise. She is a judge and coach at global FinTech events and competitions and a conference keynote speaker. Susanne leads a global community of 130,000 FinTech entrepreneurs, investors, and financial services professionals (www. fintechcircle.com). Follow Susanne on LinkedIn and on Twitter/Instagram @ SusanneChishti @FINTECHCircle @FTC_Institute.

Steven R. O'Hanlon is the CEO and president of Numerix, the leading FinTech provider of innovative capital markets technology solutions and real-time intelligence applications for trading and risk management. As a dedicated visionary, Mr. O'Hanlon leads Numerix with the mission of disrupting existing technologies and business processes via leading-edge software, giving clients a strategic advantage in their markets and enabling them to win today and tomorrow. His primary objective as an award-winning entrepreneur and FinTech leader is to push boundaries to create breakthrough solutions that help clients better manage their risk, and thus ultimately helping create a safer capital markets industry.

Mr. O'Hanlon joined Numerix in 2002 and was named president and COO in 2004. He has driven the transformation of the company from a firm without vision, with a widely disparate product line, and with a presence in only five locations, to a global analytics software company operating from a single platform with a presence in 26 countries and equal revenue distribution across the Americas, EMEA, and the APAC regions.

Mr. O'Hanlon propelled his business from a small analytic firm to a global leader of financial analytics software to the foremost FinTech company in the area of pricing and risk management.

Through Numerix's continued investment in innovative technologies, unrivaled analytic capabilities, and a customer-centric solution selling approach, the company has been firmly planted as the most prolific and dominant leader in both risk and pricing. To date, the company has been recognized with more than 200 global awards, including being named one of the fastest growing companies in North America by *Inc.* Magazine's 500|5000 and Deloitte's Technology Fast 500™.

Mr. O'Hanlon has participated in seven start-ups, has actively negotiated the sale of several companies for nearly $500 million, and has contributed to three successful IPOs.

Brendan Bradley is currently nonexecutive chairman (Fregnan and iPushPull) on the advisory board (FINTECH Circle, HUBX, Limeglass, RISE Financial Technologies, and Waymark Tech) for many early-stage FinTech firms as well as cofounder of Seismic Foundry, a seed-stage venture capital group. With all these firms, he is focused on developing new ideas around changing market structure, regulation, and technology as an investor, entrepreneur, and consultant.

Prior to this, he was an executive board member and CIO at Eurex, the largest European derivatives exchange, where he was responsible for championing and "brokering" new ideas, both internally and externally, and looking for new opportunities within the changing market environment. He has worked within the financial services industry for more than 30 years, focusing on business and product development, and played a major part in the development of the European futures and options industry with LIFFE, DTB, and Eurex.

James Jockle is CMO and executive vice president, Global Marketing & Corporate Communications for Numerix. In this role, Mr. Jockle leads the company's global marketing and corporate communications efforts, spanning a diverse set of solutions and audiences. He oversees integrated marketing communications to clients in the largest global financial markets and to the Numerix partner network through the company's branding, electronic marketing, research, events, public relations, advertising, and relationship marketing.

Prior to joining Numerix, he served as managing director of Global Marketing and Communications for Fitch Ratings. During his tenure at Fitch, Mr. Jockle built the firm's public relations program, oversaw investor relations, and led marketing and communications plans for several acquisitions. Prior to Fitch, Mr. Jockle was a member of the communications team at Moody's Investors Service.

Dawn Patrick is both the COO and executive vice president of Global Operations for Numerix, the leading provider of innovative capital markets technology solutions and real-time intelligence applications for trading and risk management. As COO, Ms. Patrick oversees the company's day-to-day operations. In this capacity, she touches every department requiring operational oversight and leads the focus on cost reduction, forecasting, and departmental efficiencies. As head of Global Field Operations, she oversees global customer support, quality assurance, IT, human resources, internal application support, training, and field operations. She has received several industry accolades since 2014.

Prior to joining Numerix in 2004, Ms. Patrick worked with Incognito Software, where she streamlined operations and constructed a customer-centric, self-service environment. She was also vice president of Customer Service and Operations at Net Exchange. In addition, Ms. Patrick was part of the senior management team responsible for the successful IPO at Register.com, the first DNS Registrar to successfully register domain names to the international registry.

Ms. Patrick began her career as an entrepreneur in the San Francisco Bay area, where she owned and operated two retail stores and a small manufacturing company for 13 years. The experience she gained running her own businesses, at a time when there were few female entrepreneurs, informed her approach to management in the larger corporate world.

Dedication

We would like to dedicate this book to everybody who is interested in the future of finance. To those who have been part of the financial sector for a long time and know it's time to change. And to those who use financial solutions, either privately as consumers or as corporate buyers, and expect more in terms of customer experience, ease of use, and value add.

So no matter whether you're a newbie, a FinTech start-up founder, a FinTech investor, a financial services professional, or a user of financial services, this book is for you.

Authors' Acknowledgments

From Susanne and Brendan: Our global FINTECH Circle community of more than 130,000 followers and members is keen to learn about the future of finance. Nothing is more exciting than meeting FinTech start-ups that have developed cutting-edge solutions and helping them to scale, or equally working with large financial institutions and helping them to innovate and change their internal culture by enabling them to upskill their management teams. FinTech is an opportunity for all of us, and we would like to thank all FinTech entrepreneurs, investors, coeditors, and coauthors of our *FinTech Book* (published by Wiley, too) and large financial institutions who have inspired us personally to cowrite this book. As a reader of this Wiley book, you can become a member on fintechcircle.com/membership-registration/ and join our research panel online at fintechcircle.com/research-panel/.

From Steve O'Hanlon and the Numerix team: Numerix wishes to thank and acknowledge all those internal supporters and contributors like Satyam Kancharla, Chief Strategy Officer and Executive Vice President of Numerix; Chris Etienne, Senior Vice President of Global Support; and Ben Meyvin, Senior Vice President of Global Services, and all those external partners and contributors like Ron Coleman, professor at Marist College and inventor who was part of the team at IBM that brought us Deep Blue, who is just one of the end users in over 300 companies that inform our understanding of the FinTech industry and of its place in the future.

Publisher's Acknowledgments

Senior Acquisitions Editor: Tracy Boggier

Dummifier: Faithe Wempen

Project Manager: Michelle Hacker

Development Editor: Georgette Beatty

Copy Editor: Jennette ElNaggar

Proofreader: Debby Butler

Technical Editor: Keith Bear, Fellow, Centre for Alternative Finance, Judge Business School, University of Cambridge

Production Editor: Siddique Shaik

Cover Image: Fintech icon © monsitj/iStock.com, Currency symbol © AdresiaStock/Shutterstock

Take dummies with you everywhere you go!

Whether you are excited about e-books, want more from the web, must have your mobile apps, or are swept up in social media, dummies makes everything easier.

Find us online!

dummies.com

dummies
A Wiley Brand

Leverage the power

Dummies is the global leader in the reference category and one of the most trusted and highly regarded brands in the world. No longer just focused on books, customers now have access to the dummies content they need in the format they want. Together we'll craft a solution that engages your customers, stands out from the competition, and helps you meet your goals.

Advertising & Sponsorships

Connect with an engaged audience on a powerful multimedia site, and position your message alongside expert how-to content. Dummies.com is a one-stop shop for free, online information and know-how curated by a team of experts.

- Targeted ads
- Video
- Email Marketing

- Microsites
- Sweepstakes sponsorship

20 MILLION PAGE VIEWS EVERY SINGLE MONTH

15 MILLION UNIQUE VISITORS PER MONTH

43% OF ALL VISITORS ACCESS THE SITE VIA THEIR MOBILE DEVICES

700,000 NEWSLETTER SUBSCRIPTIONS TO THE INBOXES OF

300,000 UNIQUE INDIVIDUALS EVERY WEEK

# of dummies

Custom Publishing

Reach a global audience in any language by creating a solution that will differentiate you from competitors, amplify your message, and encourage customers to make a buying decision.

- Apps
- Books
- eBooks
- Video
- Audio
- Webinars

Brand Licensing & Content

Leverage the strength of the world's most popular reference brand to reach new audiences and channels of distribution.

For more information, visit dummies.com/biz

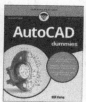

Learning Made Easy

ACADEMIC

9781119293576
USA $19.99
CAN $23.99
UK £15.99

9781119293637
USA $19.99
CAN $23.99
UK £15.99

9781119293491
USA $19.99
CAN $23.99
UK £15.99

9781119293460
USA $19.99
CAN $23.99
UK £15.99

9781119293590
USA $19.99
CAN $23.99
UK £15.99

9781119215844
USA $26.99
CAN $31.99
UK £19.99

9781119293378
USA $22.99
CAN $27.99
UK £16.99

9781119293521
USA $19.99
CAN $23.99
UK £15.99

9781119239178
USA $18.99
CAN $22.99
UK £14.99

9781119263883
USA $26.99
CAN $31.99
UK £19.99

Available Everywhere Books Are Sold

dummies.com

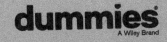

Small books for big imaginations

GETTING STARTED WITH Coding
Get Creative with Code!
Candile McClue, PhD

9781119177173
USA $9.99
CAN $9.99
UK £8.99

MODDING Minecraft
Build Your Own Minecraft Mods!
Sarah Guthals, PhD
Stephen Foster, PhD
Lindsey Handley, PhD

9781119177272
USA $9.99
CAN $9.99
UK £8.99

MAKING YouTube VIDEOS
Star in Your Own Video!
Nick Willoughby

9781119177241
USA $9.99
CAN $9.99
UK £8.99

DESIGNING Digital Games
Create Games with Scratch!
Derek Breen

9781119177210
USA $9.99
CAN $9.99
UK £8.99

GETTING STARTED WITH Raspberry Pi
Program Your Raspberry Pi!
Richard Wentk

9781119262657
USA $9.99
CAN $9.99
UK £6.99

EXPERIMENTING WITH Science
Think, Test, and Learn!

9781119291336
USA $9.99
CAN $9.99
UK £6.99

CREATING Digital Animations
Animate Stories with Scratch!

9781119233527
USA $9.99
CAN $9.99
UK £6.99

GETTING STARTED WITH Engineering
Think Like an Engineer!

9781119291220
USA $9.99
CAN $9.99
UK £6.99

WRITING Computer Code
Learn the Language of Computers!
Chris Minnick and Eva Holland

9781119177302
USA $9.99
CAN $9.99
UK £8.99

Unleash Their Creativity

dummies.com

dummies
A Wiley Brand